Leopold Stokowski
1882-1977

Discography
Concert register

compiled by John Hunt

CONTENTS

Published 1996 by John Hunt
Designed by John Hunt
Printed by Short Run Press, Exeter

ISBN 0 952827 5 9
Copyright 1996   John Hunt

ACKNOWLEDGEMENT

This publication has been made possible by contributions from the following sponsor subscribers:

Richard Ames, New Barnet
Stathis Arfanis, Athens
Yoshihiro Asada, Osaka
Jack Atkinson, Tasmania
J.M. Blyth, Darlington
A. Brandmair, Munich
J. Camps-Ros, Barcelona
Edward Chibas, Caracas
F. De Vilder, Bussum
Richard Dennis, Greenhithe
John Derry, Newcastle-upon-Tyne
Erik Dervos, London
Hans-Peter Ebner, Milan
Shuntaro Enatsu, Miyakonojo City
Henry Fogel, Chicago
Peter Fulop, Toronto
Philip Goodman, London
Jean-Pierre Goossens, Luxembourg
Johann Gratz, Vienna
Peter Hamann, Bochum
Michael Harris, London
Donald Hodgman, Riverside CT
Martin Holland, Sale
Bodo Igesz, New York
Richard Igler, Vienna
Eugene Kaskey, New York
Shiro Kawai, Tokyo
Detlef Kissmann, Solingen
Eric Kobe, Lucerne
John Larsen, Mariager
Ernst Lumpe, Soest
John Mallinson, Hurst Green
Carlo Marinelli, Rome
Finn Moeller Larsen, Virum
Philip Moores, Stafford
Bruce Morrison, Gillingham
W. Moyle, Ombersley
Alan Newcombe, Hamburg
Hugh Palmer, Chelmsford
Laurence Pateman, London
Tully Potter, Billericay
Yves Saillard, Mollie-Margot
Helger Steinhauff, Stemwede
Yoshihiro Suzuki, Tokyo
H.A. Van Dijk, Apeldoorn
Hiromitsu Wada, Chiba
Urs Weber, St Gallen
Nigel Wood, London
G. Wright, Romford
A. Greenburgh, New Barnet

=*the*=
LEOPOLD STOKOWSKI
=*society*=

A Londoner by birth and an American by naturalisation, Leopold Stokowski was of Polish and Irish extraction, and was born on 18 April 1882 in Upper Marylebone Street (now New Cavendish Street). He attended Marylebone School and at the age of 13 entered the Royal College of Music. He became a Fellow of the Royal College of Organists, took his Bachelor of Music Degree at Queen's College, Oxford, and from 1902-1905 was a noted organist and choirmaster at St. James's Church, Piccadilly.

In 1905 he left for America to take up another church appointment at St. Bartholomew's in New York City. By now he had taken up conducting - initially with small ensembles, theatre groups and so on - whilst continuing his studies in Europe. His 'official' conducting debut came in Paris with the Colonne Orchestra in Paris in 1909, and the following week he appeared at the Queen's Hall, London, with the New Symphony Orchestra.

That same year he was appointed conductor of the Cincinnati Orchestra, and in 1912 he left to take over the Philadelphia Orchestra. Stokowski's quarter-of-a-century in Philadelphia was one of the most celebrated in the annals of 20th-century music, since he took a small provincial ensemble and turned it into one of the greatest orchestras in the world. The recorded evidence on Stokowski's 78s made between the two World Wars makes it clear that there were few, if any, other orchestras at that time to match its precision, virtuosity, tone-colour, string sound and impeccable intonation.

In Philadelphia, Stokowski championed the living composer with countless premieres: he introduced to American audiences Mahler's 8th Symphony, Stravinsky's *Rite of Spring*, Schoenberg's *Gurrelieder*, Alban Berg's *Wozzeck*, several of the symphonies of Sibelius and Shostakovitch, and many other modern works. Much of Rachmaninov's music was premiered by Stokowski in Philadelphia, and he was a staunch advocate of many 20th-century composers - such as Richard Strauss, Falla, Prokoviev, Scriabin, Copland, Varese, and countless others. In addition to his conducting activities he was a noted transcriber for the orchestra of music originally written in other forms, and is especially famous for his orchestrations of Bach's keyboard works.

At the end of the 1930s, Stokowski left Philadelphia to form the All-American Youth Orchestra and co-conduct the NBC Symphony Orchestra with Toscanini. By this time he had appeared in a few films (notably Walt Disney's *Fantasia*) and during the war years he also founded the New York City Symphony Orchestra and Hollywood Bowl Symphony Orchestra. During the late 1940s he was a chief guest conductor with the New York Philharmonic, and from 1951 began a new career abroad, with frequent guest appearances conducting the world's finest orchestras. In 1963 he made his debut at the Henry Wood 'Proms' in London, his concerts there including a memorable performance of Mahler's *Resurrection* Symphony.

From 1955-1961, Stokowski was Music Director of the Houston Symphony Orchestra, and in 1962 he founded the American Symphony Orchestra in New York. Following his resignation from the ASO in 1972 he settled in England, and until his death in 1977 he made notable recordings for Decca "Phase-4", RCA, Pye, Desmar, Philips and CBS.

Two years after his death, The Leopold Stokowski Society was founded, designed to perpetuate Stokowski's memory by encouraging the reissue of his recordings (many have now appeared on the RCA, Biddulph, Pearl and Dutton Laboratories labels), and bringing to the attention of present-day conductors the famous "Stokowski Transcriptions". Several CDs of these have now been issued, including "Stokowski's Symphonic Bach", "Stokowski Encores", and "Stokowski's Mussorgsky" on Chandos (Matthias Bamert/BBC Philharmonic), and selections of Stokowski Transcriptions on Telarc (Erich Kunzel/Cincinnati Orchestra) and EMI (Wolfgang Sawallisch/Philadelphia Orchestra).

The Society's regular magazine "*Toccata*" includes articles on Stokowski and reviews reissues of his recordings. Annual Social Meetings are held during April (the month of Stokowski's birth) to which eminent Guest Speakers are invited. The most recent of these have included musicians and broadcasters Bernard Keeffe, John Amis, Jon Tolansky and Rob Cowan, along with conductor Geoffrey Simon (who has recorded several Stokowski Transcriptions) and the noted record producer and conductor Charles Gerhardt. For its 1997 Annual Social Meeting, the Society has invited Sir Edward Heath to be Guest Speaker, on a special occasion marking the 20th Anniversary of Stokowski's death.

During its early years, the Society produced a series of LPs exclusively for its Members. These have now become Collector's Items, though a few are still available. The Society also produced its first CD in 1993, entitled "Stokowski conducts Philadelphia Rarities". This compendium of rare 78s was received with such critical acclaim that it was reissued on Cala Records (CACD 0501). The Cala Records/Stokowski Society's follow-up was of previously unissued Stokowski 78s entitled "First Releases" (CACD 0502), whilst a third CD devoted to Stokowski's recordings with the NBC Symphony Orchestra of Russian Music (1941-42) is a Spring 1996 release (CACD 0505). Also in preparation as an Autumn 1996 release is a coupling of the Hollywood Bowl Symphony Orchestra recording of Tchaikovsky's "Pathetique" Symphony (1945), coupled with the 1944 New York City Symphony Orchestra set of Richard Strauss's "Death and Transfiguration".

Membership of **The Leopold Stokowski Society** (to which cheques should be made payable) is available at £15.00 per annum for the UK; $30.00 for the USA; £20.00 overseas (ie: Europe, Australia, Japan). Please send your subscription to: Mr Dennis Davis, Flat B, 23 Grantbridge Street, London N1 8LJ

Leopold Stokowski

Discography compiled
by John Hunt

LEOPOLD STOKOWSKI: THE DISCOGRAPHY

"Here is a man who puts the evidence of his ears
above that of the printed page"

Thus wrote Roger Wimbush in the pages of
Gramophone back in 1963, summing up the
achievement of a man who was already, in his
lifetime, a legend of both concert hall and
recording studio. Those famous Stokowski
transcriptions, sometimes scorned by the purists
but much loved by the general public, seemed to
have been written particularly with the recording
studio in mind, so well balanced and so
distinctively coloured were they, as if by a
master technician.

My own recollection of attending Stokowski
concerts in the 1960s and 1970s is of a special
sense of occasion, anticipation that we were
about to experience something far above the
ordinary. Stokowski shared with Beecham, Karajan
and certain other giants of the period, a special
charisma. Like those same colleagues, he also
felt at home in the recording studio, with its
endless possibilities for manipulating a musical
performance to give the best possible effect.

I was delighted when the Leopold Stokowski
Society asked me to compile this guide through
the Maestro's recorded output. As in the case
of the other musical greats to whom I have devoted
single volumes, it seemed fitting not only to
include the many live and unofficial recordings
which are now available to avid collectors and
which help immeasurably in rounding out the
musical picture of the artist, but also to go
one step further and to essay a list of as
many of the conductor's public appearances as
is possible. For both projects I leaned heavily
on the material which Edward Johnson and other
members of the Stokowski Society were able to
make available. This included previous attempts
at discographies and concert listings by, among
others, Brian Plumb and Jim Cartwright. My
greatest thanks must, however, go to Edward
Johnson for guiding me through the material and
answering my many queries (any errors which
remain are entirely mine).

The problem for a layman listener, especially one
who did not experience the Stokowski magic in a
concert hall, is to distinguish between a
composer's original score and the added nuance
and richness which it might receive when
arranged or transcribed by Leopold Stokowski.

In this discography I have simply marked with an asterisk in the title those works which have been recorded in the conductor's own arrangement or transcription. However, that does not necessarily mean that other works have not been edited or embellished from time to time, as was equally the custom with Stokowski's contemporary Willem Mengelberg - and even the purist Arturo Toscanini! Stokowski also sometimes gave his transcriptions descriptive titles which differed from the music's original title. I have retained these descriptions for identification purposes, but in the case of the Wagner transcriptions, for example, have felt it necessary to give the description by which the pieces are best known today. As an example, today's sophisticated Wagnerian would take the description "Finale to Götterdämmerung" to mean the entire closing or Immolation scene, whereas Stokowski uses it to denote the 4-minute orchestral postlude which follows after Brünnhilde has finished her peroration.

An aspect of Stokowski's work not fully covered in this volume is his contribution to the American motion picture industry. Apart from the pioneering soundtrack to Disney's **Fantasia** and the almost complete movement from Tchaikovsky's Fifth Symphony in the film **Carnegie Hall**, Stokowski did participate in a variety of capacities in numerous other cinematographic enterprises.

The discography is arranged in the standard manner for my series of discographies, that is alphabetically by composer, and divided into three columns. The first column gives the city, month and year in which a recording took place (sometimes recordings were spread over periods of days, months or, in certain cases, years, making it impossible always to be more specific anyway). In this first column a preceding "L" indicates a recording of a live, as opposed to a studio, performance. The second column contains details of orchestra and soloists. The third, and most important, column gives original catalogue numbers followed by important re-issues in the various main territories and in the main different formats (78,45,LP,CD). For Victor and Columbia 78rpm sets the <u>set</u> number is given: individual disc numbers are normally only given if a set number was not allocated. I am always glad to hear from collectors who can add to the information.

Stokowski enthusiasts will soon be marking the
20th anniversary of his death, and I hope that
this volume will be a useful companion for them.
In the meantime I can think of no better
summing-up than the words of Roger Wimbush in
that 1963 article:

"Stokowski knows as much about the concert halls
and studios of the world as its music. He never
ceases to experiment in the placing of his
orchestra, even to the individual stance of a
double-bass player. Yet this man, whose physical
presence is so arresting and whose concerts
represent the epitome of glamour and panache,
tells us that music is best simply heard and not
seen at all. His ideal, in fact, is the
gramophone record. Apart from Sir Landon Ronald,
probably no man has done more to promote the
gramophone as a purveyor of music, and during the
great formative years of recorded music he had at
his disposal the Philadelphia Orchestra, which he
had brought to an incomparable and highly
individual state. Since the 1920s he has recorded
the standard nineteenth century repertory, in some
cases several times over, and his records have
seldom failed to make a definite impact".

John Hunt

ADOLPHE ADAM (1803-1856)

Giselle, selection

New York May 1950	His SO	78: Victor DM 1394 45: Victor WDM 1394 LP: Victor LM 1083

ISAAC ALBENIZ (1860-1909)

Fête-Dieu à Seville (Ibéria)*

Philadelphia September 1928	Philadelphia Orchestra	78: Victor 7158 78: HMV D 1888
West Ham July 1976	National PO	LP: CBS 34543/73589

FIRKET AMIROV (1922-1984)

Azerbaijan Mugam

Houston March 1959	Houston SO	LP: Everest LPBR 3032/SDBR 3032 CD: Panthéon D 1032X

JOHANN SEBASTIAN BACH (1685–1750)

Adagio (Organ Toccata, Adagio and Fugue in C)*

Camden NJ October 1933	Philadelphia Orchestra	78: Victor M 236/M 243 78: HMV DB 2335 CD: Pearl GEMMCDS 9098

Air from Suite No 3*

Philadelphia January 1936	Philadelphia Orchestra	78: Victor M 401 78: HMV DA 1605 CD: Pearl GEMMCDS 9098
New York July 1941	All American SO	78: Columbia (USA) X 220
New York May 1958	His SO	LP: Capitol P 8458/SP 8458 LP: EMI SXLP 30174 CD: EMI CDM 769 0722/CDM 565 9122
London April 1974	LSO	LP: RCA ARL1-0880/GL 42921 CD: RCA/BMG 09026 612672/09026 626052

Andante from Violin Sonata No 3*

New York July 1941	All American SO	78: Columbia (USA) X 541 CD: Music and Arts CD 845

Arioso from Cantata No 156*

New York July 1941	All American SO	78: Columbia (USA) X 541
New York November 1941	NBC SO	78: Victor 18498 78: HMV DB 6150
London April 1974	LSO	LP: RCA ARL1-0880/GL 42921 CD: RCA/BMG 09026 612672/09026 626052

Aus der Tiefe rufe ich*

Camden NJ March 1930	Philadelphia Orchestra	78: Victor 7553 78: HMV DB 1789 LP: Dell' Arte DA 9001 CD: Pearl GEMMCDS 9098

Bourrée from English Suite No 2*

Philadelphia January 1936	Philadelphia Orchestra	78: HMV DA 1639 CD: Pearl GEMMCDS 9098 <u>DA 1639 was never actually issued</u>
New York March 1950	His SO	78: Victor DM 1512 45: Victor ERA 69 LP: Victor LM 1133 LP: HMV BLP 1074 CD: RCA/BMG GD 60922
New York February 1958	His SO	LP: Capitol P 8489/SP 8489 LP: EMI MFP 2062

Brandenburg Concerto No 2

Philadelphia September 1928	Philadelphia Orchestra	78: Victor M 59 78: HMV D 1708-1710 LP: Dell' Arte DA 9001

Brandenburg Concerto No 5

Philadelphia February 1960	Philadelphia Orchestra	LP: Columbia (USA) ML 5713/MS 6313 LP: CBS 30061/33228

Chaconne from Violin Partita No 2*

Camden NJ April 1934	Philadelphia Orchestra	78: Victor M 243 78: HMV DB 2541-2543 CD: Pearl GEMMCDS 9098
New York March 1950	His SO	78: Victor DM 1512 LP: Victor LM 1133 CD: RCA/BMG GD 60922
London April 1974	LSO	LP: RCA ARL1-0880/GL 42921 CD: RCA/BMG 09026 612672/09026 626052

Christ lag in Todesbanden*

Camden NJ April 1931	Philadelphia Orchestra	78: Victor 7437 78: HMV DB 1952 CD: Pearl GEMMCDS 9098

Ein' feste Burg ist unser Gott*

Philadelphia April 1939	Philadelphia Orchestra	78: Victor 1692 CD: Pearl GEMMCDS 9098 <u>Catalogue number 1692 also used for the shortened version recorded in 1933 (see below)</u>
New York July 1941	All American SO	78: Columbia (USA) X 219/12903
New York February 1958	His SO	LP: Capitol P 8694/P 8489/SP 8694/SP 8489 LP: EMI MFP 2062 LP: Angel 60235 CD: EMI CDM 769 0722
London April 1974	LSO	LP: RCA ARL1-0880/GL 42921 CD: RCA/BMG 09026 612672/09026 626052

Ein' feste Burg ist unser Gott, shortened version*

Camden NJ October 1933	Philadelphia Orchestra	78: Victor 1692 78: HMV DB 2453 <u>Catalogue number 1692 also used for the full version recorded in 1939 (see above)</u>

Es ist vollbracht (Johannes-Passion)*

Camden NJ October 1934	Philadelphia Orchestra	78: Victor 8764 78: HMV DB 2762
Philadelphia December 1940	Philadelphia Orchestra	78: Victor M 963 CD: Pearl GEMMCDS 9098

First movement from Trio Sonata No 1*

Philadelphia November 1939	Philadelphia Orchestra	78: Victor M 963 78: HMV DB 6260 CD: Pearl GEMMCDS 9098

Fugue in C minor (Wohltemperiertes Klavier Book 1)*

Camden NJ April 1934	Philadelphia Orchestra	78: Victor 1985/M 243 78: HMV DB 2453 LP: RCA Camden CAL 120 CD: Pearl GEMMCDS 9098

Ich ruf' zu dir, Herr Jesu Christ*

Philadelphia October 1927	Philadelphia Orchestra	78: Victor 6786/M 530 78: HMV D 1464 LP: Dell' Arte DA 9001 CD: Pearl GEMMCDS 9098
Philadelphia November 1939	Philadelphia Orchestra	78: Victor M 963
LNew York January 1949	NYPSO	LP: New York Philharmonic NYP 821-822
Philadelphia February 1960	Philadelphia Orchestra	LP: Columbia (USA) ML 5713/MS 6313/MGP 17 LP: CBS 30061/33228

Jesu bleibet meine Freude (Cantata No 147)*

New York August 1950	His SO	78: Victor 12-3159 78: HMV DB 21570 45: Victor 49-3159 45: HMV 7ER 5004/7R 170 LP: Victor LM 1176/LM 1877 CD: RCA/BMG GD 60922
London 1961	New SO Luboff Choir	LP: Victor LM 2593/LSC 2593/VCS 7007 LP: Quintessence PMC 7019 CD: RCA/BMG GD 89297/09026 625992 This arrangement by Luboff
New York April 1967	His SO	LP: Bach Guild 70696 LP: Vanguard 363/701-702/707-708 CD: Vanguard 363 This arrangement by Schickele

Jesus Christus, Gottessohn (Oster-Oratorium)*
also described as Chorale from the Easter Oratorio

Philadelphia April 1937	Philadelphia Orchestra	78: Victor M 401 CD: Pearl GEMMCDS 9098
New York August 1950	His SO	LP: Victor LM 2042/LM 1176 CD: RCA/BMG GD 60922
L Prague September 1972	Czech PO	LP: Decca PFS 4278 LP: London SPC 21096 CD: Decca 421 6392/448 9462

Komm süsser Tod (Schemellis Gesangbuch)*

Camden NJ October 1933	Philadelphia Orchestra	78: Victor M 236/M 243 78: Victor DB 2274 CD: Pearl GEMMCDS 9098
New York July 1941	All American SO	78: Columbia (USA) X 220
New York July 1950	His SO	78: Victor 12-3087 45: Victor 49-3087 LP: Victor LM 1176/LRM 7033 LP: HMV BLP 1074 CD: RCA/BMG GD 60922
New York February 1958	His SO	LP: Capitol P 8489/SP 8489 LP: EMI MFP 2062 LP: Angel 60235 CD: EMI CDM 769 0722
London April 1974	LSO	LP: RCA ARL1-0880/GL 42921 CD: RCA/BMG 09026 612672/09026 626052

Mein Jesu, was für Seelenweh' (Schemellis Gesangbuch)*

Philadelphia November 1936	Philadelphia Orchestra	78: Victor M 401 78: HMV DB 3405 CD: Pearl GEMMCDS 9098
New York April 1941	All American SO	78: Columbia (USA) 19004
New York March 1950	His SO	78: Victor DM 1512 45: Victor ERB 52 LP: Victor LM 1133/LM 1875 LP: HMV ALP 1387
New York August 1957	His SO	LP: Capitol P 8415/SP 8415 LP: Angel 6094 CD: EMI CDM 769 0722/CDM 565 9122
L Prague September 1972	Czech PO	LP: Decca PFS 4278 LP: London SPC 21096 CD: Decca 421 6392/448 9462

Nun komm der Heiden Heiland*

Camden NJ April 1934	Philadelphia Orchestra	78: Victor 8494/M 243 78: HMV DB 2274 CD: Pearl GEMMCDS 9098
LNew York January 1949	NYPSO	LP: New York Philharmonic NYP 821-822
Philadelphia February 1960	Philadelphia Orchestra	LP: Columbia (USA) ML 5713/MS 6313/MGP 17 LP: CBS 30061/33228

O Haupt voll Blut und Wunden (Matthäus-Passion)*
also described as My soul is athirst

Camden NJ June 1922	Choir	Victor unpublished <u>Experimental recording described as</u> <u>unspecified chorale from Matthäus-Passion</u>
Philadelphia November 1936	Philadelphia Orchestra	78: Victor M 401 78: HMV DB 3405 CD: Pearl GEMMCDS 9098

Organ Fugue in G minor "Great"*

Camden NJ April 1934	Philadelphia Orchestra	78: Victor 1728 CD: Pearl GEMMCDS 9098

Organ Fugue in G minor "Little"*

Camden NJ March 1931	Philadelphia Orchestra	78: Victor 7437 78: HMV DB 1952 CD: Pearl GEMMCDS 9098
New York November 1940	All American SO	78: Columbia (USA) M 451/11992
New York July 1950	His SO	78: HMV DB 21570 45: Victor WDM 1569/ERA 69 45: HMV 7ER 5004/7R 170 LP: Victor LM 1176 CD: RCA/BMG GD 60922
New York February 1958	His SO	LP: Capitol P 8489/P 8673/SP 8673/SP 8489 LP: EMI MFP 2062 LP: Angel 60235 CD: EMI CDM 769 0722
LNew York February 1968	American SO	CD: Japanese Stokowski Society LSCD 23-24
London April 1974	LSO	LP: RCA ARL1-0880/GL 42921 CD: RCA/BMG 09026 612672/09026 626052
LVence July 1975	Rouen Chamber Orchestra	CD: Japanese Stokowski Society LSCD 23-24 Stokowski's final public appearance

Organ Prelude and Fugue No 3 in E minor*

Philadelphia December 1937	Philadelphia Orchestra	78: Victor M 698/M 963 CD: Pearl GEMMCDS 9098

Passacaglia and Fugue in C minor*

Philadelphia May 1929	Philadelphia Orchestra	78: Victor M 59 78: HMV D 1702-1703 LP: Victor VCM 7101 LP: Dell' Arte DA 9001
Philadelphia November 1936	Philadelphia Orchestra	78: Victor M 401 78: HMV DB 3252-3253 CD: Pearl GEMMCDS 9098
New York July 1941	All American SO	78: Columbia (USA) X 216
LNew York December 1949	NYPSO	LP: Japanese Stokowski Society JLSS 0019
New York March 1950	His SO	78: Victor DM 1517 LP: Victor LM 1133/LRM 7033 LP: HMV BLP 1074
New York February 1958	His SO	LP: Capitol P 8489/SP 8489 LP: EMI MFP 2062 LP: Angel 60235 CD: EMI CDM 769 0722
LChicago March 1966	Chicago SO	LP: Japanese Stokowski Society JLSS 0020
Geneva August 1969	International Festival Youth Orchestra	LP: Audio Visual Enterprises AVE 30696
L Prague September 1972	Czech PO	LP: Decca PFS 4278 LP: London SPC 21096 CD: Decca 421 6392/448 9462

One of the pre-war versions of Passacaglia and Fugue also appears on CD Grammo Grammofono AB 78586

Prelude from Violin Partita No 3*

New York July 1941	All American SO	78: Columbia (USA) 11983
New York August 1957	His SO	LP: Capitol P 8415/SP 8415 CD: EMI CDM 769 0722/CDM 565 9122
London 1974	LSO	LP: RCA ARL1-0880 CD: RCA/BMG 09026 612672/09026 626052

Prelude in B minor (Wohltemperiertes Klavier Book 1)*

Philadelphia May 1929	Philadelphia Orchestra	78: Victor 7316 78: HMV D 1938/D 1995 LP: Dell' Arte DA 9001 CD: Pearl GEMMCDS 9098
New York March 1950	His SO	LP: Victor LM 2042 CD: RCA/BMG 60922
LVence July 1975	Rouen Chamber Orchestra	CD: Japanese Stokowski Society LSCD 23-24 Stokowski's final public appearance

Prelude in E flat minor (Wohltemperiertes Klavier Book 1)*

Philadelphia October 1927	Philadelphia Orchestra	78: Victor 6786 78: HMV D 1464 LP: Dell' Arte DA 9001 CD: Pearl GEMMCDS 9098
New York July 1941	All American SO	78: Columbia (USA) X 541
L Prague September 1972	Czech PO	LP: Decca PFS 4278 LP: London SPC 21096 CD: Decca 421 6392/448 9462

Sarabande from English Suite No 3*

Camden NJ April 1934	Philadelphia Orchestra	78: Victor M 243 78: HMV DB 2275 CD: Pearl GEMMCDS 9098

Sarabande from Violin Partita No 1*

Philadelphia November 1936	Philadelphia Orchestra	78: Victor M 401 CD: Pearl GEMMCDS 9098
New York February 1958	His SO	LP: Capitol P 8489/SP 8489 LP: EMI MFP 2062 LP: Angel 60235 CD: EMI CDM 769 0722

Schafe können sicher weiden (Cantata No 208)*

New York August 1950	His SO	78: Victor 12-3159 45: Victor 49-3159 45: HMV 7ER 5004/7R 170 LP: Victor LM 1176/LM 1877 CD: RCA/BMG GD 60922
London 1961	New SO Luboff Choir	LP: Victor LM 2593/LSC 2593/VCS 7007 LP: Quintessence PMC 7019 CD: RCA/BMG GD 89297/09026 625992
New York April 1967	His SO	LP: Bach Guild 70696 LP: Vanguard 363/701-702/707-708 CD: Vanguard 363

Siciliano from Violin and Clavier Sonata No 4*

Camden NJ October 1933	Philadelphia Orchestra	78: Victor M 243 78: HMV DB 2275 CD: Pearl GEMMCDS 9098
New York March 1950	His SO	78: Victor DM 1512 45: Victor ERA 244 LP: Victor LM 1133/LM 1875 LP: HMV ALP 1387

Sinfonia from Weihnachtsoratorium*

Philadelphia April-May 1929	Philadelphia Orchestra	78: Victor 7142 78: HMV D 1741 CD: Pearl GEMMCDS 9098
New York February 1958	His SO	LP: Capitol P 8489/SP 8489 LP: EMI MFP 2062 LP: Angel 60235 CD: EMI CDM 769 0722
New York April 1967	His SO	LP: Bach Guild 70696 <u>This version is performed in the original</u> <u>instrumentation</u>

Toccata and Fugue in D minor*

Philadelphia April 1927	Philadelphia Orchestra	78: Victor 6751 78: HMV D 1428 LP: Victor VCM 7101 LP: Dell' Arte DA 9001 CD: Pearl GEMMCDS 9098 CD: Magic Talent CD 48002
Camden NJ November 1934	Philadelphia Orchestra	78: Victor 8697/M 1064 78: HMV DB 2572 CD: Pearl GEMMCD 9488
LStockholm May 1939	Stockholm PO	LP: Orfeus 1-73-1
Philadelphia 1939	Philadelphia Orchestra	Fantasia soundtrack recording LP: Top Rank 30-003 LP: Disneyland WDX 101 LP: Buena Vista BVS 101 CD: Buena Vista CD 020 VHS Video: Buena Vista D211 322
New York July 1941	All American SO	78: Columbia (USA) X 219
New York March 1947	His SO	78: Victor 11-9653 45: Victor 49-0263 45: HMV 7RF 136 LP: Victor LM 2042/LRM 7033 LP: HMV BLP 1074 CD: RCA/BMG GD 60922
New York February 1957	His SO	LP: Capitol P 8399/P 8694/SP 8694/SP 8399 LP: EMI SMFP 2145 LP: Angel 60235 CD: EMI CDM 565 6142/CDM 769 0722
L Tokyo 1965	Japan PO	CD: Platz (Japan) P23G-535
L Prague September 1972	Czech PO	LP: Decca PFS 4278 LP: London SPC 21096 LP: IMP IMPX 9033 CD: Decca 421 6392/448 9462

One of the pre-war versions of the Toccata and Fugue also appears on CD
Grammofono AB 78586

Wachet auf, ruft uns die Stimme (Cantata No 140)*

| London April 1974 | LSO | LP: RCA ARL1-0880/GL 42921 CD: RCA/BMG 09026 612672/09026 626052 |

Wir glauben all' an einen Gott*

Philadelphia May 1929	Philadelphia Orchestra	78: Victor M 59 78: HMV D 1710 LP: Dell' Arte DA 9001 CD: Pearl GEMMCDS 9098
New York July 1950	His SO	45: Victor WDM 1569 LP: Victor LM 1176 CD: RCA/BMG GD 60922
Philadelphia February 1960	Philadelphia Orchestra	LP: Columbia (USA) ML 5713/MS 6313/MGP 17 LP: CBS 30061/33228
L Prague September 1972	Czech PO	LP: Decca PFS 4278 LP: London SPC 21096 CD: Decca 421 6392/448 9462

SAMUEL BARBER (1910-1981)

Adagio for strings

| New York January 1957 | His SO | LP: Capitol P 8385/P 8673/SP 8673
LP: Angel 34481/6094
LP: EMI SXLP 30174
CD: EMI CDC 747 5212/CDM 565 6142 |
| L Moscow 1958 | Soviet RO | CD: Music and Arts CD 787 |

BELA BARTOK (1881-1945)

Concerto for orchestra

Houston April 1960	Houston SO	LP: Everest LPBR 6069/SDBR 3069 LP: World Records CM 36/SCM 36 LP: Hallmark SHM 590 LP: Dell' Arte DA 9013 CD: Everest EVC 9008 Dell' Arte was an LP playing at 45 rpm

Music for strings, percussion and celesta

New York December 1957- January 1958	His SO	LP: Capitol P 8507/SP 8507 LP: World Records CM 69/SCM 69 LP: Angel 34481 CD: EMI CDC 747 5218

The Miraculous Mandarin, ballet suite

LNew York December 1969	American SO	CD: Intaglio INCD 7421

Sonata for 2 pianos and percussion

New York March-April 1952	Yessin, Viola, Jones, Howard	LP: Victor LM 1727

LUDWIG VAN BEETHOVEN (1770-1827)

Symphony No 2

LChicago 1962	Chicago SO	LP: Stokowski Society LS 4

Symphony No 3 "Eroica"

London 1974	LSO	LP: RCA ARL1-0600/AGL1-5247 CD: RCA/BMG 09026 613402/09026 625142

Symphony No 5

Camden NJ 1931	Philadelphia Orchestra	Victor L 7001 LP: Stokowski Society LS 13 L 7001 was an experimental 33.1/3 rpm recording (Symphonic transcription disc)
New York April 1941	All American SO	78: Columbia (USA) M 451 CD: American Stokowski Society LSSACD 4 CD: Music and Arts CD 857
L Tokyo 1965	Japan PO	CD: Platz (Japan) P23G-535
LNew York May 1968	American SO	CD: Memories HR 4495-4497
Walthamstow September 1969	LPO	LP: Decca PFS 4197/DPA 599-600 LP: London SPC 21042 CD: Decca 430 2182

Symphony No 6 "Pastoral"

New York February 1945	New York City SO	78: Victor M 1032 LP: RCA Camden CAL 187
New York March 1954	NBC SO	LP: Victor LM 1830 LP: HMV ALP 1268 LP: Stokowski Society LS 10 Second movement LP: Victor LM 1875 LP: HMV ALP 1387 Complete performance included Stokowski's spoken commentary

Symphony No 6 "Pastoral", abridged version

Philadelphia April 1939	Philadelphia Orchestra	<u>Fantasia soundtrack recording</u> LP: Top Rank 30-003 LP: Disneyland WDX 101 LP: Buena Vista BVS 101 CD: Buena Vista CD 020/60007 VHS Video: Buena Vista D211 322

Symphony No 7

Philadelphia April 1927	Philadelphia Orchestra	78: Victor M 17 78: HMV D 1639-1643 LP: RCA Camden CAL 212 LP: Parnassus 5 LP: Stokowski Society LS 13 CD: Biddulph WHL 033 <u>M17 and WHL 033 also include Stokowski's</u> <u>outline of themes recorded at same time</u>
New York December 1958	Symphony of the Air	LP: United Artists UAS 7003/8003 LP: Quintessence PMC 7110
LBoston January 1968	Boston SO	CD: Memories HR 4495-4497
London January 1973	New Philharmonia	LP: Decca PFS 4342 LP: London SPC 21139 CD: Decca 430 2182

Symphony No 8

LChicago March 1966	Chicago SO	CD: Japanese Stokowski Society JLSS 0020 CD: Chicago Symphony Orchestra CSO 90/92

Symphony No 8, Second movement

Camden NJ May 1920	Philadelphia Orchestra	78: Victor 74661/6243 78: HMV 3-0579/DB 385 LP: Stokowski Society LS 3

Symphony No 9 "Choral"

Camden NJ April 1934	Philadelphia Orchestra & Chorus Davies, Cathcart, Betts, Lowenthal <u>Sung in English</u>	78: Victor M 236 78: HMV DB 2327-2335 CD: American Stokowski Society LSSACD 3 CD: Music and Arts CD 846 CD: Grammofono AB 78577
London September 1967	LSO LSO Chorus Harper, Watts, Young, McIntyre	LP: Decca PFS 4183/DPA 599-600 LP: London SPC 21043 CD: Decca 421 6362

Symphony No 9 "Choral", final movement

L Los Angeles 1945-1946	Hollywood Bowl SO	78: International Artists' Limited edition
LNew York April 1947	NYPSO Westminster Choir Boerner, Merriman, Dame, Duncan	LP: Japanese Stokowski Society JLSS 0019

Piano Concerto No 5 "Emperor"

New York March 1966	American SO Gould	LP: Columbia (USA) ML 6288/MS 6888/MP 3888 LP: CBS 72483/Y4 34640 CD: Sony SM3K 52632/SX17K 52562

Coriolan, Overture

London 1974	LSO	LP: RCA ARL1-0600/AGL1-5247 CD: RCA/BMG 09026 613402/09026 625142

Egmont, Overture

Camden NJ May 1919	Philadelphia Orchestra	Victor unpublished
London January 1973	New Philharmonia	LP: Decca PFS 4342/D94 D2 LP: London SPC 21139

Leonore No 3, Overture

West Ham   National PO   LP: Pye/Nixa PCNHX 6
March 1976   LP: Dell' Arte DA 9003
                                       CD: Pye/Nixa CDPCN 6
                                       CD: EMI CDM 764 1402

First movement from Moonlight Sonata*

New York   His SO   78: Victor unpublished
March 1947   CD: American Stokowski Society LSSACD 3
                                       CD: Music and Arts CD 846

Die Himmel erzählen die Ehre Gottes

London   New SO   LP: Victor LM 2593/LSC 2593
1961   Luboff Choir   CD: RCA/BMG 09026 625992
                                       Arrangement by Luboff/Stott

Turkish March (Die Ruinen von Athen)

New York   His SO   LP: Victor LM 2042
February   LP: Stokowski Society LS 18
1955   Orchestra may have been NBC SO

PAUL BEN HAIM (1897-1974)

From Israel, Suite

New York February 1959	Symphony of the Air	LP: United Artists UAL 7005/UAS 8005

THEODOR BERGER (born 1905)

Rondino giocoso

New York February 1958	His SO	LP: Capitol P 8458/SP 8458 CD: EMI CDM 565 9122

IRVING BERLIN (1888-1989)

God Bless America

New York July 1940	All American SO	78: Columbia (USA) 17204

HECTOR BERLIOZ (1803-1869)

Symphonie fantastique

London June 1968	New Philharmonia	LP: Decca PFS 4160/SDD 495 LP: London SPC 21031 CD: Decca 430 1372/448 9552
LNew York April 1970	American SO	Classical Recordings Archive of America Issued only in tape cassette format

Le carnaval romain, Overture

LPhiladelphia December 1931	Philadelphia Orchestra	LP: Bell Telephone Laboratories BTL 790 Rehearsal performance
West Ham March 1976	National PO	LP: Pye/Nixa PCNHX 6 LP: Dell' Arte DA 9003 CD: Pye/Nixa CDPCN 6 CD: EMI CDM 764 1402

Danse des sylphes (La damnation de Faust)

New York 1951	His SO	LP: Victor LM 9029
London June 1970	LSO	LP: Decca PFS 4220 LP: London SPC 21112/SPC 21059 CD: Decca 433 8762

Marche hongroise (La damnation de Faust)

Camden NJ March 1923	Philadelphia Orchestra	Victor unpublished
Philadelphia October 1927	Philadelphia Orchestra	78: Victor 6823 78: HMV D 1807 LP: Victor VCM 7101 CD: Biddulph WHL 011 CD: Grammofono AB 78586 CD: Magic Talent CD 48015
West Ham November 1975	National PO	LP: Pye/Nixa PCNHX 4 CD: Pye/Nixa CDPCN 4

GEORGES BIZET (1838-1875)

Symphony in C

New York March 1952	His SO	LP: Victor LM 1706 LP: HMV ALP 1181 LP: RCA VIC 1008
London May-June 1977	National PO	LP: CBS 34567/76673 CD: Sony MBK 44894/SBK 48264 Stokowski's final recording sessions

Carmen, abridged version

LLos Angeles July 1946	Hollywood Bowl Orchestra & Chorus Heidt, Koshetz, Vinay, Pease Sung in English	LP: Japanese Stokowski Society JLSS 11/12 CD: Eklipse EKRCD 31

Carmen, Suite

Camden NJ March 1923	Philadelphia Orchestra	Victor unpublished
Philadelphia March-May 1927	Philadelphia Orchestra	78: Victor 6873-6874 78: HMV D 1618 and D 1816 Victor L 1000 LP: American Stokowski Society LSSA 3 CD: Biddulph WHL 012 L 1000 was an experimental 33.1/3 rpm issue (Symphonic transcription disc); Acts 1 and 4 Preludes from this recording: 78: Victor 1356 78: HMV E 531
New York February 1945	New York City SO	78: Victor M 1002 78: HMV DB 9505-9508 45: Victor WDM 1002 LP: Victor LM 1069
West Ham August 1976	National PO	LP: CBS 34503/76587 CD: Sony MYK 37260/MBK 44808

Contents of the recorded Carmen Suite vary, the 1945 version being the most
extended and containing additional items from L'Arlésienne

Carmen, Act 1 Prelude

Camden NJ May 1919	Philadelphia Orchestra	78: Victor 64822/796

Carmen, Marche des contrabandiers and Garde montante

Camden NJ April 1923	Philadelphia Orchestra	78: Victor 66263-66264/1017 78: HMV DA 612

L'Arlésienne, Suite No 1

Philadelphia May 1929	Philadelphia Orchestra	78: Victor M 62 78: HMV D 1801-1803 CD: Biddulph WHL 012
New York February 1952	His SO	LP: Victor LM 1706 LP: HMV ALP 1181 LP: RCA VIC 1008 Adagietto only LP: Victor LM 1875 LP: HMV ALP 1387
West Ham August 1976	National PO	LP: CBS 34503/76587 CD: Sony MYK 37260/MBK 44808

Minuetto (L'Arlésienne, Suite No 1)

Camden NJ May 1919	Philadelphia Orchestra	Victor unpublished

L'Arlésienne, Suite No 2

New York March 1952	His SO	LP: Victor LM 1706 LP: HMV ALP 1181 LP: RCA VIC 1008
West Ham August 1976	National PO	LP: CBS 34503/76587 CD: Sony MYK 37260/MBK 44808

Pastorale (L'Arlésienne, Suite No 2)

Camden NJ January 1922	Philadelphia Orchestra	78: Victor 1113
Philadelphia May 1929	Philadelphia Orchestra	78: Victor M 61 78: HMV D 1803

ERNEST BLOCH (1880-1959)

America, An Epic Rhapsody

New York February 1960	Symphony of the Air American Concert Choir	LP: Vanguard SRV 346/VRS 1056/ VSD 2056/VSL 11020 CD: Vanguard OVC 8014

Symphony for trombone

LHouston Date uncertain	Houston SO Schuman	LP: Japanese Stokowski Society JLSS 0020

Schelomo, Hebrew Rhapsody

Philadelphia March 1940	Philadelphia Orchestra Feuermann	78: Victor M 698 78: HMV DB 5816-5818 LP: Victor LCT 14 LP: RCA Camden CAL 254 LP: Virtuosi (USA) RO32 LGR-9265 CD: Biddulph LAB 042
New York February 1959	Symphony of the Air Niekrug	LP: United Artists UAL 7005/UAS 8005 CD: EMI CMS 565 4272

LUIGI BOCCHERINI (1743-1805)

Minuetto (Quintetto in E)*

Camden NJ January 1922	Philadelphia Orchestra	78: Victor 66058/798 78: HMV 2-947
Philadelphia May 1929	Philadelphia Orchestra	78: Victor 7256 78: HMV D 1864 LP: RCA Camden CAL 120
New York February 1958	His SO	LP: Capitol P 8458/P 8650/SP 8458/SP 8650 LP: EMI SXLP 30174 CD: EMI CDM 565 9122

ALEXANDER BORODIN (1833-1887)

In the Steppes of Central Asia

New York February 1953	His SO	LP: Victor LM 1816/LRM 7056 LP: Quintessence PMC 7026

Nocturne, arranged by Sargent

New York August 1957	His SO	LP: Capitol P 8415/P 8650/SP 8650 /SP 8415 LP: EMI SXLP 30174 CD: EMI CDM 565 9122

Prince Igor, excerpt (No sleep, no rest)

LPhiladelphia January 1962	Philadelphia Orchestra London	LP: Melodram MEL 228

Polovtsian Dances (Prince Igor)*
including Dance of the Polovtsian Maidens

Philadelphia April 1937	Philadelphia Orchestra	78: Victor M 499 78: HMV DB 3232-3233 LP: RCA Camden CAL 203 CD: Dutton CDAX 8009 CD: Biddulph WHL 027
New York February 1950	His SO Chorus	78: Victor 10-4212 78: HMV DA 2073 45: Victor 49-4212/WDM 1386 LP: Victor LM 1054/LRM 7056 LP: RCA CDM 1071/VIC 1043

Polovtsian Dances (Prince Igor), arranged by Rimsky-Korsakov/Glazunov

London June 1969	RPO Chorus	LP: Decca PFS 4189 LP: London SPC 21041/SPC 21111 CD: IMP IMPX 9033 CD: Decca 417 7532/430 4102/ 433 6252/443 8962
LLondon June 1969	RPO Chorus	CD: Music and Arts CD 847

Polovtsian Dances, individual extracts*

Camden NJ October- December 1920	Philadelphia Orchestra	Victor unpublished
Camden NJ April 1922	Philadelphia Orchestra	Victor unpublished
Philadelphia April 1925	Philadelphia Orchestra	78: Victor 6514

JOHANNES BRAHMS (1833-1897)

Symphony No 1

Philadelphia April 1927	Philadelphia Orchestra	78: Victor M 15 78: HMV D 1499-1503 Victor LM 15 LP: Cameo GOCLP 9009 CD: Biddulph WHL 017-018 LM 15 was an experimental 33.1/3 rpm issue (Symphonic transcription disc); M 15 and WHL 017-018 also include Stokowski's spoken outline of themes recorded at the same time
Camden NJ October 1935- January 1936	Philadelphia Orchestra	78: Victor M 301 78: HMV DB 2874-2878 LP: RCA Camden CAL 105
New York July 1941	All American SO	CD: American Stokowski Society LSSACD 4 CD: Music and Arts CD 857
Los Angeles August 1945	Hollywood Bowl SO	78: Victor DM 1402/DV 4 45: Victor WDM 1402 LP: Victor LM 1070 DV 4 was a set of Red Seal Deluxe vinyl discs
LLondon June 1972 (14 June)	LSO	CD: Intaglio INCD 7221
LLondon June 1972 (15 June)	LSO	LP: Decca PFS 4305/OPFS 3-4 LP: London SPC 21090-21091/SPC 21131

Symphony No 1, second movement rehearsal

Stockholm April 1939	Stockholm PO	CD: Bis BISCD 424B

Symphony No 2

Philadelphia April 1929	Philadelphia Orchestra	78: Victor M 82 78: HMV D 1877-1882 LP: Stokowski Society LS 11 CD: Biddulph WHL 017-018
London April 1977	National PO	LP: CBS 35129/76667

Rehearsal sequences of Stokowski with San Francisco SO in Brahms Symphony No 2
issued on CD by Archive Documents ADCD 200-201

Symphony No 3

Philadelphia September 1928	Philadelphia Orchestra	78: Victor M 42 78: HMV D 1769-1773 LP: RCA Camden CAL 164 LP: Stokowski Society LS 1 CD: Biddulph WHL 017-018
Houston March 1959	Houston SO	LP: Everest LPBR 6030/SDBR 3030 LP: World Records T 102/ST 102 LP: Hallmark SHM 551 CD: Bescol CD 517 CD: Everest EVC 9016

Symphony No 3, third movement

Camden NJ May 1921	Philadelphia Orchestra	Victor unpublished
Camden NJ February 1921	Philadelphia Orchestra	Victor unpublished
Camden NJ April 1921	Philadelphia Orchestra	78: Victor 74722/6242

Symphony No 4

Camden NJ April 1931	Philadelphia Orchestra	78: Victor M 108 LP: Neiman Marcus DPM4-0210 M 108 published only in Chile
Camden NJ March-April 1933	Philadelphia Orchestra	78: Victor M 185 Victor LM 185 CD: Biddulph WHL 017-018 LM 185 was an experimental 33.1/3 rpm issue (Symphonic transcription disc)
New York April 1941	All American SO	78: Columbia (USA) M 452 LP: American Stokowski Society LSSA 4 CD: Music and Arts CD 845
LLondon May 1974	New Philharmonia	CD: BBC Radio Classics BBCRD 9107
Walthamstow June 1974	New Philharmonia	LP: RCA ARL1-0719 CD: RCA/BMG 09026 062

Piano Concerto No 1

LNew York	American SO	CD: American Stokowski Society LSSACD 2
October 1969	Ogdon	CD: Music and Arts CD 844
		<u>CD 844 includes rehearsal extracts</u>

Serenade No 1

New York	Symphony	LP: Decca Gold Label DCM 3205
July 1961	of the Air	LP: Varèse DL 710031/DL 10031/VC 81050
		CD: MCA Classics 9826

Menuetto (Serenade No 1)

Camden NJ	Philadelphia	78: Victor 1720
November	Orchestra	78: HMV DA 1462
1934		

Haydn Variations

LChicago	Chicago SO	LP: Stokowski Society LS 4
1962		

Academic Festival Overture

London	New Philharmonia	LP: RCA ARL1-0719
June 1974		CD: RCA/BMG 09026 625142

Tragic Overture

London	National PO	LP: CBS 35129/76667
April 1977		

Hungarian Dance No 1 *

Camden NJ May 1920	Philadelphia Orchestra	78: Victor 1113
Camden NJ November 1922	Philadelphia Orchestra	Victor unpublished
Camden NJ May 1923	Philadelphia Orchestra	Victor unpublished
Camden NJ March 1934	Philadelphia Orchestra	78: Victor 1675 78: HMV DA 1398 45: RCA Camden CAE 192 LP: RCA Camden CAL 123
Los Angeles August 1946	Hollywood Bowl SO	78: Victor 10-1302 45: Victor 49-1293
West Ham November 1975	National PO	LP: Pye/Nixa PCNHX 4 CD: Pye/Nixa CDPCN 4

Hungarian Dance No 5 *

| Camden NJ
October
1917 | Philadelphia
Orchestra | 78: Victor 64752/797
LP: Stokowski Society LS 3
Stokowski's first recording sessions |

Hungarian Dance No 6 *

| Camden NJ
October
1917 | Philadelphia
Orchestra | 78: Victor 64753/797
LP: Stokowski Society LS 3
Stokowski's first recording sessions |

HAVERGAL BRIAN (1876-1972)

Symphony No 28

| London
October
1973 | New Philharmonia | LP: Aries LP 1607
Labelled with the pseudonyms Hamburg PO/
Werner |

BENJAMIN BRITTEN (1913-1976)

Variations and Fugue on a theme of Purcell

LLondon July 1963	BBC SO	CD: Music and Arts CD 787

WILLIAM BYRD (1543-1623)

Pavan and Gigue (Fitzwilliam Virginal Book)*

Philadelphia April 1937	Philadelphia Orchestra	78: Victor 1943 78: HMV DA 1637 LP: American Stokowski Society LSSA 5
L London June 1972	LSO	LP: Decca PFS 4351 LP: London SPC 21130 CD: Decca 433 8762

THOMAS CANNING (born 1911)

Fantasy on a hymn tune of Justin Morgan

Houston April 1960	Houston SO	LP: Everest LPBR 6070/SDBR 3070 LP: World Records TP 79/PE 751 LP: Vox STGBY 515040 LP: Dell' Arte DA 9013 CD: Everest EVC 9004 DA 9013 was a 45rpm transfer

JOSEPH CANTELOUBE (1879-1957)

Chants d'Auvergne, selection

New York 1964	American SO Moffo	LP: Victor LSC 2795/LSB 4114 CD: RCA/BMG 7831-2-RG/GD 87831/ 09026 626002

MARC ANTONIO CESTI (1618-1699)

Tu moncavi a tormentarmi, crudelissima speranza*

New York February 1952	His SO	LP: Victor LM 1721/LM 1875 LP: HMV ALP 1387
New York December 1958	Symphony of the Air	LP: United Artists UAL 7001/UAS 8001 CD: EMI CMS 565 4272

EMMANUEL CHABRIER (1841-1894)

Espana

Camden NJ May 1919	Philadelphia Orchestra	78: Victor 76421/6241 78: HMV DB 384
West Ham November 1975	National PO	LP: Pye/Nixa PCNHX 4 CD: Pye/Nixa CDPCN 4 CD: EMI CDM 764 1402

ERNEST CHAUSSON (1855-1899)

Poème for violin and orchestra

LLos Angeles July 1945	Hollywood Bowl SO Seidel	CD: Eklipse EKRCD 1401

FREDERIC CHOPIN (1810–1849)

Les sylphides, selection

New York May 1950	His SO	78: Victor DM 1394 78: HMV DB 21255 45: Victor WDM 1394 LP: Victor LRM 7022/VIC 1020

Mazurka in A minor*

Philadelphia November 1937	Philadelphia Orchestra	78: Victor 1855 78: HMV DA 1638 CD: Biddulph WHL 027
Houston April 1960	Houston	LP: Everest LPBR 6070/SDBR 3070 LP: World Records TP 79 LP: Vox STGBY 515040
London June 1972	LSO	LP: Decca PFS 4351 LP: London SPC 21130 CD: Decca 433 8762

Mazurka in B flat minor*

Philadelphia December 1937	Philadelphia Orchestra	78: Victor M 841 CD: Biddulph WHL 027
West Ham July 1976	National PO	LP: CBS 34543/73589

Prelude in D minor*

Philadelphia November 1937	Philadelphia Orchestra	78: Victor 1998 78: HMV DA 1639 CD: Biddulph WHL 027 DA 1639 remained unpublished
New York 1950	His SO	LP: Victor LM 1238
Houston April 1960	Houston SO	LP: Everest LPBR 6070/SDBR 3070 LP: World Records TP 79 LP: Vox STGBY 515040
West Ham July 1976	National PO	LP: CBS 34543/73589

Prelude in E minor*

Camden NJ April 1922	Philadelphia Orchestra	Victor unpublished
Camden NJ November 1922	Philadelphia Orchestra	78: Victor 1111
New York 1950	His SO	LP: Victor LM 1238

Waltz in C sharp minor*

Houston April 1960	Houston SO	LP: Everest LPBR 6070/SDBR 3070 LP: World Records TP 79 LP: Vox STGBY 515040

JEREMIAH CLARKE (1674-1707)

Trumpet Voluntary*

Camden NJ December 1924	Philadelphia Orchestra	Victor unpublished
Los Angeles August 1946	Hollywood Bowl SO	78: Victor 11-9419 78: HMV DB 6737 LP: RCA Camden CAL 153
L London June 1972	LSO	LP: Decca PFS 4351 LP: London SPC 21130 CD: IMP IMPX 9033 CD: Decca 433 8762

AARON COPLAND (1900-1990)

Prairie Night and Celebration Dance (Billy the Kid)

New York 1947	NYPSO	LP: Columbia (USA) ML 2167

ARCANGELO CORELLI (1653-1713)

Concerto grosso in G minor "Christmas Concerto"*

New York April 1967	His SO	LP: Bach Guild 70696 LP: Vanguard SRV 363 CD: Vanguard VBD 363/OVC 8009

HENRY COWELL (1897-1965)

Persian Set

| New York | Chamber Orchestra | LP: Composers' Recordings CRI 114 |
| April 1957 | Soloists | |

Tales of our Countryside, for piano and orchestra

| New York | All American SO | 78: Columbia (USA) X 235 |
| July 1941 | Cowell | LP: American Stokowski Society LSSA 6 |

PAUL CRESTON (1906-1985)

Scherzo (Symphony No 1)

| New York | All American SO | 78: Columbia (USA) 11713 |
| July 1941 | | LP: American Stokowski Society LSSA 6 |

LUIGI DALLAPICCOLA (1904-1975)

Il prigionero

LNew York	New York City	LP: Private Edition MR 2009
1960	Opera Orchestra	
	McKnight, Cassilly,	
	Treigle	

WILLIAM DAWSON (1898-1990)

Negro Folk Symphony

New York	American SO	LP: Decca Gold Label DL 710077/DL 10077
July 1963		LP: Brunswick AXA 4520/SXA 4520
		LP: Varèse VC 81056
		CD: MCA Classics 9826

CLAUDE DEBUSSY (1862-1918)

La mer

London June 1970	LSO	LP: Decca PFS 4220/SDD 455 LP: London SPC 21059/SPC 21109 CD: Decca 417 7792

Prélude à l'après-midi d'un faune

Camden NJ November 1917	Philadelphia Orchestra	Victor unpublished
Camden NJ November 1921	Philadelphia Orchestra	Victor unpublished
Camden NJ April 1924	Philadelphia Orchestra	78: Victor 6481 78: HMV 4-0642/DB 840
Philadelphia March 1927	Philadelphia Orchestra	78: Victor 6696 78: HMV D 1768
Philadelphia March 1940	Philadelphia Orchestra	CD: Biddulph WHL 013
Philadelphia December 1940	Philadelphia Orchestra	78: Victor 17700
New York October 1949	His SO	78: Victor 12-1119 78: HMV DB 21297 45: Victor 49-0942 LP: Victor LM 1154/LRM 7024 LP: Stokowski Society LS 6
LFrankfurt May 1955	Orchestra of Hessischer Rundfunk	CD: Music and Arts CD 778
New York January 1957	His SO	LP: Capitol P 8399/P 8673/SP 8673/SP 8399 LP: Angel 6094 LP: EMI SMFP 2145 CD: EMI CDM 769 1162/CDM 565 6142
LLondon June 1972	LSO	LP: Decca OPFS 3-4/SDD 455/D94 D2/ DPA 601-602 LP: London SPC 21090-21091/SPC 21109 CD: Decca 433 8762

Nuages (Nocturnes)

Philadelphia May 1929	Philadelphia Orchestra	78: Victor M 116 78: HMV D 1614
Philadelphia November 1937	Philadelphia Orchestra	78: Victor M 630 78: HMV DB 3596 LP: RCA Camden CAL 140 CD: Biddulph WHL 013
New York October- November 1950	His SO	45: Victor WDM 1560 LP: Victor LM 1154/LM 6129 LP: Stokowski Society LS 6
London June 1957	LSO	LP: Capitol P 8520/SP 8520 LP: Angel 60104 CD: EMI CDC 747 4232
LLeipzig June 1959	Gewandhaus Orchestra	CD: Music and Arts CD 280

Fêtes (Nocturnes)

Camden NJ April 1922	Philadelphia Orchestra	Victor unpublished
Philadelphia October 1927	Philadelphia Orchestra	78: Victor 1309 78: HMV E 507
Philadelphia December 1937- April 1939	Philadelphia Orchestra	78: Victor M 630 78: HMV DA 1742 LP: RCA Camden CAL 140 CD: Biddulph WHL 013
New York October- November 1950	His SO	45: Victor WDM 1560 45: HMV 7ER 5011 LP: Victor LM 1154 LP: Stokowski Society LS 6
London June 1957	LSO	LP: Capitol P 8520/SP 8520/P 8673/SP 8673 LP: Angel 60104 CD: EMI CDC 747 4232
LLeipzig June 1959	Gewandhaus Orchestra	CD: Music and Arts CD 280

Sirènes (Nocturnes)

Philadelphia April 1939	Philadelphia Orchestra Chorus	78: Victor M 630 78: HMV DB 3981-3982 LP: RCA Camden CAL 140 CD: Biddulph WHL 013
New York October- November 1950	His SO Shaw Chorale	45: Victor WDM 1560 LP: Victor LM 1154 LP: Stokowski Society LS 6
London June 1957	LSO BBC Chorus	LP: Capitol P 8520/SP 8520 LP: Angel 60104 CD: EMI CDC 747 4232
LLeipzig June 1959	Gewandhaus Orchestra Chorus	CD: Music and Arts CD 280

Ibéria (Images pour orchestre)

Paris May 1958	Orchestre National	LP: Capitol P 8463/SP 8463 LP: Angel 60102 LP: EMI SXLP 30263 CD: EMI CDC 747 4232/CDM 565 4222
LParis May 1958	Orchestre National	CD: Music and Arts CD 778

Danse sacrée et danse profane

Camden NJ April 1931	Philadelphia Orchestra Phillips	78: Victor M 116 78: HMV DB 1642-1643 CD: Biddulph WHL 013

Childrens' Corner, Suite arranged by Caplet

New York March 1949	His SO	78: Victor DM 1327 45: Victor WDM 1327 LP: Victor LM 9/LM 9023 LP: RCA ANL1-2604
New York April 1959	Stadium SO	LP: Everest LPBR 6108/SDBR 3108/SDBR 3327 LP: World Records T 173/ST 173 CD: Everest EVC 9023 This version contains three of the movements only

Clair de lune*

Philadelphia April 1937	Philadelphia Orchestra	78: Victor 1812 78: HMV DA 1634 V-Disc 122A 45: RCA Camden CAE 188 LP: RCA Camden CAL 123
New York March 1947	His SO	78: Victor 10-1534 45: Victor 49-1009/ERA 47 45: HMV 7ER 5011 LP: Victor LM 1154 LP: Stokowski Society LS 6
New York January 1957	His SO	LP: Capitol P 8399/P 8694/SP 8694/SP 8399 LP: Angel 6094 LP: EMI SMFP 2145 CD: EMI CDM 769 1162/CDM 565 6142
West Ham July 1976	National PO	LP: CBS 34543/73589

La cathédrale engloutie*

Camden NJ April 1930	Philadelphia Orchestra	78: Victor M 116 CD: Biddulph WHL 013
London September 1965	New Philharmonia	LP: Decca LK 4766/PFS 4095/SDD 455 LP: London PM 55004/SPC 21006 CD: Decca 417 7792

Soirée dans Grenade*

Philadelphia December 1940	Philadelphia Orchestra	CD: Biddulph WHL 013
LPhiladelphia March 1962	Philadelphia Orchestra	CD: Japanese Stokowski Society LSCD 23/24
West Ham July 1976	National PO	LP: CBS 34543/73589

LEO DELIBES (1836-1891)

Sylvia, selection

| New York
May 1950 | His SO | 78: Victor DM 1394
45: Victor WDM 1394
LP: Victor LM 1083/LRY 8000
LP: HMV ALP 1133
LP: RCA VIC 1020 |

ROBERT EMMETT DOLAN (1908-1972)

A Message for Liza

| Los Angeles
August 1946 | Hollywood Bowl SO | 78: Victor 10-1302
45: Victor 49-1293 |

ARCADY DUBENSKY (1890-1966)

The Raven, melodrama for speaker and orchestra

Camden NJ	Philadelphia	78: Victor 2000-2001
December	Orchestra	Victor L 1006
1932	De Loache	CD: Stokowski Society LSCD 20
		CD: Cala CACD 0501
		L 1006 was an experimental 33.1/3 rpm
		issue (Symphonic transcription disc)

PAUL DUKAS (1865-1935)

L'apprenti sorcier

Philadelphia	Philadelphia	78: Victor M 717
November	Orchestra	78: HMV DB 3533-3534
1937		LP: RCA Camden CAL 118
		CD: Biddulph WHL 011
		CD: Pearl GEMMCD 9488
		CD: Magic Talent CD 48002
Philadelphia	Philadelphia	Fantasia soundtrack recording
April 1939	Orchestra	LP: Top Rank 30-003
		LP: Disneyland WDX 101
		LP: Buena Vista BVS 101
		CD: Buena Vista CD 020/60007
		VHS Video: Buena Vista D211 322

Fanfare (La péri)

New York	His SO	LP: Capitol P 8385/P 8673/SP 8673
February 1957		LP: Angel 6094
		CD: EMI CDM 565 6142

HENRI DUPARC (1848-1933)

Extase*

London	LSO	LP: Decca PFS 4351
June 1972		LP: London SPC 21130
		CD: Decca 433 8762

ANTONIN DVORAK (1841-1904)

Symphony No 9 "From the New World"

Philadelphia May-December 1925	Philadelphia Orchestra	78: Victor 6565-6569
Philadelphia October 1927	Philadelphia Orchestra	78: Victor M 1 78: Victor D 1893-1897 LP: RCA CRL2-0334 CD: Biddulph WHL 027
Camden NJ October 1934	Philadelphia	78: Victor M 273 78: HMV DB 2543-2547 LP: RCA Camden CAL 104/CDN 1008 LP: Supraphon 1010 3351-1010 3352 CD: Japanese Stokowski Society LSCD 25 CD: Grammofono AB 78552
New York July 1940	All American SO	78: Columbia (USA) M 416 CD: Music and Arts CD 841
New York December 1947	His SO	78: Victor M 1248/V-25 45: Victor WDM 1248 LP: Victor LM 1013
Walthamstow July 1973	New Philharmonia	LP: RCA CRL2-0334 CD: RCA/BMG 09026 626012

Symphony No 9 "From the New World", outline of themes

Philadelphia October 1927	78: Victor 6743 CD: Biddulph WHL 027 <u>Stokowski's spoken introduction to his 1927 recording of the symphony</u>

Symphony No 9 "From the New World", third movement

Camden NJ December 1917	Philadelphia Orchestra	Victor unpublished

Symphony No 9 "From the New World", second movement

Camden NJ May 1920	Philadelphia Orchestra	Victor unpublished

Serenade for strings

| London | RPO | LP: Desmar DSM 1011 |
| August 1975 | | LP: Teldec 642.631 |

Slavonic Dance No 10 in E minor

L Prague	Czech PO	LP: Decca PFS 4333/PFS 4351
September		LP: London SPC 21117/SPC 21130
1972		CD: IMP IMPX 9033
		CD: Decca 433 8762

HENRY EICHHEIM (1870–1942)

Chinese Rhapsody

| Camden NJ | Philadelphia | Victor unpublished |
| May 1923 | Orchestra | |

Japanese Nocturne

| Camden NJ | Philadelphia | Victor unpublished |
| May 1923 | Orchestra | |

Philadelphia	Philadelphia	78: Victor 7260
April 1929	Orchestra	78: HMV D 1936
		CD: Stokowski Society LSCD 20
		CD: Cala CACD 0501

Bali (Symphonic Variations)

Camden NJ	Philadelphia	78: Victor 14141–14142
November	Orchestra	CD: Stokowski Society LSCD 20
1934		CD: Cala CACD 0501

EDWARD ELGAR (1857-1934)

Enigma Variations

L Prague   Czech PO   LP: Decca PFS 4333/D94 D2
September   LP: London SPC 21136
1972   <u>Nimrod only</u>
                                LP: Decca PFS 4351
                                LP: London SPC 21112/SPC 21130
                                CD: IMP IMPX 9033
                                CD: Decca 433 8762

GEORGE ENESCU (1881-1955)

Rumanian Rhapsody No 1

New York   His SO   78: Victor 12-0069
February   78: HMV DB 6828
1947   45: Victor 49-0127
                                LP: Stokowski Society LS 17

New York   His SO   LP: Victor LM 1878
April-   LP: Quintessence PMC 7023
October
1953

New York   RCA Victor   LP: Victor LM 2471/LSC 2471/VCS 7077
March 1961   Orchestra   LP: RCA RB 16259/SB 2130/AGL1-5259
                                CD: RCA/BMG 09026 615032/09026 626022

Rumanian Rhapsody No 2

New York   His SO   LP: Victor LM 1878
April-   LP: Quintessence PMC 7023
October
1953

MANUEL DE FALLA (1876-1946)

El amor brujo

Los Angeles August 1946	Hollywood Bowl SO Merriman	78: Victor M 1089 78: HMV DB 21039-21041 45: Victor WDM 1089 LP: Victor LM 1054/VIC 1043/CDM 1071
Philadelphia February 1960	Philadelphia Orchestra Verrett	LP: Columbia (USA) MS 6147/Y 32368 LP: CBS 61288 CD: Sony MPK 46449 Stokowski's first stereo recording with the Philadelphia Orchestra
LPhiladelphia February 1960	Philadelphia Orchestra Verrett	LP: Longanesi GCL 61
LLondon 1964	BBC SO Lane	CD: Music and Arts CD 770

Danza ritual del fuego (El amor brujo)

New York July 1941	All American SO	78: Columbia (USA) 11879

El sombrero de 3 picos, Suite

San Francisco December 1953	San Francisco Symphony Orchestra	Victor unpublished

Noches en los jardines de Espana

LNew York November 1949	NYPSO Kapell	LP: New York Philharmonic NYP 821-822 LP: Discocorp MLG 71 CD: Japanese Stokowski Society LSCD 25 CD: Music and Arts CD 771

Danza espanol (La vida breve)

Philadelphia December 1928	Philadelphia Orchestra	78: Victor M 46 78: HMV DB 1949 CD: Cala CACD 0501

HAROLD FARBERMAN (born 1929)

Evolution, Section 1

New York February 1957	His SO	LP: Capitol P 8385 CD: EMI CDM 565 6142

STEPHEN FOSTER (1826-1864)

Oh Susanna!*

Philadelphia May 1929	Philadelphia Orchestra	78: Victor unpublished CD: Cala CACD 0502

CESAR FRANCK (1822-1890)

Symphony in D minor

Philadelphia October 1927	Philadelphia Orchestra	78: Victor M 22 78: HMV D 1404-1408 Victor LM 22 LP: American Stokowski Society LSSA 3 LM 22 was an experimental 33.1/3 rpm issue (Symphonic transcription disc); M 22 and LSSA 3 also include Stokowski's spoken outline of themes of the symphony recorded at the same time
Camden NJ December 1935- January 1936	Philadelphia Orchestra	78: Victor M 300 78: HMV DB 3226-3231 CD: Biddulph WHL 011
Hilversum August 1970	Hilversum RO	LP: Decca PFS 4218 LP: London SPC 21061
LHilversum August 1970	Hilversum RO	CD: Music and Arts CD 657 Third movement CD: RCA/BMG 74321 308892

Symphony in D minor, second movement

Camden NJ April 1922	Philadelphia Orchestra	Victor unpublished

Andante from Grande pièce symphonique, arranged by O'Connell

Philadelphia April 1937	Philadelphia Orchestra	78: Victor 14947 LP: American Stokowski Society LSSA 3 CD: Biddulph WHL 011

Panis angelicus*

Philadelphia January 1936	Philadelphia Orchestra	78: Victor M 300 78: HMV DB 3318 LP: American Stokowski Society LSSA 3 CD: Biddulph WHL 011

GIROLAMO FRESCOBALDI (1583-1643)

Gagliarda*

Camden NJ October 1934	Philadelphia Orchestra	78: Victor 1985 78: HMV DA 1606 LP: Americam Stokowski Society LSSA 5
New York April 1952	His SO	LP: Victor LM 1721/LM 1875 LP: HMV ALP 1387
New York December 1958	Symphony of the Air	LP: United Artists UAL 7001/UAS 8001/ UAS 8003 CD: EMI CMS 565 4272

GIOVANNI GABRIELI (1557-1612)

Sonata pian e forte (Sacrae symphoniae), arranged by Stein

New York	Symphony	LP: United Artists UAL 7001/UAS 8001
December	of the Air	CD: EMI CMS 565 4272
1958		

Canzon quarti toni a 15*; In ecclesiis benedicte Dominus*

New York	His SO	LP: Victor LM 1721
March 1952		

ALEXANDER GLAZUNOV (1865-1936)

Violin Concerto

LLondon	LSO	CD: Intaglio INCD 7221
June 1972	Marcovici	
(14 June)		
LLondon	LSO	LP: Decca OPFS 3-4
June 1972	Markovici	LP: London SPC 21090-21091
(15 June)		

Danse orientale (Scènes de ballet)

Philadelphia	Philadelphia	78: Victor 1335
May 1927	Orchestra	78: HMV E 521

REINHOLD GLIERE (1875-1956)

Symphony No 3 "Ilya Mourometz" *

Philadelphia March 1940	Philadelphia Orchestra	78: Victor M 841 45: Victor WCT 1106 LP: Victor LCT 1106 CD: Biddulph WHL 005
New York March 1957	Houston SO	LP: Capitol P 8402/SP 8402 LP: Angel 60089 CD: EMI CDM 565 0742

Russian Sailors' Dance (The Red Poppy)

Camden NJ March 1934	Philadelphia Orchestra	78: Victor 1675 78: HMV DA 1398 LP: Victor VCM 7101/VIC 6060 CD: Biddulph WHL 005 CD: Magic Talent CD 48015
New York February 1953	His SO	LP: Victor LM 1816 LP: Quintessence PMC 7026

MIKHAIL GLINKA (1804-1857)

Kamarinskaya

LLondon June 1969	RPO	CD: Music and Arts CD 847

CHRISTOPH WILLIBALD GLUCK (1714-1787)

Armide, Musette and Sicilienne*

New York	His SO	LP: Capitol P 8415/P 8650/SP 8650/SP 8415
August 1957		LP: Angel 6094
		CD: EMI CDM 565 9122

Iphigénie en Aulide, Lento*

New York	His SO	LP: Capitol P 8415/P 8650/SP 8650/SP 8415
August 1957		LP: Angel 6094
		CD: EMI CDM 565 9122

Orfeo ed Euridice, Dance of the Blessed Spirits*

Camden NJ	Philadelphia	78: Victor 74567/6238
November	Orchestra	LP: Stokowski Society LS 3
1917		
New York	His SO	LP: Capitol P 8458/P 8650/SP 8458/SP 8650
February 1958		CD: EMI CDM 565 9122

Orfeo ed Euridice, Dance of the Blessed Spirits, choral version arranged by Luboff

London	New SO	LP: Victor LM 2593/LSC 2593
1961	Luboff Choir	CD: RCA/BMG 09026 625992

ROGER GOEB (born 1917)

Symphony No 3

New York	His SO	45: Victor WDM 1727
April 1952		LP: Victor LM 1727
		LP: Composers' Recordings CRI 120

MORTON GOULD (1913–1996)

Dance Variations

San Francisco November 1953	San Francisco SO Whittemore, Lowe	LP: Victor LM 1858

Guaracha (Latin–American Symphonette No 4)

New York July 1941	All American SO	78: Columbia (USA) 11713 LP: American Stokowski Society LSSA 6

CHARLES GOUNOD (1818–1893)

Faust, Waltz

Camden NJ October 1922	Philadelphia Orchestra	Victor unpublished
Camden NJ November 1922	Philadelphia Orchestra	Victor unpublished
Camden December 1922	Philadelphia Orchestra	Victor unpublished
Camden NJ May 1923	Philadelphia Orchestra	78: Victor 66161/944 78: HMV DA 562 LP: Stokowski Society LS 3

Faust, excerpt (Vous qui faites l'endormie)

L Philadelphia January 1962	Philadelphia Orchestra London	LP: Melodram MEL 228

PERCY GRAINGER (1882-1961)

1.Country Gardens; 2.Shepherd's Hey; 3.Mock Morris; 4.Handel in the Strand;
5.Irish Tune from County Derry; 6.Molly on the shore; 7.Early one morning

New York	His SO	45: HMV 7ER 5046 (3,4,5,6)
May-	Grainger	LP: Victor LM 1238/ARL1-3059/RL 10168
November		
1950		

My Robin is to the green wood gone

New York	His SO	Victor unpublished
May 1950	Grainger	

ENRIQUE GRANADOS (1867-1916)

Goyescas, Intermezzo

New York	His SO	78: Victor 12-0470/18-0169
December		78: HMV DB 6915
1947		45: Victor 49-0882
		LP: Victor LM 9029/LM 151
		LP: Stokowski Society LS 17

EDVARD GRIEG (1843-1907)

Piano Concerto

LLos Angeles	Hollywood Bowl SO	LP: International Piano Archives IPA 508
July 1945	Grainger	

Peer Gynt, Anitra's Dance

Camden NJ	Philadelphia	78: Victor 64768/799
November	Orchestra	LP: Stokowski Society LS 3
1917		

Jeg elsker dig

New York	Melchior	LP: Ed Smith EJS 322
1963	American SO	

CHARLES GRIFFES (1884-1920)

The White Peacock (Roman Sketches)

New York   NYPSO   78: Columbia (USA) 19012
November   LP: Columbia (USA) ML 2167
1947

FRANZ GRUBER (1787-1863)

Stille Nacht, heilige Nacht

Camden NJ   Stokowski Chorus   Victor unpublished
June 1922   Experimental recording: versions recorded
                                            with and without Stokowski playing organ

GEORGE FRIDERIC HANDEL (1685-1759)

Alcina, Tamburino*

New York   His SO   LP: Capitol P 8458/SP 8458
February 1958   LP: EMI SXLP 30174
                                            CD: EMI CDM 565 9122

Concerto in B flat

LNew York   NYPSO   LP: New York Philharmonic NYP 821-822
November   Landowska   LP: Discocorp BWS 720
1949   CD: Japanese Stokowski Society LSCD 25

Messiah, selections

London   LSO   LP: Decca LK 4840/PFS 4113/SPA 284
September   LSO Chorus   LP: London SPC 21014
1966   Armstrong, Procter,   CD: IMP IMPX 9007
                 Bowen, Cameron   CD: Decca 433 8742

Messiah, Pastoral symphony*

Camden NJ March 1930	Philadelphia Orchestra	78: Victor 7316 78: HMV D 1938 LP: RCA Camden CAL 120 CD: Cala CACD 0502
New York March 1947	His SO	78: Victor 11-9837 45: Victor 49-0974/ERA 119

Music for the Royal Fireworks

New York April 1961	RCA Victor Orchestra	LP: Victor LM 2612/LSC 2612/VICS 1513 LP: RCA RB 6522/SB 6522/AGL1-2704/VL42054 LP: Contour CCV 5002 CD: RCA/BMG 7817-2-RV/09026 626052

Overture in D minor (Chandos Anthem No 2)*

Camden NJ December 1935	Philadelphia Orchestra	78: Victor 1798 78: HMV DA 1556 LP: American Stokowski Society LSSA 5

Serse, Largo*

Camden NJ May 1919	Philadelphia Orchestra	Victor unpublished Co-arranger was Cailliet
London 1961	New SO Luboff Choir	LP: Victor LM 2593/LSC 2593/VCS 7077 LP: Quintessence PMC 7019 CD: RCA/BMG 09026 625992 This version arranged by Luboff/Stott

Water Music, Suite*

Camden NJ April 1934	Philadelphia Orchestra	78: Victor 8550-8551 78: HMV DB 2528-2529 LP: American Stokowski Society LSSA 5 Some sections revert to the standard Harty arrangement
New York April 1961	RCA Victor Orchestra	LP: Victor LM 2612/LSC 2612/VCS 7077 LP: RCA RB 6522/SB 6522/VICS 1513/ AGL1-2704/VL 42054 LP: Contour CCV 5002 CD: RCA/BMG 7817-2-RV/09026 625992 Different selection and arrangements to the 1934 recording

LOU HARRISON (born 1917)

Suite for violin, piano and small orchestra

New York October 1952	His SO A.& M.Ajemian	LP: Victor LM 1785 LP: Composers' Recordings CRI 114

JOSEF HAYDN (1732-1809)

Symphony No 53 "L'imperiale"

New York May 1949	His SO	78: Victor DM 1352 LP: Victor LM 1073 LP: Stokowski Society LS 18

Andante cantabile (String Quartet op 3 no 5)*

Camden NJ December 1924	Philadelphia Orchestra	Victor unpublished
Philadelphia May 1929	Philadelphia Orchestra	78: Victor 7256 78: HMV D 1864/D 1995 LP: RCA Camden CAL 120
Los Angeles August 1946	Hollywood Bowl SO	78: Victor 11-9419 78: HMV DB 6737
West Ham November 1975	National PO	LP: Pye/Nixa PCNHX 4 CD: Pye/Nixa PCPCN 4

PAUL HINDEMITH (1895-1963)

Piano Concerto

Camden NJ	Philadelphia	Victor unpublished
December	Orchestra	
1932	Nortch	

Violin Concerto

L New York	New York City SO	LP: Town Hall S 32
January	Gross	
1945		

GUSTAV HOLST (1874-1934)

The Planets

Hollywood	Los Angeles PO	LP: Capitol P 8389/SP 8389
September 1956	Wagner Chorale	LP: Angel 60175
		LP: EMI SMFP 2134
		CD: EMI CDM 565 4232

ENGERLBERT HUMPERDINCK (1854-1921)

Hänsel und Gretel, Overture

New York	His SO	78: Victor 12-1321
September		78: HMV DB 21256
1949		45: Victor 49-1376
		45: HMV 7ER 5016
		LP: Victor LM 2042

Hänsel und Gretel, Evening Prayer arranged by Luboff

London	New SO	LP: Victor LM 2593/LSC 2593
1961	Luboff Choir	LP: Quintessence PMC 7019
		CD: RCA/BMG 09026 625992

JACQUES IBERT (1890-1962)

Escales

New York 1951	His SO	LP: Victor LM 9029/LM 6129 LP: Stokowski Society LS 17
Paris May 1958	Orchestre National	LP: Capitol P 8463/SP 8463 LP: Angel 60102 LP: EMI SXLP 30263 CD: EMI CDM 565 4222
LParis May 1958	Orchestre	CD: Music and Arts CD 778

MIKHAIL IPPOLITOV-IVANOV (1859-1935)

Procession of the Sardar (Caucasian Sketches)

Philadelphia October 1927	Philadelphia Orchestra	78: Victor 1335 78: HMV E 521 LP: RCA VCM 7101/VIC 6060 LP: RCA Camden CAL 123 CD: Biddulph WHL 005 CD: Magic Talent CD 48015
West Ham November 1975	National PO	LP: Pye/Nixa PCNHX 4 CD: Pye/Nixa CDPCN 4 CD: EMI CDM 764 1402

In the Village (Caucasian Sketches)

Philadelphia May 1925	Philadelphia Orchestra	78: Victor 6514 CD: Biddulph WHL 005
New York November 1947	NYPSO	78: Columbia (USA) M 729

In a Mountain Pass; March of the Caucasian Chiefs (Caucasian Sketches)

Camden NJ April 1922	Philadelphia Orchestra	Victor unpublished

CHARLES IVES (1874–1954)

Symphony No 4

New York April 1965	American SO Schola Cantorum	LP: Columbia (USA) ML 6175/MS 6775 LP: CBS 72403/77424 CD: Sony MPK 46726

Orchestral Set No 2

London June 1970	LSO	LP: Decca PFS 4203 LP: London SPC 21060 CD: Decca 433 0172/448 9562
LLondon June 1970	LSO	CD: Intaglio INCD 742 CD: Music and Arts CD 787

The Unanswered Question

LTokyo July 1965	Japan PO	CD: Music and Arts CD 787

Robert Browning Overture

New York December 1966	American SO	LP: Columbia (USA) ML 6415/MS 7015 LP: CBS 72646 CD: Sony MPK 46726

4 Songs for chorus and orchestra

New York October 1967	American SO and Chorus	LP: CBS M4-32504 CD: Sony MPK 46726

WERNER JOSTEN (1885–1963)

Concerto sacro I-II

New York	American SO	LP: Composers' Recordings CRI 100
1965	Del Tredici	CD: Composers' Recordings CRI 597

Canzona seria

New York	American SO	LP: Composers' Recordings CRI 267
March 1971		CD: Composers' Recordings CRI 597

Jungle, tone poem

New York	American SO	LP: Composers' Recordings CRI 267
March 1971		CD: Composers' Recordings CRI 597

ROBERT KELLY (born 1916)

Sunset Reflections (Adironack Suite)

New York	NBC SO	78: Victor unpublished
November		CD: Cala CACD 0502
1941		

FRANCIS SCOTT KEY (1779–1843)

The Star-spangled Banner, march*

New York	All American SO	78: Columbia (USA) 17204
July 1940		

ARAM KHACHATURIAN (1903–1978)

Symphony No 2 "The Bell"

New York December 1958	Symphony of the Air	LP: United Artists UAL 7001/UAS 8001 CD: EMI CMS 565 4273

Symphony No 3

Chicago February 1968	Chicago SO	LP: RCA LSC 3067/SB 6804/GL 42923 CD: RCA/BMG 09026 625162

Masquerade, Suite

New York November 1947	NYPSO	78: Columbia (USA) M 729 LP: Columbia (USA) ML 4071

OTTO KLEMPERER (1885–1973)

Merry Waltz (Das Ziel)

LLondon May 1974	New Philharmonia	CD: BBC Radio Classics BBCRD 9107

ZOLTAN KODALY (1882–1967)

Hary Janos, Suite

Budapest February· 1967	Hungarian RO	LP: Stokowski Society LS 2 CD: Music and Arts CD 771

Te Deum

New York 1968	Youth Performers' Orchestra & Chorus Soloists	LP: Audio EC 68006 CD: Music and Arts CD 771

EDOUARD LALO (1823-1892)

Symphonie espagnole

LNew York January 1947	NYPSO Thibaud	LP: Discocorp IGI 373

KURT LEIMER (1922-1974)

Piano Concerto No 4

New York March 1959	Symphony of the Air Leimer	LP: EMI 1C 063 29030

ANATOL LIADOV (1885-1914)

8 chants populaires russes

Camden NJ March 1934	Philadelphia Orchestra	78: Victor 1681/8491 78: HMV DA 1415/DB 2443 45: RCA Camden CAE 256 CD: Pearl GEMMCD 9031 CD: Iron Needle IN 1334 <u>1681 and DA 1415 contained only Légende des oiseaux, Berceuse and Ronde</u>

4 chants populaires russes

LLondon June 1969	RPO	CD: Music and Arts CD 847

Dance of the Amazon

Camden NJ December 1924	Philadelphia Orchestra	78: Victor 1112 LP: Stokowski Society LS 3

FRANZ LISZT (1811-1886)

Les Préludes

New York December 1947	His SO	78: Victor DM 1277 45: Victor WDM 1277 LP: Victor LM 1073 LP: Stokowski Society LS 8

Hungarian Rhapsody No 1

New York February 1955	NBC SO	LP: Victor LM 1878 LP: Quintessence PMC 7023

Hungarian Rhapsody No 2

Camden NJ May 1920	Philadelphia Orchestra	78: Victor 74647/6236
Philadelphia November 1926- March 1927	Philadelphia Orchestra	78: Victor 6652 78: HMV D 1296 LP: Victor VCM 7101/VIC 6060 CD: Biddulph WHL 027 CD: Grammofono AB 78552 CD: Magic Talent CD 48015
Philadelphia November 1936	Philadelphia Orchestra	78: Victor 14422 78: HMV DB 3086
New York July 1941	All American SO	78: Columbia (USA) 11646
New York February 1955	NBC SO	LP: Victor LM 1878 LP: Quintessence PMC 7023
New York March 1961	RCA Victor Orchestra	LP: Victor LM 2471/LSC 2471/VCS 7077 LP: RCA RB 16259/SB 2130/AGL1-5259 CD: RCA/BMG 09026 615032/09026 626022

Hungarian Rhapsody No 3

New York February 1955	NBC SO	LP: Victor LM 1878 LP: Quintessence PMC 7023

CHARLES LOEFFLER (1861-1935)

A Pagan Poem

New York	His SO	LP: Capitol P 8433/SP 8433
January 1958		LP: Angel 60080
		CD: EMI CDM 565 0742

JEAN-BAPTISTE LULLY (1632-1687)

Alceste, Prelude*

Camden NJ	Philadelphia	78: Victor 7424
April 1930	Orchestra	78: HMV DB 1587
		LP: American Stokowski Society LSSA 5

Thésée, March*

Camden NJ	Philadelphia	78: Victor 7424
April 1930	Orchestra	78: HMV DB 1587
		LP: American Stokowski Society LSSA 5
New York	His SO	LP: Victor LM 1721
April 1952		

Triomphe de l'amour, Notturno*

Camden NJ	Philadelphia	78: Victor 7424
April 1930	Orchestra	78: HMV DB 1587
		LP: American Stokowski Society LSSA 5
New York	His SO	LP: Victor LM 1721/LM 1875
April 1952		LP: HMV ALP 1387

WITOLD LUTOSLAWSKI (1913-1994)

Symphony No 1

LWarsaw	Warsaw PO	CD: Preludio PRL 2156
1959		

EDWARD MACDOWELL (1860-1908)

Suite No 2

Camden NJ December 1932	Philadelphia Orchestra	Victor unpublished

GUSTAV MAHLER (1860-1911)

Symphony No 2 "Resurrection"

LLondon July 1963	LSO Choruses Woodland, Baker	LP: Penzance PR 19 CD: Intaglio INCD 7491 CD: Music and Arts CD 885
LPhiladelphia November 1967	Philadelphia Orchestra Choruses Tyler, Godoy	CD: Japanese/American Stokowski Society LSCD 26 CD: Memories HR 4495-4497 CD: Hunt CDGI 749
Walthamstow July-August 1974	LSO Choruses M.Price, Fassbaender	LP: RCA ARL2-0852/GL 85392 CD: RCA/BMG 09026 625062

Symphony No 8 "Symphony of a Thousand"

LNew York April 1950	NYPSO Choruses Yeend, Graf, Williams, Lipton, Bernhardt, Conley, Alexander, London	LP: Penzance PR 19 CD: Music and Arts CD 280

FRANK MARTIN (1890-1974)

Petite symphonie concertante

New York December 1957	His SO	LP: Capitol P 8507/SP 8507 LP: World Records CM 69/SCM 69 CD: EMI CDM 565 8682

HARL MCDONALD (1899–1955)

Concerto for 2 pianos and orchestra

Philadelphia April 1937	Philadelphia Orchestra Behrend, Kelberine	78: Victor M 557 78: HMV DB 5700–5702 CD: Stokowski Society LSCD 20 CD: Cala CACD 0501

Dance of the Workers (Festival of the Workers)

Philadelphia November 1935	Philadelphia Orchestra	78: Victor 8919 78: HMV DB 2913 CD: Stokowski Society LSCD 20 CD: Cala CACD 0501

Legend of the Arkansas Traveller

Philadelphia March 1940	Philadelphia Orchestra	78: Victor 18069 LP: RCA Camden CAL 238 CD: Stokowski Society LSCD 20 CD: Cala CACD 0501

Rhumba (Symphony No 2)

Camden NJ November 1935	Philadelphia Orchestra	78: Victor 8919 78: HMV DB 2913 LP: RCA Camden CAL 238 CD: Stokowski Society LSCD 20 CD: Cala CACD 0501

GIAN CARLO MENOTTI (born 1911)

Sebastian, ballet suite

New York September 1954	NBC SO	LP: Victor LM 1858/ARL1-2715 CD: RCA/BMG 09026 625172

FELIX MENDELSSOHN-BARTHOLDY (1809-1847)

Symphony No 4 "Italian"

London May-June 1977	National PO	LP: CBS 34567 CD: Sony MBK 44894 <u>Stokowski's final recording sessions</u>

A Midsummer Night's Dream, Scherzo

Camden NJ November 1917	Philadelphia Orchestra	78: Victor 74560/6238
LPhiladelphia December 1931	Philadelphia Orchestra	LP: Bell Telephone Laboratories BTL 7901
New York July 1941	All American SO	78: Columbia (USA) 11983 CD: Music and Arts CD 845

A Midsummer Night's Dream, Wedding March

Camden NJ March 1923	Philadelphia Orchestra	Victor unpublished

OLIVIER MESSIAEN (1908-1992)

L'Ascension, 4 meditations for orchestra

New York November 1947- February 1949	NYPSO	78: Columbia (USA) MM 893 LP: Columbia (USA) ML 4214
London June 1970	LSO	LP: Decca PFS 4203 LP: London SPC 21060 CD: Decca 448 9552
LLondon June 1970	LSO	CD: Intaglio INCD 7421 CD: Music and Arts CD 787

Hymne au Saint Sacrement

LFrankfurt May 1955	Orchestra of Hessischer Rundfunk	CD: Music and Arts CD 770

DARIUS MILHAUD (1892-1974)

Concerto for percussion and small orchestra

LBaden-Baden May 1955	Südwestfunk Orchestra	CD: Music and Arts CD 778

JOSEPH LA MONACA

Saltarello

Philadelphia October 1935	Philadelphia Orchestra	CD: Cala CACD 0502

CLAUDIO MONTEVERDI (1567-1643)

Vespro della beata Vergine, extracts*

Illinois 1951-1952	University Orchestra & Chorus Stewart, Clark, Miller, Foote	LP: University of Illinois CRS 1

Orfeo*

LNew York 1960	New York City Opera Orchestra and Chorus Raskin, Souzay	LP: Private edition MR 2009

WOLFGANG AMADEUS MOZART (1756-1791)

Symphony No 40, third movement

Camden NJ	Philadelphia	78: Victor 74609/6243
May 1919	Orchestra	78: HMV DB 385
		LP: Stokowski Society LS 3

Piano Concerto No 20

Geneva	International	LP: Audio Visual Enterprises AVE 30696
August 1969	Festival Youth	
	Orchestra	
	Di Carla	

Piano Concerto No 21

LNew York	NYPSO	LP: MJA 1967
February	Hess	
1949		

Sinfonia concertante for wind

Philadelphia	Philadelphia	78: Victor M 760
December	Orchestra	78: HMV DB 10118-10121
1940	Tabuteau, Portnoy,	LP: RCA Camden CAL 213
	Schoenbach, Jones	

Serenade for 13 wind instruments

New York	Soloists of	LP: Vanguard VRS 1158/VSD 71158
May 1966	American SO	LP: World Records T 898/ST 898
		CD: Vanguard OVC 8009

German Dance No 3 "Sleigh Ride"

| New York March 1949 | His SO | 78: Victor 10-1487 45: Victor 49-0553/ERA 119 LP: Victor LM 1238 LP: Stokowski Society LS 18 |

Turkish March (Piano Sonata No 11)*

| New York February 1955 | His SO | LP: Victor LM 2042 LP: Stokowski Society LS 18 <u>Orchestra may have been NBC SO</u> |

Don Giovanni, Overture*

| West Ham March 1976 | National PO | LP: Pye/Nixa PCNHX 6 LP: Dell' Arte DA 9003 CD: Pye/Nixa CDPCN 6 CD: EMI CDM 764 1402 |

Le nozze di Figaro, excerpt (Non più andrai)

| LPhiladelphia January 1962 | Philadelphia Orchestra London | LP: Melodram MEL 228 |

MODEST MUSSORGSKY (1839-1881)

Boris Godunov arranged Rimsky-Korsakov, scenes

San Francisco	San Francisco SO	45: Victor WDM 1764
December	SF Opera Chorus	LP: Victor LM 1764
1952	Rossi-Lemeni	LP: Dell' Arte DA 9002
	Mason, Cauwet	

Rehearsal sequence (possibly for this recording) issued on CD by
Archive Documents ADCD 200-201

Symphonic synthesis on Boris Godunov*

Philadelphia	Philadelphia	78: Victor M 391
November	Orchestra	78: HMV DB 3244-3246
1936		LP: RCA Camden CAL 140
		LP: Stokowski Society LS 14
		CD: Dutton CDAX 8009
New York	All American SO	78: Columbia (USA) M 516
July 1941		
LBoston	Boston SO	CD: Memories HR 4495-4497
January		
1968		
Geneva	Suisse Romande	LP: Decca PFS 4181/SDD 456/SPA 142
September	Orchestra	LP: London SPC 21032/SPC 21110
1968		LP: Musical Heritage MHS 827052
		CD: Castle CCD 107
		CD: Decca 443 8962

Khovantschina, Act 1 Prelude and Dance of the Persian Slaves*

New York	His SO	LP: Victor LM 1816
February		LP: Quintessence PMC 7026
1953		

Khovantschina, Act 4 Entr'acte*

Camden NJ	Philadelphia	78: Victor 6336
November	Orchestra	78: HMV DB 599
1922		
Philadelphia	Philadelphia	78: Victor M 53
October	Orchestra	78: HMV D 1427
1927		LP: Stokowski Society LS 14
		CD: Grammofono AB 78552
		CD: Dutton CDAX 8009

Khovantschina Act 4 Entr'acte/concluded

New York February 1953	His SO	LP: Victor LM 1816 LP: Quintessence PMC 7026
West Ham November 1975	National PO	LP: Pye/Nixa PCNHX 4

Night on Bare Mountain*

Philadelphia April 1939	Philadelphia Orchestra	<u>Fantasia soundtrack recording</u> LP: Top Rank 30-003 LP: Disneyland WDX 101 LP: Buena Vista BVS 101 CD: Buena Vista CD 020/60007 VHS Video:
Philadelphia December 1940	Philadelphia Orchestra	78: Victor 17900 78: HMV DB 5900 45: Victor 49-0722 LP: Victor VCM 7101 LP: RCA Camden CAL 118 LP: Stokowski Society LS 14 CD: Dutton CDAX 8009 CD: Pearl GEMMCD 9488 CD: Grammofono AB 78586 CD: Magic Talent CD 48002
New York February 1953	His SO	LP: Victor LM 1816 LP: Quintessence PMC 7026
LLondon September 1964	LSO	CD: Seven Seas KICC 2076 CD: Music and Arts CD 765/CD 657
London June 1967	LSO	LP: Decca LK4927/PFS 4139/PFS 4260/SDD 456 LP: London SPC 21026/SPC 21110 LP: Musical Heritage MHS 827052 LP: Readers Digest RDS 9019/GMEL 8A-S9 CD: Castle CCD 107 CD: IMP IMPX 9033 CD: Decca 430 1372/430 4162/ 433 6252/443 8962
LLondon June 1969	RPO	CD: Music and Arts CD 847

Pictures at an Exhibition*

Philadelphia November 1939	Philadelphia Orchestra	78: Victor M 706 78: HMV DB 5827-5830 LP: Stokowski Society LS 14 CD: Dutton CDAX 8009
New York July 1941	All American SO	78: Columbia (USA) M 511
LPhiladelphia March 1962	Philadelphia Orchestra	CD: Japanese Stokowski Society LSCD 23/24
LLondon July 1963	BBC SO	CD: Seven Seas KICC 2076 CD: Music and Arts CD 765 Great Gate of Kiev CD: Japanese Stokowski Society LSCD 23/24
London September 1965	New Philharmonia	LP: Decca LK 4766/PFS 4095/SDD 456/ SPA 159/VIV 26 LP: London PM 55004/SPC 21006/STS 15558 CD: Castle CCD 107 CD: Decca 443 8982

Hut on Fowl's Legs and Great Gate of Kiev (Pictures, Ravel orchestration)

New York February 1957	His SO	LP: Capitol P 8385/P 8694/SP 8694 LP: Angel 6094 CD: EMI CDM 565 6142

Pictures at an Exhibition, extracts in the Ravel orchestration

LPhiladelphia 1931-1932	Philadelphia Orchestra	LP: Bell Telephone Laboratories BTL 7901

Sorochinsky Fair, excerpt (Parassia's Dream)

LLos Angeles July 1945	Hollywood Bowl SO Koshetz	CD: Eklipse EKRCD 31

CARL NIELSEN (1865-1931)

Symphony No 2 "The Four Temperaments"

| LCopenhagen
August 1967 | Danish RO | LP: Poco DLP 8407 |

OTTOKAR NOVACEK (1866-1900)

Perpetuum mobile*

Philadelphia December 1940	Philadelphia Orchestra	78: Victor 18069 LP: RCA Camden CAL 123
New York July 1941	All American SO	78: Columbia (USA) 11879
West Ham July 1976	National PO	LP: CBS 34543/73589

JACQUES OFFENBACH (1819-1880)

Barcarolle (Les contes d'Hoffmann)*

| Los Angeles
July 1945 | Hollywood Bowl SO | 78: Victor 11-9174
78: HMV DB 10130
LP: RCA Camden CAL 153 |

CARL ORFF (1895-1982)

Carmina burana

| Houston
April 1958 | Houston SO
Choruses
Babikian, Hager,
Gardner | LP: Capitol P 8470/SP 8470
LP: World Records T 793/ST 793
LP: Angel 60236
LP: EMI CFP 40311
CD: EMI CDM 565 2072 |

NICCOLO PAGANINI (1782-1840)

Moto perpetuo, arranged by Lavagnino

New York August 1957	His SO	LP: Capitol P 8415/P 8650/SP 8650/SP 8415 LP: EMI SXLP 30174 CD: EMI CDM 565 9122

GIOVANNI PALESTRINA (1524-1594)

Adoramus te*

Camden NJ November 1934	Philadelphia Orchestra	78: Victor M 508/M 963 78: HMV DA 1606/DB 6260 LP: American Stokowski Society LSSA 5
New York March 1952	Unaccompanied Chorus	LP: Victor LM 1721
New York December 1958	Symphony of the Air	LP: United Artists UAL 7001/UAS 8001/ UAS 8003 CD: EMI CMS 565 4272

O bone Jesu

New York March 1952	Unaccompanied Chorus	LP: Victor LM 1721

ANDRZEJ PANUFNIK (1914-1991)

Universal Prayer

London September 1970	Halsey Singers Cantelo, Watts, Mitchinson, Stalman	LP: Unicorn RHS 305 According to Gramophone Classical Catalogue 1995 this recording remains available on tape cassette DKPC 9049

VINCENT PERSICHETTI (1915-1987)

March (Divertimento for Band)

New York January 1957	His SO	LP: Capitol P 8385 CD: EMI CDM 565 6142

AMILCARE PONCHIELLI (1834-1886)

Dance of the Hours (La Gioconda)*

Philadelphia April 1939	Philadelphia Orchestra	Fantasia soundtrack recording LP: Top Rank 30-003 LP: Disneyland WDX 101/DQ 1243 LP: Buena Vista BVS 101 CD: Buena Vista CD 020/60007 VHS Video: Buena Vista D211 322

FRANCIS POULENC (1899-1963)

Concert champêtre for harpsichord and orchestra

LNew York November 1949	NYPSO Landowska	LP: International Piano Archive IPA 106-107

SERGEI PROKOFIEV (1891-1953)

Symphony No 5

Moscow   USSR RO   LP: MK 1551/MK 04408/BR 14050
June 1958

Symphony No 6

LNew York   NYPSO   LP: New York Philharmonic NYP 821-822
December
1949

Piano Concerto No 3

LNew York   NYPSO   LP: Melodram MEL 228
February   Kapell   CD: Music and Arts CD 769
1949   MEL 228 incorrectly labelled NBC SO

Alexander Nevsky, cantata

LHilversum   Hilversum RO   CD: Music and Arts CD 252/CD 831
1970   and Chorus   Also unpublished video recording
                 Sante   (not approved by Stokowski)

Cinderella, ballet suite

New York   Stadium SO   LP: Everest LPBR 6016/LPBR 6108/
October   SDBR 3016/SDBR 3108
1958   LP: World Records T 173/ST 173
                                        LP: Concert Hall SMSC 2533
                                        CD: Bescol CD 519
                                        CD: Priceless D 22697
                                        CD: Everest EVC 9023

Infernal Scene, March and Prince and the Princess (L'amour des 3 oranges)

New York November 1941	NBC SO	78: Victor 18497 78: HMV DB 6151 LP: American Stokowski Society LSSA 4 March only CD: Cala CACD 0505

Peter and the Wolf

New York July 1941	All American SO Rathbone	78: Columbia (USA) M 477 LP: Columbia (USA) ML 4038/CL 171/P 14204
New York 1959	Stadium SO Keeshan	LP: Everest LPBR 6043/SDBR 3043 CD: Bescol CD 519 Everest also contains the music without the over-dubbed narration;this latter version also used as basis for a French language edition narrated by Pierre Tcherina and published on Mode Laser CD 670027

Romeo and Juliet, ballet suite

New York October 1954	NBC SO	LP: Victor LM 2117/ARL1-2715 CD: RCA/BMG 09026 625172

Romeo and Juliet, 3 excerpts

LBaden-Baden May 1955	Südwestfunk Orchestra	CD: Music and Arts CD 831

The Ugly Duckling

New York 1959	Stadium SO Resnik	LP: Everest LPBR 6108/SDBR 3108 LP: World Records T 173/ST 173 CD: Bescol CD 519

GIACOMO PUCCINI (1858-1924)

Turandot

LNew York March 1961	Metropolitan Opera Orchestra & Chorus Nilsson, Moffo, Corelli, Giaiotti	LP: Metropolitan Opera special issue LP: HRE Records HRE 229 LP: Accord ACC 15.0038 CD: Metropolitan Opera MET 16 CD: Datum 12301 CD: Memories HR 4535-4536

Madama Butterfly, Act 2 Entr'acte

Camden NJ December 1924	Philadelphia Orchestra	Victor unpublished

Tosca, excerpt (Vissi d'arte)

LPhiladelphia January 1962	Philadelphia Orchestra Nilsson	LP: Melodram MEL 228

HENRY PURCELL (1658-1695)

When I am laid in earth (Purcell Suite)*

New York August 1950	His SO	78: Victor 12-3087 45: Victor 49-3087 LP: Victor LM 1875
LLondon May 1954	BBC SO	VHS Video: Teldec 4509 950383 Laserdisc: Teldec 4509 950386
London August 1975	RPO	LP: Desmar DSM 1011 LP: Teldec 642.631

Hornpipe from King Arthur (Purcell Suite)

New York February 1958	His SO	LP: Capitol P 8458/SP 8458 LP: Angel 6094 CD: EMI CDM 565 9122

SERGEI RACHMANINOV (1873-1943)

Symphony No 2

LLos Angeles 1946	Hollywood Bowl SO	LP: Discocorp LSSA 28 CD: Music and Arts CD 769

Symphony No 3

West Ham April-May 1975	National PO	LP: Desmar DES 1007/DSM 1007

Piano Concerto No 2

Camden NJ January 1924- December 1924	Philadelphia Orchestra Rachmaninov	LP: RCA ARM3-0260 CD: RCA/BMG 09026 612652 <u>2nd and 3rd movements</u> 78: HMV DB 747-749 78: Victor 89166-89171/8064-8066 <u>Side 3 of original 78rpm recording does</u> <u>not survive (this represents concluding</u> <u>part of first movement); for LP and CD</u> <u>issues it is therefore replaced by the</u> <u>corresponding section from the 1929</u> <u>recording</u>
Philadelphia April 1929	Philadelphia Orchestra Rachmaninov	78: Victor M 58 78: HMV DB 1333-1337/DB 7427-7431 45: Victor WCT 18 LP: Victor LCT 1014/LSB 4011 LP: HMV ALP 1630/CSLP 517 LP: RCA ARM3-0296/AVM 30296 CD: Pickwick PK 524 CD: RCA/BMG 5997-2-RC/09026 612652
Los Angeles September 1945	Hollywood Bowl SO Rubinstein	Victor unpublished

Piano Concerto No 2, second movement and part of third movement

Camden NJ December 1923	Philadelphia Orchestra Rachmaninov	Victor unpublished

Rhapsody on a theme of Paganini

Camden NJ December 1934	Philadelphia Orchestra Rachmaninov	78: Victor M 250 78: HMV DB 2426-2428 45: Victor WCT 1118 LP: Victor LCT 1118/LSB 4013 LP: HMV CSLP 509 LP: RCA ARM3-0296 CD: Pickwick PK 524 CD: Fidelio 8822-3EB3 CD: RCA/BMG 6659-2-RC/09026 612652

Georgian Melody*

LLos Angeles July 1945	Hollywood Bowl SO Koshetz	CD: Eklipse EKRCD 31

Prelude in C sharp minor*

LNew York 1960	American SO	LP: Discocorp LSSA 228
LPrague September 1972	Czech PO	LP: Decca PFS 4351 LP: London SPC 21130 CD: Decca 433 8762

Vocalise

New York February 1953	His SO	LP: Victor LM 2042 LP: Stokowski Society LS 17
New York August 1957	His SO	LP: Capitol P 8415/P 8650/SP 8650/SP 8415 LP: EMI SXLP 30174 CD: EMI CDM 565 9122 Arrangement by Dubensky
New York 1964	American SO Moffo	LP: RCA LSC 2795/SB 6804/GL 42923 CD: RCA/BMG 7831-2-RG/GD 87831/ 09026 626002 Arrangement by Dubensky
West Ham April-May 1975	National PO	LP: Desmar DES 1007/DSM 1007

MAURICE RAVEL (1875–1937)

Alborada del gracioso

Paris May 1958	Orchestre National	LP: Capitol P 8463/P 8694/SP 8694 LP: Angel 60102 LP: EMI SXLP 30263 CD: EMI CDC 747 4232/CDM 565 4222
LParis May 1958	Orchestre National	CD: Music and Arts CD 778

Boléro

New York July 1940	All American SO	78: Columbia (USA) X 174 CD: Music and Arts CD 841

Daphnis et Chloé, second suite

London June 1970	LSO LSO Chorus	LP: Decca PFS 4220 LP: London SPC 21059/SPC 21112 CD: Decca 417 7792

Fanfare (L'éventail de Jeanne)

Hilversum August 1970	Hilversum RO	LP: Decca PFS 4218/SPA 159 LP: London SPC 21061

Rapsodie espagnole

Camden NJ March 1934	Philadelphia Orchestra	78: Victor 8282-8283 78: HMV DB 2367-2368 LP: RCA Camden CAL 118 CD: Biddulph WHL 013
London July 1957	LSO	LP: Capitol P 8520/SP 8520 LP: Angel 60104 CD: EMI CDC 747 4232/CDM 565 4222
LLeipzig June 1959	Gewandhaus Orchestra	CD: Music and Arts CD 280
LLondon May 1974	New Philharmonia	CD: BBC Radio Classics BBCRD 9107

OTTORINO RESPIGHI (1879-1936)

Pini di Roma

New York December 1958	Symphony of the Air	LP: United Artists UAL 7001/UAS 8001 CD: EMI CMS 565 4272/CDM 565 9212

SILVESTRE REVUELTAS (1899-1940)

Sensemaya

New York December 1947	His SO	78: Victor 12-0470/18-0169 78: HMV DB 6915 45: Victor 49-0882 LP: Stokowski Society LS 17

NIKOLAY RIMSKY-KORSAKOV (1844-1908)

Scheherazade

Philadelphi October 1927	Philadelphia Orchestra	78: Victor M 23 78: HMV D 1436-1440 CD: Biddulph WHL 010
Camden NJ October- November 1934	Philadelphia Orchestra	78: Victor M 269 78: HMV DB 2522-2527
London May-June 1951	Philharmonia	LP: HMV ALP 1339 LP: Victor LM 1732 LP: Stokowski Society LS 12
LPhiladelphia February 1962	Philadelphia Orchestra	LP: Longanesi GCL 68 CD: Frequenz 041.017
London September 1964	LSO	LP: Decca LK 4658/PFS 4062 LP: London PM 55002/SPC 21005 CD: Castle CCD 102 CD: Decca 417 7532
London February- March 1975	RPO	LP: RCA ARL1-1182/AGL1-5213 CD: RCA/BMG 7743-2-RV/VD 87743/ 09026 625042

Scheherazade, The Sea and Sinbad's Ship

Philadelphia May 1927	Philadelphia Orchestra	CD: Biddulph WHL 010

Scheherazade, The Young Prince and Princess

Camden NJ October- December 1920	Philadelphia Orchestra	Victor unpublished
Camden NJ March 1921	Philadelphia Orchestra	78: Victor 74691/6246

Scheherazade, Festival at Bagdad

Camden NJ May 1919	Philadelphia Orchestra	78: Victor 74593/6246

Russian Easter Festival Overure

Philadelphia January 1929	Philadelphia Orchestra	78: Victor 7018-7019 78: HMV D 1676-1677 L 7002 LP: Victor VCM 7101/VIC 6060 LP: RCA Camden CAL 163 CD: Biddulph WHL 010 L 7002 was an experimental 33.1/3 rpm issue (Symphonic transcription disc)
New York April 1942	NBC SO Moscona	78: Victor M 937 78: HMV DB 6173-6174 CD: Cala CACD 0505
LLucerne August 1951	Lucerne Festival Orchestra	CD: Relief CR 1882
New York February 1953	His SO Moscona	LP: Victor LM 1816 LP: Quintessence PMC 7026
Chicago February 1968	Chicago SO	LP: RCA LSC 3067/SB 6804/VCS7077/GL42923 CD: RCA/BMG GD 60206/09026 604872/ 09026 625042

Rehearsal sequence from Russian Easter Festival Overture with Rossi-Lemeni/
San Francisco SO issued on CD by Archive Documents ADCD 200-201

Capriccio espagnol

London January 1973	New Philharmonia	LP: Decca PFS 4333 LP: London SPC 21117 CD: Decca 417 7532/430 4102/433 6252

The Flight of the Bumble Bee (Tsar Sultan)

New York July 1941	All American SO	78: Columbia (USA) 19005
West Ham July 1976	National PO	LP: CBS 34543/73589

Dance of the Tumblers (The Snow Maiden)

| Camden NJ | Philadelphia | 78: Victor 74849/6431 |
| March 1923 | Orchestra | LP: Stokowski Society LS 3 |

Ivan the Terrible (The Maid of Pskov), Act 3 Prelude

Philadelphia	Philadelphia	78: Victor M 717
April 1939	Orchestra	78: HMV DB 6039
		CD: Biddulph WHL 010
West Ham	National PO	LP: CBS 34543/73589
July 1976		

The Tsar's Bride, excerpt (Ivan Sergeivich, come into the garden!)

| LLos Angeles | Hollywood Bowl SO | CD: Eklipse EKRCD 31 |
| July 1945 | M.Koshetz | |

The Nightingale and the Rose

| LLos Angeles | Hollywood Bowl SO | CD: Eklipse EKRCD 31 |
| July 1945 | M.Koshetz | |

GIOACHINO ROSSINI (1792-1868)

Guilleaume Tell, Overture

Camden NJ	Philadelphia	Victor unpublished
March 1923	Orchestra	
West Ham	National PO	LP: Pye/Nixa PCNHX 6
March 1976		LP: Dell' Arte DA 9003
		CD: Pye/Nixa CDPCN 6
		CD: EMI CDM 764 1402

CAMILLE SAINT-SAENS (1835-1921)

Samson et Dalila, excerpts (Arrêtez, o mes frères!; Printemps qui commence;
Amour, viens aider ma faiblesse!; La victoire facile; Se pourrait-il?;
C'est toi/Mon coeur s'ouvre à ta voix; Vois ma misère!; Bacchanale;
Gloire à Dagon!)

New York September 1954	NBC SO Shaw Chorale Stevens, Peerce, Merrill	45: Victor WDM 1848 LP: Victor LM 1848 LP: HMV ALP 1308 LP: Stokowski Society LS 15 La victoire facile is only on WDM 1848 and LS 15

Samson et Dalila, Bacchanale

Camden NJ October- December 1920	Philadelphia Orchestra	78: Victor 74671/6241 78: HMV DB 384
Philadelphia November 1927	Philadelphia Orchestra	78: Victor 6823 78: HMV D 1807 LP: Victor VCM 7101 CD: Biddulph WHL 012 CD: Magic Talent CD 48002

One of these versions also appears on CD Grammofono AB 78586

Le carnaval des animaux

Philadelphia September 1929	Philadelphia Orchestra Barabini, Montgomery	78: Victor M 71 78: HMV D 1992-1994 CD: Biddulph WHL 012
Philadelphia November 1939	Philadelphia Orchestra S.Levin, Behrend	78: Victor M 785 78: HMV DB 5942-5944 LP: Victor VCM 7101 LP: RCA Camden CAL 100 Side 3 of the original recording was re-made in 1941 without the participation of Stokowski

Danse macabre

Camden NJ March 1923	Philadelphia Orchestra	Victor unpublished
Philadelphia April 1925	Philadelphia Orchestra	78: Victor 6505 78: HMV D 1121 Thought to be the first electrical recording of a full symphony orchestra
Philadelphia January 1936	Philadelphia Orchestra	78: Victor 14162 78: HMV DB 3077 LP: Victor VCM 7101/VIC 6060 LP: RCA Camden CAL 254 CD: Grammofono AB 78552 CD: Biddulph WHL 012 CD: Magic Talent CD 48002 Grammofono incorrectly dated 1928
West Ham November 1975	National PO	LP: Pye/Nixa PCNHX 4 CD: Pye CDPCN 4

ERIK SATIE (1866–1925)

Gymnopédies 1 and 3 , orchestrated by Debussy

Philadelphia December 1937	Philadelphia Orchestra	78: Victor 1965 78: HMV DA 1688 LP: Stokowski Society LSSA 3 CD: Biddulph WHL 011 CD: Magic Talent CD 48015

AHMED ADNAN SAYGUN (born 1907)

Yunus Emre, oratorio

New York November 1958	Symphony of the Air Choruses	LP: RW 3967–3968

ARNOLD SCHOENBERG (1874-1951)

Verklärte Nacht

New York February 1952	His SO	LP: Victor LM 1739/LM 2117 LP: HMV ALP 1205
New York August 1957	His SO	LP: Capitol P 8433 LP: Angel 60080 CD: EMI CDC 747 5212
L New York November 1960	Symphony of the Air	CD: Library of Congress CLC 2

Gurrelieder

LPhiladelphia 9 April 1932	Philadelphia Orchestra Choruses Vreeland, Bampton, Althouse, Betts, Robofsky, De Loache	LM 127 CD: Pearl GEMMCDS 9066 LM 127 was an experimental 33.1/3 rpm issue (Symphonic transcription disc); both issues contain Stokowski's spoken outline of themes recorded in May 1932 with piano illustrations played by Artur Rodzinski
LPhiladelphia 11 April 1932	Philadelphia Orchestra Choruses Vreeland, Bampton, Althouse, Betts, Robofsky, De Loache	78: Victor M 127/DM 127 78: HMV DB 1769-1782 LP: Victor LCT 6012/AVM2-2017 CD: Nuova Era HMT 90025-90026 Excerpts CD: Magic Talent CD 48015 M 127 and DB 1769 also contain shortened version of Stokowski's outline of themes detailed under 9 April performance
LPhiladelphia March 1961	Philadelphia Orchestra Choruses Soloists include Rankin, Zambrana, Petrak	Unpublished radio broadcast
LEdinburgh August 1961	LSO Choruses Brouwenstijn, Rankin, McCracken, Lanigan, Robinson, Lidell	Unpublished radio broadcast

Gurrelieder, Song of the Wood Dove

New York November 1949	NYPSO Lipton	LP: Columbia (USA) ML 2140

FRANZ SCHUBERT (1797–1828)

Symphony No 8 "Unfinished"

Camden NJ December 1923	Philadelphia Orchestra	Victor unpublished
Camden NJ January 1924	Philadelphia Orchestra	Victor unpublished
Camden NJ April 1924	Philadelphia Orchestra	78: Victor 74894-74899/6459-6461 78: HMV DB 792-794 <u>Stokowski's first published recording of</u> <u>a complete symphony</u>
Philadelphia April 1927	Philadelphia Orchestra	78: Victor M 16 78: HMV D 1779-1781 L 11645-11646 LP: Parnassus 5 CD: Biddulph WHL 033 <u>L 11645-11646 was an experimental 33.1/3</u> <u>rpm issue (Symphonic transcription disc)</u>
New York July 1941	All American SO	78: Columbia (USA) M 485
Walthamstow September 1969	LPO	LP: Decca PFS 4197/D94 D2 LP: London SPC 21042 CD: King (Japan) K30Y 1538

Rosamunde, Overture

New York September 1952	His SO	LP: Victor LM 1730 LP: HMV ALP 1193 LP: Stokowski Society LS 18
West Ham March 1976	National PO	LP: Pye/Nixa PCNHX 6 LP: Dell' Arte DA 9003 CD: Pye/Nixa CDPCN 6 CD: EMI CDM 764 1402

Rosamunde, Ballet music No 2

Philadelphia May 1927	Philadelphia Orchestra	CD: Biddulph WHL 033 Longer version with repeats
Philadelphia October 1927	Philadelphia Orchestra	78: Victor 1312 LP: RCA Camden CAL 123 CD: Biddulph WHL 033
New York September 1952	His SO	LP: Victor LM 1730 LP: HMV ALP 1193 LP: Stokowski Society LS 18

Rosamunde, Entr'acte No 3*

New York September 1952	His SO	LP: Victor LM 1730 LP: HMV ALP 1193 LP: Stokowski Society LS 18 Stokowski's version includes an interpolation from Schubert's Impromptu in B flat D935

Moment musical No 3*

Camden NJ January 1922	Philadelphia Orchestra	78: Victor 66098/799
Philadelphia April 1927	Philadelphia Orchestra	78: Victor 1312 45: RCA Camden CAE 188 LP: RCA Camden CAL 123 CD: Biddulph WHL 033
Los Angeles July 1945	Hollywood Bowl SO	78: Victor 11-9174 78: HMV DB 10130
New York October 1970	American SO	CD: Japanese Stokowski Society LSCD 23/24
London June 1972	LSO	LP: Decca PFS 4351 LP: London SPC 21130 CD: IMP IMPX 9033 CD: Decca 433 8762

German Dances D783, selection*
described by Stokowski as Tyrolean Dances

New York December 1944	New York City SO	CD: Cala CACD 0502

New York June 1949	His SO	78: Victor 10-1519 45: Victor 49-0814/ERA 67 45: HMV 7ER 5043 LP: Victor LM 1238 LP: Stokowski Society LS 18

German Dance No 3 (German Dances D783)*
described by Stokowski as Viennese Dance

Camden NJ October 1922	Philadelphia Orchestra	Victor unpublished
Camden NJ November 1922	Philadelphia Orchestra	Victor unpublished
Camden NJ December 1922	Philadelphia Orchestra	78: Victor 74814

Ave Maria*

Philadelphia April 1939	Philadelphia Orchestra Chorus & soloist	<u>Fantasia soundtrack recording</u> LP: Top Rank 30-003 LP: Disneyland WDX 101 LP: Buena Vista BVS 101 CD: Buena Vista CD 020/60007 VHS Video: Buena Vista D211 322

Ständchen*

Philadelphia October 1935	Philadelphia	CD: Cala CACD 0502

ROBERT SCHUMANN (1810-1856)

Symphony No 2

New York   His SO   45: Victor WDM 1614
July 1950   LP: Victor LM 1194
                                            LP: Stokowski Society LS 8

Cello Concerto

New York   NYPSO   CD: Arlecchino ARL 169
November 1949   Fournier

Träumerei*

New York   All American SO   78: Columbia (USA) 11982
July 1941   LP: American Stokowski Society LSSA 6

THOMAS SCOTT (1912-1961)

From the Sacred Harp

New York   NYPSO   V-Disc 896
January   <u>Includes spoken introduction by composer</u>
1949

ALEXANDER SCRIABIN (1872-1915)

Le poème de l'extase

Camden NJ March 1932	Philadelphia Orchestra	78: Victor M 125 78: HMV DB 1706-1707 L 11616-11617 CD: Pearl GEMMCD 9066 L 11616-11617 was an experimental 33.1/3 rpm issue (Symphonic transcription disc)
Houston March 1959	Houston SO	LP: Everest LPBR 6032/SDBR 3032 LP: Concert Hall SMSC 2533 CD: Philips (USA) 422 3062 CD: Pantheon D 1032X
LLondon June 1969	RPO	CD: Music and Arts CD 847
LPrague September 1972	Czech PO	LP: Decca PFS 4333/D94 D2 LP: London SPC 21117/SPC 21136 CD: Decca 443 8982

Prometheus, poème du feu

Camden NJ March 1932	Philadelphia Chorus S.Levin	78: Victor M 125 78: HMV DB 1708-1709 L 11616-11617 CD: Pearl GEMMCD 9066 L11616-11617 was an experimental 33.1/3 rpm issue (Symphonic transcription disc)

Prometheus, extract

LPhiladelphia March 1932	Philadelphia S.Levin	LP: Bell Telephone Laboratories BTL 7901

Etude in C sharp minor*

New York December 1944	New York City SO	78: Victor unpublished CD: Cala CACD 0502
New York April 1971	American SO	LP: Vanguard VCS 10095 CD: Vanguard OVC 8012

DMITRI SHOSTAKOVICH (1906-1975)

Symphony No 1

Camden NJ November 1933	Philadelphia Orchestra	78: Victor M 192 78: HMV DB 2203-2207 LM 192 CD: Pearl GEMMCDS 9044 LM 192 was an experimental 33.1/3 rpm issue (Symphonic transcription disc)
New York December 1958	Symphony of the Air	LP: United Artists UAL 7004/UAS 8004 CD: EMI CMS 565 4272

Symphony No 5

Philadelphia April 1939	Philadelphia Orchestra	78: Victor M 619 78: HMV DB 3991-3996 LP: American Stokowski Society LSSA 4 CD: Pearl GEMMCDS 9044 CD: Dutton CDAX 8017
New York October 1958	Stadium SO	LP: Everest LPBR 6010/SDBR 3010 LP: World Records T 281/ST 281 CD: Priceless D 22697 CD: Philips (USA) 422 3062
LPrague 1961	Czech PO	CD: Preludio PR 2156
LLondon September 1964	LSO	CD: Seven Seas KICC 2076 CD: Music and Arts CD 765 CD: BBC Radio Classics 15656 91542

Symphony No 6

Philadelphia December 1940	Philadelphia Orchestra	78: Victor M 867 CD: Dell' Arte CDDA 9023 CD: Dutton CDAX 8017
Chicago February 1968	Chicago SO	LP: RCA LSC 3133/SB 6839/AGL1-5063 CD: RCA/BMG 09026 625162

Symphony No 7 "Leningrad"

LNew York   NBC SO   CD: Pearl GEMMCDS 9044
December
1942

Symphony No 10

LChicago   Chicago SO   LP: Japanese Stokowski Society JLSS 0021
March 1966   CD: Chicago Symphony Orchestra CSO 90/12

Symphony No 11 "Year 1905"

Houston   Houston SO   LP: Capitol 8448/8700
April 1958   LP: Angel 60228
                               LP: Everest SDBR 3310
                               LP: World Records T776-777/ST776-777
                               LP: Angel 34446
                               CD: EMI CDC 747 4192/CDM 565 2062

Moscow   Moscow Radio SO   CD: Russian Disc RDCD 15100
1958

The Age of Gold, ballet suite

Chicago   Chicago SO   LP: RCA LSC 3133/SB 6839/AGL1-5063
February   CD: RCA/BMG 09026 625162
1968   Polka
                               LP: RCA VCS 7077

Lady Macbeth of Mzensk, Entr'acte

New York   Symphony   LP: United Artists UAL 7004/UAS 8004
December   of the Air   CD: EMI CMS 565 4272
1958

Prelude in E flat minor*

Camden NJ December 1935	Philadelphia Orchestra	78: Victor M 192/M 291 78: HMV DB 2884 LP: American Stokowski Society LSSA 4 CD: Pearl GEMMCDS 9044 CD: Dutton CDAX 8002
New York November 1940	All American SO	78: Columbia (USA) 12903/M 446
LScheveningen June 1951	Residentie Orkest	CD: Residentie Orkest 90th anniversary album
New York December 1958	Symphony of the Air	LP: United Artists UAL 7004/UAS 8004 CD: EMI CMS 565 4272
LLondon June 1969	RPO	CD: Music and Arts CD 847
West Ham July 1976	National PO	LP: CBS 34543/73589

JEAN SIBELIUS (1865–1957)

Symphony No 1

New York July 1950	His SO	78: Victor DM 1497 78: HMV DB 21264-21267 45: Victor WDM 1497 LP: Victor LM 1125 LP: HMV ALP 1210 LP: Stokowski Society LS 16
West Ham November 1976	National PO	LP: CBS 34548/76666

Symphony No 2

New York September 1954	NBC SO	LP: Victor LM 1854 LP: HMV ALP 1440 LP: Dell' Arte DA 9002

Symphony No 4

Camden NJ February 1932	Philadelphia Orchestra	78: Victor M 160 L 11638-11639 LP: Victor SRS 3001 CD: Dell' Arte CDDA 9023 <u>L 11638-11639 was an experimental 33.1/3 rpm issue (Symphonic transcription disc)</u>

Symphony No 7

New York September 1940	All American SO	78: Columbia (USA) unpublished LP: American Stokowski Society LSSA 6 CD: Music and Arts CD 841

Violin Concerto

Camden NJ December 1934	Philadelphia Orchestra Heifetz	Victor unpublished

Berceuse (The Tempest)

Philadelphia November 1937	Philadelphia Orchestra	78: Victor 14726 78: HMV DB 3534 45: RCA Camden CAE 188 LP: RCA Camden CAL 123 CD: Dell' Arte CDDA 9023
New York March 1950	His SO	78: Victor 12-1191 78: HMV DB 21334 45: Victor 49-1168 45: HMV 7R 101 45: Electrola 7RW 137 LP: Victor LM 1238/LRM 7024 LP: Stokowski Society LS 16

Girl with roses (Swan White)

New York November 1947	NYPSO	78: Columbia (USA) M 806

Finlandia

Camden NJ March-April 1921	Philadelphia Orchestra	78: Victor 74698/6366 78: HMV DB 599
Camden NJ April 1930	Philadelphia Orchestra	78: Victor 7412 78: HMV DB 1584 L 11656 45: RCA Camden CAE 101 LP: Victor VCM 7101 LP: RCA Camden CAL 120 L 11656 was an experimental 33.1/3 rpm issue (Symphonic transcription disc)
New York May 1957	His SO	45: Capitol FAP 48399/SFP 48399 LP: Capitol P 8399/SP 8399 LP: Angel 6094 LP: EMI MFP 2145 CD: EMI CDM 565 6142

A version of Finlandia, incorrectly dated April 1928, appears on CD Magic
Talent CD 48015

Swan of Tuonela

Philadelphia May 1929	Philadelphia Orchestra	78: Victor 7380 78: HMV D 1997 L 11656 LP: Victor VCM 7101 CD: Grammofono AB 78586 CD: Magic Talent CD 48015 L 11656 was an experimental 33.1/3 rpm issue (Symphonic transcription disc)
New York December 1947	His SO	78: Victor 12-0585 78: HMV DB 21555 45: Victor 49-0461 LP: Victor LM 9029/LM 151/LRM 7024 LP: Stokowski Society LS 16
New York May 1957	His SO	45: Capitol FAP 48399/SFP 48399 LP: Capitol P 8399/P 8673/SP 8399/SP 8673 LP: Angel 6094 LP: EMI SMFP 2145 CD: EMI CDM 565 6142
West Ham November 1976	National PO	LP: CBS 34548/76666

Valse triste

Philadelphia January 1936	Philadelphia Orchestra	78: Victor 14726 78: HMV DB 3318/DB 6009 45: RCA Camden CAE 188 LP: RCA Camden CAL 123 CD: Dell' Arte CDDA 9023
New York October 1949	His SO	78: Victor 12-1191 78: HMV DB 21334 45: Victor 49-1168 45: HMV 7R 101 45: Electrola 7RW 137 LP: Victor LM 1238/LRM 7024 LP: Stokowski Society LS 16

BEDRICH SMETANA (1824-1884)

The Moldau (Ma Vlast)

New York March 1961	RCA Victor Orchestra	LP: Victor LM 2471/LSC 2471/VCS 7077 LP: RCA RB 16259/SB 2130/AGL1-5259 CD: RCA/BMG 09026 615032/09026 626012

The Bartered Bride, Overture

New York March 1961	RCA Victor Orchestra	LP: Victor LM 2471/LSC 2471 LP: RCA RB 16259/SB 2130/AGL1-5259 CD: RCA/BMG 09026 615032/09026 626012

JOHN PHILIP SOUSA (1854-1932)

El capitan, March

Camden NJ March 1930	Philadelphia Orchestra	78: Victor 1441 78: HMV E 556 CD: Japanese Stokowski Society LSCD 23/24 CD: Cala CACD 0501 CD: Stokowski Society LSCD 20 CACD 0501 and LSCD 20 have different takes

Manhattan Beach, March

Philadelphia September 1929	Philadelphia Orchestra	78: Victor unpublished CD: Stokowski Society LSCD 20

Stars and Stripes forever, March

Philadelphia September 1929	Philadelphia Orchestra	78: Victor 1441 78: HMV E 556 CD: Japanese Stokowski Society LSCD 23/24 CD: Stokowski Society LSCD 20
West Ham November 1975	National PO	LP: Pye/Nixa PCNHX 4 CD: EMI CDM 764 1402 This version arranged by Stokowski

Stars and Stripes forever, rehearsal extract

New York November 1963	American SO	CD: Japanese Stokowski Society LSCD 23/24

WILLIAM GRANT STILL (1895-1978)

Scherzo (Afro-American Symphony)

New York November 1940	All American SO	78: Columbia (USA) 11992 LP: American Stokowski Society LSSA 6

EDGAR STILLMAN-KELLEY (1867-1944)

Alice in Wonderland, Suite

Camden NJ December 1924	Philadelphia Orchestra	Victor unpublished

LEOPOLD STOKOWSKI (1882-1977)

Balance Test March

Philadelphia May 1929	Philadelphia Orchestra	CD: Cala CACD 0502

Reveries

New York ca. 1969	American SO	CD: Japanese Stokowski Society LSCD 23/24

JOHANN STRAUSS II (1825–1899)

An der schönen blauen Donau, waltz

New York January– February 1955	His SO	45: Victor ERA 259 LP: Victor LM 2042 This recording may be with NBC SO and also exist in an unpublished stereo edition
New York February 1957	His SO	LP: Capitol P 8399/P 8694/SP 8399/SP 8694 LP: Angel 6094 LP: EMI SMFP 2145

An der schönen blauen Donau, standard abbreviated version

Camden NJ May 1919	Philadelphia Orchestra	78: Victor 74627/6237
Philadelphia June 1926	Philadelphia Orchestra	78: Victor 6584 78: HMV D 1218
Philadelphia April 1939	Philadelphia Orchestra	78: Victor 15425 78: HMV DB 3821 LP: Victor LM 6074
New York September 1949	His SO	78: Victor 12-1160 78: HMV DB 21346 45: Victor 49-1076/WDM 1438 45: HMV 7R 169 45: HMV (Italy) 7RQ 182

Du und du (Fledermaus Waltz) *

Los Angeles August 1946	Hollywood Bowl SO	78: Victor 10-1310 45: Victor 49-0279/ERA 67

G'schichten aus dem Wienerwald, waltz

New York January– February 1955	His SO	45: Victor ERA 259 LP: Victor LM 2042 This recording may be with NBC SO and also exist in an unpublished stereo edition
West Ham November 1975	National PO	LP: Pye/Nixa PCNHX 4 CD: Pye/Nixa CDPCN 4

G'schichten aus dem Wienerwald, standard abbreviated version

Camden NJ May 1920	Philadelphia Orchestra	Victor unpublished
Philadelphia June 1926	Philadelphia Orchestra	78: Victor 6584 78: HMV D 1218
Philadelphia April 1939	Philadelphia Orchestra	78: Victor 15425 78: HMV DB 3821 LP: Victor LM 6074 LP: RCA Camden CAL 153/CFL 103
New York September 1949	His SO	78: Victor 12-1160 78: HMV DB 21346 45: Victor 49-1076 45: HMV 7R 169 45: HMV (Italy) 7RQ 182

RICHARD STRAUSS (1864-1949)

Dance of the 7 veils (Salome)

Camden NJ November- December 1921	Philadelphia Orchestra	78: Victor 74729-74730/6240 78: HMV DB 383
Philadelphia May 1929	Philadelphia Orchestra	78: Victor 7259-7260 78: HMV D 1935-1936 LP: RCA Camden CAL 254
Philadelphia April 1937	Philadelphia Orchestra	78: Victor unpublished CD: Cala CACD 0502
New York October 1958	Stadium SO	LP: Everest LPBR 6023/SDBR 3023 LP: World Records T 108/ST 108/PE 751 CD: Priceless D 1323X CD: Bescol CD 538 CD: Everest EVC 9004

Don Juan

New York October 1958	Stadium SO	LP: Everest LPBR 6023/SDBR 3023 LP: World Records T 108/ST 108/PE 751 CD: Priceless D 1323X CD: Bescol CD 538 CD: Everest EVC 9004

Gavotte (Suite for winds)

New York	His SO	LP: Capitol P 8385/SP 8385
February 1957		CD: EMI CDM 565 6142

Till Eulenspiegels lustige Streiche

New York	Stadium SO	LP: Everest LPBR 6023/SDBR 3023
October		LP: World Records T 108/ST 108/PE 751
1958		CD: Priceless D 1323X
		CD: Bescol CD 538
		CD: Everest EVC 9004

Tod und Verklärung

Camden NJ	Philadelphia	78: Victor M 217
April 1934	Orchestra	78: HMV DB 2324-2326
		CD: RCA/BMG 09026 609292

New York	All American SO	78: Columbia (USA) M 492
July 1941		CD: Music and Arts CD 845

New York	New York City SO	78: Victor M 1006
December		78: HMV DB 6320-6322
1944		LP: RCA Camden CAL 189
		LP: Stokowski Society LS 5
		CD: Cala CACD 0506

IGOR STRAVINSKY (1882–1972)

Fireworks

Camden NJ November 1922	Philadelphia Orchestra	78: Victor 1112 LP: Stokowski Society LS 3 CD: Pearl GEMMCD 9031 CD: Dutton CDAX 8002

L'histoire du soldat

1966	Instrumental ensemble Milhaud, Aumont, Singher	**Complete version in French** LP: Vanguard VRS 1165/VSD 71165 LP: World Records T 858/ST 859 LP: Festival Classique FC 442 CD: Vanguard VCS 10121/OVC 8004/SVC 1 **Complete version in English** LP: Vanguard VRS 1166/VSD 71166 **Instrumental sections only** LP: Vanguard VSD 707-708 CD: Vanguard OVC 8013

Le sacre du printemps

Philadelphia September 1929– March 1930	Philadelphia Orchestra	78: Victor M 74 78: HMV D 1919-1922 LP: RCA DPM2-0534 LP: Dell' Arte DA 9005 CD: RCA/BMG 09026 613942 CD: Pearl GEMMCD 9488 CD: Magic Talent CD 48002

Le sacre du printemps, abridged version

Philadelphia April 1939	Philadelphia Orchestra	Fantasia soundtrack recording LP: Top Rank 30-003 LP: Disneyland WDX 101 LP: Buena Vista BVS 101 CD: Buena Vista CD 030/60007 VHS Video: Buena Vista D211 322

L'oiseau de feu, Ballet suite

Camden NJ October 1924	Philadelphia Orchestra	Victor unpublished
Camden NJ October-December 1924	Philadelphia Orchestra	78: Victor 6492-6493 78: HMV DB 841-842
Philadelphia October 1927	Philadelphia Orchestra	78: Victor M 53 LP: RCA DPM2-0534 LP: Dell' Arte DA 9005 CD: Biddulph WHL 005
Camden NJ November-December 1935	Philadelphia Orchestra	78: Victor M 291 78: HMV DB 2882-2884 CD: Pearl GEMMCD 9031 CD: Dutton CDAX 8002
New York April 1941	All American SO	78: Columbia (USA) M 446
New York April 1942	NBC SO	78: Victor M 933 CD: Cala CACD 0505
New York May-June 1950	His SO	78: HMV DM 1421 45: Victor WDM 1421 LP: Victor LM 9029/LM 44/LM 6113
Berlin May 1957	BPO	LP: Capitol P 8407/SP 8407 LP: Angel 60229 LP: EMI CFP 134 CD: EMI CDM 769 1162/CDM 565 2072 Excerpt LP: Capitol P 8673/SP 8673
London June 1967	LSO	LP: Decca LK 4927/PFS 4139 LP: London SPC 21026 LP: Musical Heritage MHS 827052 CD: Decca 443 8982

Pastorale*

Camden NJ November 1934	Philadelphia Orchestra	78: Victor 1998 CD: Pearl GEMMCD 9031 CD: Dutton CDAX 8002
London June 1969	RPO	LP: Decca PFS 4189/SPA 159 LP: London SPC 21041
LLondon June 1969	RPO	CD: Music and Arts CD 847

Petrushka

| Philadelphia April–November 1937 | Philadelphia Orchestra | 78: Victor M 574/M 1064
78: HMV DB 3511-3514
LP: RCA Camden CAL 203
LP: RCA DPM2-0534
CD: Pearl GEMMCD 9031
CD: Dutton CDAX 8002
CD: RCA/BMG 09026 613942 |
| New York June-July 1950 | His SO | LP: Victor LM 1175
LP: HMV ALP 1240 |

Petrushka, Ballet suite

Berlin May 1957	BPO	LP: Capitol P 8407/SP 8407 LP: Angel 60229 LP: EMI CFP 134 CD: EMI CDM 769 1162/CDM 565 4232
LPhiladelphia December 1962	Philadelphia Orchestra	LP: Longanesi GCL 57
LBudapest February 1967	Budapest SO	LP: Stokowski Society LS 2

Petrushka rehearsal sequence with the Japan Philharmonic Symphony Orchestra during Stokowski's 1965 visit published on Japanese CD Platz P23G-535

PIOTR TCHAIKOVSKY (1840-1893)

Symphony No 4

Philadelphia September- December 1928	Philadelphia Orchestra	78: Victor M 48 78: HMV DB 1793-1797 CD: Pearl GEMMCD 9120
New York November 1941	NBC SO	78: Victor M 880/DM 880 LP: American Stokowski Society LSSA 1 CD: Cala CACD 0505
New York April 1971	American SO	LP: Vanguard VCS 10095 CD: Vanguard OVC 8012

Symphony No 4, third movement

Camden NJ March 1921	Philadelphia Orchestra	Victor unpublished
New York January 1957	His SO	LP: Capitol P 8385/P 8673/SP 8385/SP 8673 LP: Angel 6094 CD: EMI CDM 565 6142

Symphony No 5

Camden NJ November 1934	Philadelphia Orchestra	78: Victor M 253 78: HMV DB 2548-2553 LP: RCA Camden CAL 201 CD: Biddulph WHL 015
LHamburg July 1952	NDR Orchestra	LP: Movimento musica 01.041 CD: Frequenz 041.011
New York February 1953	His SO	LP: Victor LM 1780
London September 1966	New Philharmonia	LP: Decca LK 4882/PFS 4129/SDD 493 LP: London SPC 21017 CD: Decca 433 6872
Geneva August 1973	International Youth Festival Orchestra	LP: Cameo Classics GOCLP 9007

Symphony No 5, second movement

Camden NJ March 1923	Philadelphia Orchestra	Victor unpublished
Camden NJ April 1923	Philadelphia Orchestra	78: Victor 74846-74848/6430-6431
New York February 1947	His SO	78: Victor 11-9574 45: Victor 49-0296 Abridged version described as "Themes from second movement" and recorded for soundtrack of the film "Carnegie Hall"

Symphony No 6 "Pathétique"

New York November 1940	All American SO	78: Columbia (USA) M 432
Los Angeles July 1945	Hollywood Bowl SO	78: Victor M 1105 LP: RCA Camden CAL 152 LP: RCA CFL 100/CFL 104 LP: Stokowski Society LS 9 CD: Cala CACD 0506
London September 1973	LSO	LP: RCA ARL1-0426 LP: Grandi interpreti GIM 10 CD: RCA/BMG 09026 626022

Symphony No 6 "Pathétique", second movement

Camden NJ May 1919	Philadelphia Orchestra	Victor unpublished

Symphony No 6 "Pathétique", third movement

Camden NJ December 1917	Philadelphia Orchestra	Victor unpublished
Camden NJ October- December 1920	Philadelphia Orchestra	Victor unpublished
Camden NJ February 1921	Philadelphia Orchestra	Victor unpublished
Camden NJ March 1921	Philadelphia Orchestra	78: Victor 74713/6242

1812 Overture

Camden NJ April 1930	Philadelphia Orchestra	78: Victor 7499-7500 78: HMV DB 1663-1664 CD: Biddulph WHL 015
London June 1969	RPO Grenadiers Band Choruses	LP: Decca PFS 4189/SDD 454 LP: London SPC 21041/SPC 21108 CD: Decca 430 4102/433 6252/443 8962
LLondon June 1969	RPO Grenadiers Band Choruses	CD: Music and Arts CD 847

Andante cantabile from String Quartet No 1*

New York January 1958	His SO	LP: Capitol P 8458/P 8650/SP 8458/SP 8650 LP: EMI SXLP 30174 CD: EMI CDM 565 9122

Capriccio italien

Philadelphia January 1929	Philadelphia Orchestra	78: Victor 6949-6950 78: HMV D 1739-1740 L 7002 CD: Pearl GEMMCD 9120 <u>L 7002 was an experimental 33.1/3 rpm</u> <u>issue (Symphonic transcription disc)</u>
Brent December 1973	LPO	LP: Philips 6500 766 CD: Philips 438 3862/442 7452

Casse noisette, Ballet suite

Philadelphia November 1926	Philadelphia Orchestra	78: Victor M 3 78: HMV D 1214-1216 L 7004 Excerpts LP: Supraphon 1010 3351-1010 3352 L 7004 was an experimental 33.1/3 rpm issue (Symphonic transcription disc)
Camden NJ November- December 1934	Philadelphia Orchestra	78: Victor M 265 78: HMV DB 2540-2542 45: RCA Camden CAE 187 LP: RCA Camden CAL 100/CFL 102 CD: Pearl GEMMCD 9488
Philadelphia April 1939	Philadelphia Orchestra	Fantasia soundtrack recording LP: Top Rank 30-003 LP: Disneyland WDX 101/DQ 1243 LP: Buena Vista BVS 101 CD: Buena Vista CD 020/60007 VHS Video: Buena Vista D211 322 This version omits the Overture
New York May-June 1950	His SO	78: Victor DM 1468 45: WDM 1468 LP: Victor LM 9023/LM 46/ANL1-2604 LP: HMV ALP 1193 Excerpts 78: HMV DB 21547 45: Victor 49-3346/WDM 1394/49-0553 45: HMV 7ER 5016/7RF 195 LP: Victor LM 1083/VIC 1020 LP: HMV ALP 1133
Brent December 1973	LPO	LP: Philips 6500 766/6570 027 CD: Philips 442 7452 Waltz of the flowers CD: Philips 438 3862

One of the pre-war versions of Casse noisette Suite also appears on
CD Grammofono AB 78586

Casse noisette, Waltz of the flowers

Camden NJ February 1921	Philadelphia	Victor unpublished

Casse noisette, Russian Dance

Camden NJ October 1917	Philadelphia Orchestra	Victor unpublished

Casse noisette, Dance of the Sugar Plum Fairy

Camden NJ October 1917	Philadelphia Orchestra	Victor unpublished
New York March 1949	His SO	78: Victor 10-1487 45: Victor 49-0533

Casse noisette, Dance of the Reeds

Camden NJ February 1921	Philadelphia Orchestra	Victor unpublished
Camden NJ April 1921	Philadelphia Orchestra	Victor unpublished
Camden NJ February 1922	Philadelphia Orchestra	78: Victor 66128/798

Chant sans paroles*

Camden NJ November 1922	Philadelphia Orchestra	Victor unpublished
Camden NJ December 1922	Philadelphia Orchestra	Victor unpublished
Camden NJ April 1924	Philadelphia Orchestra	78: Victor 1111
Philadelphia December 1928	Philadelphia Orchestra	78: Victor M 71/M 192 78: HMV D 1994/DB 2207 LP: American Stokowski Society LSSA 1 CD: Pearl GEMMCD 9120 CD: Biddulph WHL 015
London June 1972	LSO	LP: Decca PFS 4351 LP: London SPC 21130 CD: IMP IMPX 9033

Eugene Onegin, Tatiana's Letter scene

New York	His SO	LP: Victor LM 142
February	Albanese	LP: HMV BLP 1075
1951		CD: RCA/BMG GD 60384

Eugene Onegin, Waltz

Brent	LPO	LP: Philips 6500 766
December		CD: Philips 442 7452
1973		

Eugene Onegin, Polonaise

New York	His SO	LP: Victor LM 2042
October 1953		

Brent	LPO	LP: Philips 6500 766
December		CD: Philips 442 7452
1973		

Francesca da Rimini

New York	NYPSO	78: Columbia (USA) M 806
November		LP: Columbia (USA) ML 4071/ML 4381/P14137
1947		LP: Columbia 33CX 1030

New York	Stadium SO	LP: Everest LPBR 6011/SDBR 3011
October		LP: World Records T 98/ST 98
1958		LP: Top Rank 35-014
		LP: Dell' Arte DA 9006
		CD: Priceless D 25327
		CD: Dell' Arte CDDA 9006
		DA 9006 was a 45 rpm LP issue

Brent	LSO	LP: Philips 6500 921
October		CD: Philips 442 7452
1974		

Hamlet

New York October 1958	Stadium SO	LP: Everest LPBR 6011/SDBR 3011 LP: World Records T 98/ST 98 LP: Top Rank 35-014 LP: Dell' Arte DA 9006 CD: Priceless D 25327 CD: Dell' Arte CDDA 9006 DA 9006 was a 45 rpm LP issue

Humoresque*

New York July 1941	All American SO	78: Columbia (USA) 19005 CD: Cala CACD 0505
New York April 1942	NBC SO	78: Victor M 933
Los Angeles August 1945	Hollywood Bowl SO	78: Victor 11-9187 LP: RCA Camden CAL 153
New York February 1953	His SO	LP: Victor LM 1774
West Ham July 1976	National PO	LP: CBS 34543/73589

Hymn of Praise (Cherubic Hymn No 1)*

Camden NJ June 1922	Choir	Victor unpublished Experimental recording

Marche slave

Philadelphia May 1925	Philadelphia Orchestra	78: Victor 6513 78: HMV D 1046
New York April 1942	NBC SO	CD: Cala CACD 0502
Los Angeles August 1945	Hollywood Bowl SO	78: Victor 11-9388 LP: RCA Camden CAL 153

London
June 1967
	LSO	LP: Decca LK 4927/PFS 4139/D94 D2/
		    SDD 454/SPA 159
		LP: London SPC 21026
		LP: Musical Heritage MHS 827052
		CD: IMP IMPX 9033
		CD: Decca 421 6342/430 4102/
		    433 6252/443 8962

LLondon June 1972	LSO	LP: Decca OPFS 3-4 LP: London SPC 21090-21091 With introductory speech by Stokowski

Pater noster (Church Song No 3)*

Camden NJ June 1922	Choir	Victor unpublished Experimental recording: versions made both with and without Stokowski playing organ
London 1961	New SO Luboff Choir	LP: Victor LM 2593/LSC 2593 CD: RCA/BMG 09026 625992 This version arranged by Luboff

Romeo and Juliet

Philadelphia September 1928	Philadelphia Orchestra	78: Victor M 46 78: HMV D 1947-1949 CD: Pearl GEMMCD 9120
New York December 1944	New York City SO	78: Victor unpublished CD: Cala CACD 0502
New York November 1949	NYPSO	78: Columbia (USA) M 898 LP: Columbia (USA) ML 4273/ML 4381 LP: Columbia 33CX 1030
LScheveningen June 1951	Hague Residentie Orchestra	CD: Music and Arts CD 831
LPhiladelphia February 1962	Philadelphia Orchestra	LP: Longanesi GCL 57
LLugano August 1968	Swiss-Italian RO	CD: Ermitage ERM 139
Geneva September 1968	Suisse Romande Orchestra	LP: Decca PFS 4181/SDD 454 LP: London SPC 21032/SPC 21108 LP: Musical Heritage MHS 827052 CD: Decca 433 6872/448 9502

Serenade for strings

Brent October 1974	LSO	LP: Philips 6500 921/6570 027 CD: Philips 442 7452

Waltz (Serenade for strings)

New York November 1949	NYPSO	78: Columbia (USA) M 898

The Sleeping Beauty, selections

Los Angeles August 1945	Hollywood Bowl SO	Victor unpublished
New York November 1947	His SO	78: Victor M 1205/V 16 78: HMV DB 9499-9504 45: Victor WDM 1205 LP: Victor LM 1010 LP: HMV ALP 1002 LP: Pathé FALP 133 LP: American Stokowski Society LS 7
New York February- April 1953	His SO	LP: Victor LM 1774
West Ham May 1976	National PO	LP: CBS 34560/44560/76665

The 1953 and 1976 recordings are drawn largely from the material in the
ballet often entitled Aurora's Wedding, in the arrangement by Diaghilev;
Iron Needle CD IN 1334 has published Music from the Sleeping Beauty dated 1934
but this must be the 1947 or 1953 recordings

The Sleeping Beauty, Ballet suite

London September 1965	New Philharmonia	LP: Decca LK 4807/PFS 4083/SDD 454/SPA 159 LP: London PM 55006/SPC 21008 CD: Decca 430 1402/448 9502

Solitude*

Philadelphia April 1937	Philadelphia Orchestra	78: Victor 14947/M 710 CD: Biddulph WHL 015
New York July 1941	All American SO	78: Columbia (USA) 11982
New York 1942	NBC SO	CD: Cala CACD 0502
Los Angeles July 1945	Hollywood Bowl SO	78: Victor 11-9187 LP: RCA Camden CAL 153
New York February 1953	His SO	LP: Victor LM 1774
West Ham November 1975	National PO	LP: Pye/Nixa PCNHX 4 CD: Pye/Nixa CDPCN 4 CD: EMI CDM 764 1402

Swan Lake, Acts 2 and 3

New York   NBC SO   LP: Victor LM 1894
November   LP: HMV ALP 1443
1954-   LP: Quintessence PMC 7007
January 1955

Swan Lake, Ballet suite

London   New Philharmonia   LP: Decca LK 4807/PFS 4083/SPA 159
September   LP: London PM 55006/SPC 21008
1965   CD: Decca 430 1402/448 9502

Swan Lake, Dance of the Cygnets and Queen of the Swans

New York   His SO   78: Victor DM 1394
May 1950   45: Victor WDM 1394
                                LP: Victor LM 1083/VIC 1020
                                LP: HMV ALP 1133

AMBROISE THOMAS (1811-1896)

Gavotte (Mignon)

Camden NJ   Philadelphia   78: Victor 66172/944
March 1923   Orchestra   78: HMV DA 562

Philadelphia   Philadelphia   78: Victor M 116
May 1929   Orchestra   78: HMV DB 1643
                                CD: Biddulph WHL 011
                                CD: Magic Talent CD 48015
                                Biddulph and Magic Talent incorrectly
                                dated 1937

VIRGIL THOMSON (1896-1989)

The Plow that broke the Plains, suite

Los Angeles August 1946	Hollywood Bowl SO	78: Victor M 1116 CD: RCA/BMG 09026 681632
New York January 1961	Symphony of the Air	LP: Vanguard VRS 1071/VSD 2095/VBD 385/ VSD 707-708 CD: Vanguard OVC 8013/SVC 1

The River, suite

New York January 1961	Symphony of the Air	LP: Vanguard VRS 1071/VSD 2095/VBD 385 CD: Vanguard OVC 8013/SVC 1

The Mother of us all, Symphonic suite

LNew York March 1950	NYPSO	LP: New York Philharmonic NYP 821-822

JOAQUIN TURINA (1882-1949)

La oracion del torero

New York February 1958	His SO	LP: Capitol P 8458/P 8694/SP 8694 LP: Angel 6094/34481 LP: EMI SXLP 30174

Gypsy Dance (The Sacred Mountain)

Philadelphia April 1937	Philadelphia Orchestra	CD: Stokowski Society LSCD 20 CD: Cala CACD 0501

RALPH VAUGHAN WILLIAMS (1872-1958)

Symphony No 6, original version

New York February 1949	NYPSO	78: Columbia (USA) M 838 LP: Columbia (USA) ML 4214 LP: CBS 61432 CD: Sony SMK 58933

Symphony No 8

LLondon September 1964	BBC SO	CD: Music and Arts CD 770 CD: BBC Radio Classics 15656 91312

Scherzo (Symphony No 8)

New York February 1957	His SO	LP: Capitol P 8385 CD: EMI CDM 565 6142

Fantasia on Greensleeves

New York February 1949	NYPSO	78: Columbia (USA) M 838 LP: Columbia (USA) BM 13 LP: Japanese Stokowski Society JLSS 0019

Fantasia on a theme by Thomas Tallis

LNew York March 1948	NYPSO	LP: Japanese Stokowski Society JLSS 0019
New York September 1952	His SO	LP: Victor LM 1739 LP: HMV ALP 1205 LP: Stokowski Society LS 17
LNew York November 1960	Symphony of the Air	CD: Library of Congress CLS 2
LLondon May 1974	New Philharmonia	CD: BBC Radio Classics BBCRD 9107
London August 1975	RPO	LP: Desmar DSM 1011 LP: Teldec 642.631

GIUSEPPE VERDI (1813-1901)

Aida, excerpt (Ciel! Mio padre!)

LPhiladelphia January 1962	Philadelphia Orchestra Nilsson, London	LP: Melodram MEL 228

La forza del destino, Overture

LPhiladelphia January 1963	Philadelphia Orchestra	LP: Japanese Stokowski Society JLSS 11/12

HEITOR VILLA-LOBOS (1887-1959)

Bachianas brasilieras No 1 "Modinha"

New York October 1958	Stadium SO	LP: Everest LPBR 6016/SDBR 3016 LP: World Records T 173/ST 173 CD: Priceless D 24924 CD: Everest EVC 9023

Bachianas brasilieras No 5

New York February 1951	His SO Albanese	LP: Victor LM 142 LP: HMV BLP 1075
New York 1964	American SO Moffo	LP: RCA LSC 2795/LSB 4114 CD: RCA/BMG 7831-2-RG/GD 87831/ 09026 626002

Uirapuru, tone poem

New York October 1958	Stadium SO	LP: Everest LPBR 6016/SDBR 3016 CD: Priceless D 24924 CD: Everest EVC 9023

ANTONIO VIVALDI (1675-1741)

Le 4 stagioni

London June 1966	New Philharmonia Bean	LP: Decca LK 4873/PFS 4124/VIV 3 LP: London SPC 21015 CD: Decca 417 0742/433 6802

Concerto grosso in D minor op 3 No 11*

Camden NJ November 1934	Philadelphia Orchestra	78: Victor 14113-14114 78: HMV DB 6047-6048 LP: Stokowski Society LSSA 5
New York February- April 1952	His SO	LP: Victor LM 1721
New York April 1967	His SO I.Kipnis	LP: Bach Guild 70696 LP: Vanguard SRV 363/VSD 707-708 CD: Vanguard OVC 8009/VBD 363 This version performed in the original instrumentation

RICHARD WAGNER (1813-1883)

Siegfried Idyll

LNew York November 1960	Symphony of the Air	CD: Library of Congress CLC 2 CD: Music and Arts CD 657

Wesendonk-Lieder

New York May 1950	His SO Farrell	78: Victor M 1233 45: Victor WDM 1233 LP: Victor LM 1066/AVM1-1413

3 Wesendonk-Lieder (Im Treibhaus; Schmerzen; Träume)*

Philadelphia December 1940	Philadelphia Orchestra Traubel	78: Victor M 872 CD: Pearl GEMMCD 9486

Schmerzen and Träume also appear on a special CD issued by the
Metropolitan Opera

Der fliegende Holländer, Overture

New York January 1949	NYPSO	LP: Columbia (USA) BM 39 LP: Japanese Stokowski Society JLSS 0019

Götterdämmerung, Dawn and Rhine Journey

New York 1949	NYPSO	LP: Columbia (USA) ML 4273
London August 1966	LSO	LP: Decca LK 4851/PFS 4116/SPA 537 LP: London SPC 21016/STS 15565 CD: Decca 421 0202/433 6392/443 9012
London November 1974	LSO	LP: RCA ARL1-1317 CD: RCA/BMG 5995-2-RC/09026 625982

Götterdämmerung, Siegfried's Death and Funeral March

Camden NJ November 1922	Philadelphia Orchestra	Victor unpublished
Camden NJ December 1922	Philadelphia Orchestra	Victor unpublished
LPhiladelphia April 1932	Philadelphia Orchestra	LP: Bell Telephone Laboratories BTL 8001
London August 1966	LSO	LP: Decca LK 4851/PFS 4116 LP: London SPC 21016/STS 15565 CD: Decca 421 0202/433 6392/443 9012
London November 1974	LSO	LP: RCA ARL1-1317 CD: RCA/BMG 5995-2-RC/09026 625982

Götterdämmerung, Brünnhilde's Immolation (Starke Scheite schichtet mir dort)

Camden NJ March- October 1933	Philadelphia Orchestra Davies	78: Victor M 188 78: HMV DB 2126-2130 LM 188 LP: Recherche 1002 CD: Pearl GEMMCDS 9076 <u>LM 188 was an experimental 33.1/3 rpm</u> <u>issue (Symphonic transcription disc)</u>
LPhiladelphia January 1962	Philadelphia Orchestra Nilsson	LP: Melodram MEL 228

Götterdämmerung Brünnhilde's Immolation, orchestral version*

LPhiladelphia April 1932	Philadelphia OrchestraL	LP: Bell Telephone Laboratories BTL 8001
London November 1974	LSO	LP: RCA ARL1-1317 CD: RCA/BMG 5595-2-RC/09026 625982

Götterdämmerung, Finale (orchestral postlude to Immolation Scene)

Camden NJ November 1922	Philadelphia Orchestra	Victor unpublished
Camden NJ December 1922	Philadelphia Orchestra	Victor unpublished
Philadelphia January 1927	Philadelphia Orchestra	78: Victor 6625 78: HMV D 1227 LP: Victor VCM 7101/VIC 6060 CD: Pearl GEMMCDS 9076 CD: Magic Talent CD 48015

Lohengrin, Prelude

Camden NJ April 1922	Philadelphia Orchestra	Victor unpublished
Camden NJ April 1924	Philadelphia Orchestra	78: Victor 6490 78: HMV DB 839
Philadelphia October 1927	Philadelphia Orchestra	78: Victor 6791 78: HMV D 1463 LP: RCA Camden CAL 120 LP: American Stokowski Society LSSA 2 CD: Pearl GEMMCD 9486
LPhiladelphia January 1962	Philadelphia Orchestra	LP: Melodram MEL 228 Incorrectly described as Act 2 Prelude

Lohengrin, Act 3 Prelude

Camden NJ May 1919	Philadelphia Orchestra	Victor unpublished
Camden NJ March 1921	Philadelphia Orchestra	Victor unpublished
Camden NJ April 1921	Philadelphia Orchestra	Victor unpublished
Philadelphia March 1940	Philadelphia Orchestra	78: Victor M 731 78: HMV DB 5853 CD: Pearl GEMMCD 9486

Die Meistersinger von Nürnberg, Overture

Philadelphia January 1936	Philadelphia Orchestra	78: Victor M 508/M 731 78: HMV DB 5852-5853 LP: American Stokowski Society LSSA 2 CD: Pearl GEMMCD 9486
LLondon June 1972	LSO	LP: Decca OPFS 3-4 LP: London SPC 21090-21091 CD: Decca 421 0202/433 6392/443 9012

Die Meistersinger von Nürnberg, Suite (Act 3 Prelude, Dance of the
Apprentices and Entry of the Masters)*

Barking October 1973	RPO	LP: RCA ARS1-0498 CD: RCA/BMG 5995-2-RC/09026 612682/ 09026 625982

Die Meistersinger von Nürnberg, Act 3 Prelude

Camden NJ March 1931	Philadelphia Orchestra	78: Victor 1584 78: HMV DA 1291

Parsifal, Prelude

Philadelphia November 1936	Philadelphia Orchestra	78: Victor M 421 78: HMV DB 3269-3270 LP: RCA Camden CAL 163 CD: Pearl GEMMCD 9448

Parsifal, Good Friday Music

Philadelphia November 1936	Philadelphia Orchestra	78: Victor M 421 78: HMV DB 3271-3272 LP: RCA Camden CAL 163 CD: Pearl GEMMCD 9448
New York September 1952	His SO	LP: Victor LM 1730 LP: Stokowski Society LS 5
Houston March 1959	Houston SO	LP: Everest LPBR 6031/SDBR 3031 LP: World Records TP 79 LP: Hallmark SHM 541 LP: Top Rank 40-007 LP: Vox STGBY 515040 CD: Everest EVC 9024

Parsifal, Symphonic synthesis from Act 3*

Camden NJ April 1934	Philadelphia Orchestra	78: Victor 8617-8618 78: HMV DB 2272-2273 CD: Pearl GEMMCD 9448
New York September 1952	His SO	LP: Victor LM 1730 LP: Stokowski Society LS 5
Houston March 1959	Houston SO	LP: Everest LPBR 6031/SDBR 3031 LP: World Records TP 79 LP: Hallmark SHM 541 LP: Vox STGBY 515040 LP: Top Rank 40-007 CD: Everest EVC 9024

Parsifal, extracts (Weh! Weh!..to Schlafen ich muss; Ha! Kühner!..to Traute, teuerste Mutter; War dir fremd noch der Schmerz..to end of Act 2; Enthüllet den Gral!..to end of Act 3)

LPhiladelphia March- April 1933	Philadelphia Orchestra Various choirs Bampton, Steel, Eddy, Tcherkassky, Treash	LP: Ed Smith UORC 280

Parsifal, Transformation music

Camden NJ May 1923	Philadelphia Orchestra	Victor unpublished

Das Rheingold, Orchestral extracts (Prelude, Song of the Rhinemaidens, Alberich steals the Gold, Erda's Warning and Entrance of the Gods into Valhalla)*

Camden NJ March 1933	Philadelphia Orchestra	78: Victor M 179 78: HMV DB 1976-1978 L 11643-11644 CD: Pearl GEMMCDS 9076 L 11643-11644 was an experimental 33.1/3 rpm issue (Symphonic transcription disc)

Das Rheingold, Orchestral extracts (Alberich steals the Gold and Erda's Warning)*

Camden NJ May 1923	Philadelphia Orchestra	Victor unpublished

Das Rheingold, Entrance of the Gods into Valhalla*

| New York
December
1960 | Symphony
of the Air
Arroyo, Ordassy,
Parker | LP: Victor LM 1336/LSC 2555/VCS 7077
LP: RCA RB 16279/SB 2148/VICS1301/
AGL1-1338/GL 11336
LP: Camden Classics CCV 5005
CD: RCA/BMG 09026 625972 |
| London
August 1966 | LSO | LP: Decca LK 4851/PFS 4116/SPA 537
LP: London SPC 21016/STS 15565
CD: Decca 421 0202/433 6392/443 9012 |

Rienzi, Overture

Camden NJ May 1919	Philadelphia Orchestra	78: Victor 74602/6239 78: HMV 3/0520-0521/DB 382
Philadelphi November 1926- January 1927	Philadelphia Orchestra	78: Victor 6624-6625 78: HMV D 1226-1227 LP: Cameo Classics GOCLP 9009H
New York August 1947	NYPSO	LP: Columbia (USA) ML 2153 LP: Columbia 33C 1026
LPhiladelphia January 1962	Philadelphia Orchestra	LP: Melodram MEL 228
Barking October 1973	RPO	LP: RCA ARS1-0498 CD: RCA/BMG 09026 612682/09026 625972

**Siegfried, extracts (1.The Wanderer questions Mime; 2.Nothung! Nothung!;
3.Forest murmurs; 4.Final duet, beginning at Ob jetzt ich dein?)***

| Camden NJ
November
1934 | Philadelphia
Orchestra
Davies (4),
Jagel (2,4) | 78: Victor M 441/DM 441
LP: Recherche LP 1002 (4)
CD: Pearl GEMMCDS 9076 |

Siegfried, Forest murmurs

LPhiladelphia April 1932	Philadelphia Orchestra	LP: Bell Telephone Laboratories BTL 8001
Los Angeles August 1946	Hollywood Bowl SO	78: Victor 11-9418 78: HMV DB 21238 LP: RCA Camden CAL 153
London August 1966	LSO	LP: Decca LK 4851/PFS 4116 LP: London SPC 21016/STS 15565 CD: Decca 421 0202/433 6392/443 9012

Tannhäuser, Overture

Camden NJ May 1919	Philadelphia Orchestra	Victor unpublished
Camden NJ March 1921	Philadelphia Orchestra	Victor unpublished
Camden NJ November- December 1921	Philadelphia Orchestra	78: Victor 74758-74759-74768/6244-6478 78: HMV DB 386-387 LP: Stokowski Society LS 3

Tannhäuser, Overture and Venusberg Music

Philadelphia September 1929- March 1930	Philadelphia Orchestra	78: Victor M 78 78: HMV D 1905-1907 L 11669-11670 L 11669-11672 was an experimental 33.1/3 rpm issue (Symphonic transcription disc)
Philadelphia December 1937	Philadelphia Orchestra	78: Victor M 530 78: HMV DB 3775-3777 CD: Pearl GEMMCD 9448
New York February 1950	His SO Chorus	78: Victor DM 1383 45: Victor WDM 1383 LP: Victor LM 1066 LP: Stokowski Society LS 19
New York December 1960- April 1961	Symphony of the Air Chorus	LP: Victor LM 1336/LSC 2555 LP: RCA RB 16279/SB 2148/VICS 1301/ AGL1-1338/GL 11336 LP: Contour CCV 5005 LP: Quintessence PMC 7019 CD: RCA/BMG 09026 615032/09026 625972 Quintessence incorrectly describes orchestra as RCA Victor SO

Tannhäuser, Act 3 Prelude

Philadelphia January 1936	Philadelphia Orchestra	78: Victor M 530 78: HMV DB 3254-3255 CD: Pearl GEMMCD 9448
New York February 1950	His SO	78: Victor DM 1383 45: Victor WDM 1383 LP: Victor LM 1066

Tannhäuser, Entry of the Guests

Camden NJ April 1923	Philadelphia Orchestra	Victor unpublished
Camden NJ December 1923	Philadelphia Orchestra	Victor unpublished
Camden NJ April 1924	Philadelphia Orchestra	78: Victor 6478 LP: Stokowski Society LS 3
New York April 1966	Metropolitan Opera Orchestra & Chorus	LP: MRF Records MRF 7 Farewell gala in Old Metropolitan Opera House; includes brief speech by Stokowski

Tannhäuser, Pilgrims' Chorus

London 1961	New SO Luboff Choir	LP: Victor LM 2593/LSC 2593/VCS 7077 LP: Quintessence PMC 7019 CD: RCA/BMG GD 89293/09026 625992 Arranged by Luboff/Stott

Tristan und Isolde, Prelude

Camden NJ February 1922	Philadelphia Orchestra	Victor unpublished
Camden NJ April 1922	Philadelphia Orchestra	Victor unpublished
Camden NJ October 1922	Philadelphia Orchestra	Victor unpublished
Philadelphia April- November 1937	Philadelphia Orchestra	78: Victor 15202-15203/M 508 CD: Pearl GEMMCD 9486

Tristan und Isolde, Prelude and Liebestod

New York   New York City SO   Victor unpublished
February
1945

LPhiladelphia   Philadelphia   LP: Melodram MEL 228
January   Orchestra   This LP set separates Prelude from
1962   Liebestod

Barking   RPO   LP: RCA ARS1-0498
October   CD: RCA/BMG 5995-2-RC/09026 612682/
1973   09026 625982

Tristan und Isolde, Symphonic synthesis (Prelude, Act 2 Liebesnacht and
Liebestod)*

Camden NJ   Philadelphia   78: Victor M 154
April 1932   Orchestra   78: HMV DB 1911-1914
                                     L 11636-11637
                                     L 11636-11637 was an experimental 33.1/3
                                     rpm issue (Symphonic transcription disc)

New York   His SO   LP: Victor LM 1174
1950   LP: Stokowski Society LS 19

LNew York   American SO   CD: Memories HR 4495-4497
May 1969

Tristan und Isolde, Symphonic synthesis (Liebesnacht and Liebestod)*

Philadelphia   Philadelphia   78: Victor M 508
December   Orchestra   78: HMV DB 3087-3089
1935-   LP: American Stokowski Society LSSA 2
April 1939   CD: Pearl GEMMCD 9486

New York   All American SO   78: Columbia (USA) M 427
November
1940

Philadelphia   Philadelphia   LP: Columbia (USA) ML 5471/MS 6147/MGP 17
February   Orchestra   LP: CBS Y 32368/61288
1960   LP: Philips SCFL 107

Tristan und Isolde, Act 3 Prelude

New York April 1961	Symphony of the Air	LP: Victor LM 1336/LSC 2555/VICS 1301 LP: RCA RB 16279/SB 2148/AGL1-1338/ GL 11336 LP: Camden Classics CCV 5005 CD: RCA/BMG 09026 615032/09026 625972

Tristan und Isolde, Liebestod*

LPhiladelphia December 1931	Philadelphia Orchestra	LP: Bell Telephone Laboratories BTL 7901

Die Walküre, extracts (1.Siegmund comforts Sieglinde; 2.Ride of the Valkyries; 3.War es so schmählich?)*

Camden NJ April 1934	Philadelphia Orchestra Davies (3)	78: Victor M 248 78: HMV DB 2470-2471 CD: Pearl GEMMCD 9076 <u>Victor and HMV sets also include Wotan's Farewell and Magic Fire Music (see separate entry)</u>

Die Walküre, Ride of the Valkyries*

Camden NJ March 1921	Philadelphia Orchestra	78: Victor 74684/6245 78: HMV 3-0632/DB 387
LPhiladelphia April 1932	Philadelphia Orchestra	LP: Bell Telephone Laboratories BTL 8001 <u>Recording as published is incomplete</u>
New York December 1960	Symphony of the Air Arroyo, Ordassy, Yarick, Allen, Okerson, Sarfaty, Verrett, Parker	LP: Victor LM 1336/LSC 2555/VCS 7077 LP: RCA RB 16279/SB 2148/AGL1-1338/ GL 11336 LP: Camden Classics CCV 5005 CD: RCA/BMG GD 89293/09026 625972
London August 1966	LSO	LP: Decca LK 4851/PFS 4116/SPA 537 LP: London SPC 21016/SPC 21074/STS 15565 CD: IMP IMPX 9033 CD: Decca 421 0202/433 6392/443 9012

Die Walküre, Wotan's Farewell and Magic Fire music*

| Camden NJ
April 1934 | Philadelphia
Orchestra
Tibbett | 78: Victor M 248
78: HMV DB 2472-2473
CD: RCA/BMG GD 87808
CD: Pearl GEMMCDS 9076 |

Die Walküre, Magic Fire music*

Camden NJ May 1920	Philadelphia Orchestra	Victor unpublished
Camden NJ April 1921	Philadelphia Orchestra	Victor unpublished
Camden NJ November- December 1921	Philadelphia Orchestra	78: Victor 74736/6245 78: HMV 3-0723/DB 387
LPhiladelphia April 1932	Philadelphia Orchestra	LP: Bell Telephone Laboratories BTL 8001 Recording as published is incomplete
Philadelphia April 1939	Philadelphia Orchestra	78: Victor 15800 78: HMV DB 3942 45: RCA Camden CAE 101 LP: Victor VCM 7101 LP: RCA Camden CAL 120 CD: Pearl GEMMCDS 9076 CD: Magic Talent CD 48015
New York November 1947	NYPSO	78: Columbia (USA) M 301 LP: Columbia (USA) ML 2153 LP: Columbia 33C 1026
Houston April 1960	Houston SO	LP: Everest LPBR 6070/SDBR 3070 LP: World Records TP 79 LP: Vox STGBY 515040 CD: Priceless D 1323X CD: Everest EVC 9024
Barking October 1973	RPO	LP: ARS1-0498 CD: RCA/BMG 09026 616682/09026 625972

BEN WEBER (born 1916)

Symphony on poems of William Blake

New York October 1952	His SO Galfour	LP: Victor LM 1785 LP: Composers' Recordings CRI 120

CARL MARIA VON WEBER (1786-1826)

Invitation to the Dance*

Camden NJ May 1919	Philadelphia Orchestra	78: Victor 74598/6237 <u>Arrangement by Weingartner</u>
Philadelphia May 1927	Philadelphia Orchestra	78: Victor 6643 78: HMV D 1285/DB 3699 LP: Stokowski Society LS 1 CD: Grammofono AB 78552 <u>Arrangement by Berlioz</u>
LPhiladelphia December 1931	Philadelphia Orchestra	LP: Bell Telephone Laboratories BTL 7901 <u>Arrangement by Berlioz</u>
Philadelphia April 1937	Philadelphia Orchestra	78: Victor 15189 78: HMV DB 3699 45: RCA Camden CAE 192 LP: RCA Camden CAL 123/CAL 282 LP: Supraphon 1010 3351-1010 3352 <u>Arrangement by Berlioz/Stokowski;</u> <u>Supraphon incorrectly dated 1935</u>
New York December 1940	All American SO	78: Columbia (USA) 11481 <u>Arrangement by Berlioz/Stokowski</u>
New York May 1950	His SO	LP: Victor LM 1083/VIC 1020 LP: HMV ALP 1133 <u>Arrangement by Berlioz/Stokowski</u>

MISCELLANEOUS OR TRADITIONAL

Deep river

| London | New SO | LP: Victor LM 2593/LSC 2593 |
| 1961 | Luboff Choir | CD: RCA/BMG 09026 625992 |

Doxology (Old 100th)

| London | New SO | LP: Victor LM 2593/LSC 2593 |
| 1961 | Luboff Choir | CD: RCA/BMG 09026 625992 |

Etenraku, 8th century Japanese Ceremonial Prelude, arranged by Kunoye

Camden NJ	Philadelphia	78: Victor 14142
November	Orchestra	CD: Stokowski Society LSCD 20
1934		CD: Cala CACD 0501

La Marseillaise

| LPhiladelphia | Philadelphia | CD: Cala CACD 0502 |
| October 1935 | Orchestra | |

O come all ye faithful*

Camden NJ	Choir	Victor unpublished
June 1922		Experimental recording: versions made with
		and without Stokowski playing organ

Russian Christmas music*, sometimes attributed to Ippolitov-Ivanov

Camden NJ October 1934	Philadelphia Orchestra	78: Victor 1692 Re-recorded in 1939 with same catalogue number
New York February 1947	His SO	78: Victor 11-9837 45: Victor 49-0974/ERA 119

Ancient Liturgical melodies (Veni, creator spiritus; Veni, Emanuel)*

Camden NJ April 1934	Philadelphia Orchestra	78: Victor 1789 78: HMV DA 1551 CD: Stokowski Society LSCD 20 CD: Cala CACD 0501

SELECTION OF PUBLISHED SPEECH RECORDINGS BY LEOPOLD STOKOWSKI

Stokowski introduces a broadcast of music from Wagner's Ring

New York   CD: Pearl GEMMCDS 9076
January 1932

Speech to audience at the end of Bell Telephone sessions

Philadelphia   LP: Bell Telephone Laboratories BTL 8001
April 1932

Speech to audience at Farewell gala in the Old Metropolitan Opera House

New York   LP: MRF Records MRF 7
April 1966

Stokowski talks about his Bach transcriptions

1962   CD: Pearl GEMMCDS 9098

Television interview

Budapest   LP: Stokowski Society LS 2
February 1967

Radio interview

Copenhagen   LP: Poco DLP 8407
August 1967

Unspecified speech

1972   CD: Japanese Stokowski Society LCSD 23/24

Stokowski introduces performance of Tchaikovsky's Marche slave

London   LP: Decca OPFS 3-4
June 1972   LP: London SPC 21090-21091

ROYAL ALBERT HALL
Sunday 10 February at 7.30 p.m.

LONDON SYMPHONY ORCHESTRA

Principal Conductor
André Previn

Leaders
Hugh Bean
John Brown

Patron : Her Majesty the Queen

STOKOWSKI

BEETHOVEN
Coriolan Overture
Symphony No. 8
Symphony No. 3 "Eroica"

Royal
Albert
Hall

£2.00   £1.50   £1.00   80p   50p

(standing)

Tickets on sale at
Royal Albert Hall Box
Office (01-589 8212)

Presented in association
with the London Orchestral
Concert Board

Leopold Stokowski

Concert register

compiled by John Hunt

LEOPOLD STOKOWSKI: THE CONCERT REGISTER

My thanks goes again to Edward Johnson and other
Stokowski Society members and contributors for
giving the impetus for this partial listing of
Leopold Stokowski's public appearances in the
role of conductor.

We hoped at the outset to present a virtually
complete listing of the Maestro's activities over
a 68-year period, but it transpired during the
work that a number of gaps in our knowledge just
stubbornly refused to be filled. Particularly
unfortunate is the apparent absence from the
Philadelphia Orchestra's own archive of programme
details for a number of seasons in the late 1930s.

I would estimate that we have probably been able
to assemble a listing amounting to about
seventy-five percent of Stokowski's work in
concert halls and opera houses worldwide.

A remarkable Stokowski achievement not mentioned
in the introduction to the discography itself is
his pioneering work in introducing new music,
giving premiere performances of countless scores,
many of which have gone on to become established
twentieth-century classics. Because of space
restrictions in the concert listing itself, a
separate listing of the works given their first
world or American performances by Stokowski
follows at the end. Suffice it here to note
what must be Stokowski's most fitting monument:
Mahler (US premieres of 2 works), Prokofiev
(US premieres of 3 works), Rachmaninov (World
premieres of 4 works, and US premiere of 1 more),
Schoenberg (World premieres of 2 works, and US
premieres of 4 more), Shostakovich (US premieres
of 5 works), Sibelius (US premieres of 4 works),
Stravinsky (US premieres of 6 works).

Ealing, 16–17 November 1904
Wekerlin La laitière de Trainon
Nicolai Die lustigen Weiber Overture
Elgar Salut d'amour
Délibes Waltz from Coppélia
This comprised the interval music for a production of the play "Woodbarrow Farm" by Jerome K. Jerome; other similar engagements were probably carried out by Stokowski during this period, when he was organist at St. James' Piccadilly

Paris, 12 May 1909
Colonne Orchestra
Samaroff
Tchaikovsky March (Symphony No 6)
Tchaikovsky Piano Concerto No 1
Ippolitov-Ivanov Caucasian Sketches
Stokowski's official conducting début; concert also included items performed by the singers Litvinne and Samkov not accompanied by Stokowski

London, 18 May 1909
New Symphony Orchestra
MacMillen
Beethoven Coriolan Overture
Lalo Symphonie espagnole
Saint-Saens Violin Concerto No 3
Ippolitov-Ivanov Caucasian Sketches

Cincinnati, 26–27 November 1909
Cincinnati Orchestra
Mozart Zauberflöte Overture
Beethoven Symphony No 5
Weber Freischütz Overture
Wagner Siegfried Idyll
Wagner Ride of the Valkyries

Ohio Northern University,
30 November 1909
Cincinnati Orchestra
Handel Messiah

St Mary's, 1 December 1909 (afternoon)
Cincinnati Orchestra
Details as for 30 November

Piqua, 1 December 1909 (evening)
Cincinnati Orchestra
Details as for 30 November

Oberlin, 2–3 December 1909
Cincinnati Orchestra
Details as for 30 November

Cincinnati, 10–11 December 1909
Cincinnati Orchestra
Powell
Ippolitov-Ivanov Caucasian Sketches
Tor Aulin Violin Concerto No 3
Tchaikovsky Symphony No 6

Cincinnati, 17–18 December 1909
Cincinnati Orchestra
Koerner
Brahms Symphony No 3
Mendelssohn Hebrides Overture
Smetana The Moldau
Vocal items by Beethoven & Brahms

Cincinnati, 7–8 January 1910
Cincinnati Orchestra
Wüllner
Strauss Tod und Verklärung
Liszt Les Préludes
Items with vocal declamation by Schubert, Schumann and Schillings

Cincinnati, 21–22 January 1910
Cincinnati Orchestra
Rachmaninov
Schubert Symphony No 9
Rachmaninov Piano Concerto No 2
Wagner Fliegende Holländer Overture

Dayton, 28 January 1910
Cincinnati Orchestra
Kreisler
Sibelius Symphony No 1
Beethoven Violin Concerto
Beethoven Leonore No 3 Overture

Concert on 31 January reported as
containing Gliere Sirenen

Cincinnati, 4-5 February 1910
Details as for 28 January

Cincinnati, 11 February 1910
Cincinnati Orchestra
Weber Freischütz Overture
Wagner Lohengrin Act 3 Prelude
Grieg Peer Gynt Suite
Ippolitov-Ivanov Caucasian Sketches,
   excerpt
Programme also included piano solos
by Rubinstein, Chopin & Mendelssohn
played by Maude Allan

Cincinnati, 18-19 February 1910
Cincinnati Orchestra
Busoni
Bach Suite No 3
Haydn Symphony No 100
Liszt Piano Concerto No 1
Rimsky-Korsakov Scheherazade

Cincinnati, 23 February 1910
Cincinnati Orchestra
Elman

Columbus, 28 February 1910
Cincinnati Orchestra
Heermann
Gluck/Mottl Ballet Suite
Brahms Violin Concerto
Beethoven Symphony No 3

Cincinnati, 4-5 March 1910
Details as for 28 February

Muncis, 7 March 1910
Cincinnati Orchestra
Bizet L'Arlésienne Suite No 1
Debussy Nuages et fêtes (Nocturnes)
MacDowell Indian Suite
Programme also included vocal items

St Mary's, 8 March 1910
Details as for 7 March

Cleveland, 9 March 1910
Cincinnati Orchestra
Sembrich
Programme as for 7 March

Wooster, 10 March 1910
Details as for 7 March

Akron, 11 March 1910
Details as for 7 March

Findlay, 12 March 1910
Details as for 7 March

Cincinnati, 18-19 March 1910
Cincinnati Orchestra
Kirkby-Lunn
Programme as for 7 March

Columbus, 28 March 1910
Cincinnati Orchestra
Carreno
Wagner Lohengrin Prelude
Tchaikovsky Piano Concerto No 1
Sibelius Swan of Tuonela
Tchaikovsky Symphony No 5

Dayton, 29 March 1910
Details as for 28 March

Cincinnati, 1-2 April 1910
Details as for 28 March

Cincinnati, 10 May 1910
Cincinnati Orchestra
Gluck/Mottl Ballet Suite
Wagner Parsifal Prelude
Wagner Lohengrin Act 3 Prelude
Tchaikovsky Symphony No 6

Connersville, 11-12 May 1910
Details as for 10 May

Other works noted as having been
performed during the Cincinnati
1909-1910 touring season include
Beethoven Symphony No 9, Gounod
Mireille Overture, Saint-Saens
Violin Concerto No 3 and Cello
Concerto, Tchaikovsky Sérénade
mélancholique and Weber's aria
Ozean du Ungeheuer (Oberon)

Cincinnati, 26-27 November 1910
Cincinnati Orchestra
Beethoven Symphony No 7
Wagner Tristan Prelude and Liebestod
Weber Oberon Overture
Vocal items by Saint-Saens & Wagner

Cincinnati, 9-10 December 1910
Cincinnati Orchestra
Schumann Symphony No 2
Goldmark Violin Concerto
Liszt Tasso
Smetana Bartered Bride Overture

Cincinnati, 16-17 December 1910
Cincinnati Orchestra
Strauss programme
Don Juan
Dance of the 7 veils (Salome)
Love Scene (Feuersnot)
Tod und Verklärung

Cincinnati, 6-7 January 1911
Cincinnati Orchestra
Glinka Ruslan and Ludmila Overture
Rachmaninov Isle of the Dead
Rubinstein Piano Concerto in D
Tchaikovsky Symphony No 4

Cincinnati, 15 January 1911
Cincinnati Orchestra
Elgar Pomp & Circumstance March No 1
Weber Aria from Der Freischütz
Tchaikovsky Casse noisette Suite
Saint-Saens Danse macabre
Wagner Tannhäuser Overture

Cincinnati, 20-21 January 1911
Cincinnati Orchestra
Schubert Rosamunde Overture
Beethoven Symphony No 8
Tchaikovsky Violin Concerto
Dukas L'apprenti sorcier

Cincinnati, 29 January 1911
Cincinnati Orchestra
Dvorak Carnival Overture
Sibelius Valse triste
Chopin Piano Concerto No 1
Grieg Peer Gynt Suite
Huber Serenata
Liszt Hungarian Rhapsody
Wagner Kaisermarsch

Cincinnati, 3-4 February 1911
Cincinnati Orchestra
Sgambati Symphony in D
Sinigaglia Le baruffe chiozotte Ov.
Rossini Barbiere di Siviglia Overture
Vocal items by Puccini and Verdi

Cincinnati, 12 February 1911
Cincinnati Orchestra
Nicolai Die lustigen Weiber Overture
Longfellow King Robert of Sicily
Weber Invitation to the Dance
Mendelssohn Midsummer Night's Dream
Wagner Ride of the Valkyries

Cincinnati, 17-18 February 1911
Cincinnati Orchestra
Beethoven Coriolan Overture
Mozart Symphony No 40
Bohlmann Lyric Tone Poem
Scharwenka Piano Concerto in F
Wagner Meistersinger Overture

Cincinnati, 26 February 1911
Cincinnati Orchestra
Meyerbeer Coronation March
German 3 Dances from Henry VIII
Saint-Saens Bacchanale
Wagner Lohengrin Prelude
Vocal items by Mozart and Bizet

Cincinnati, 3-4 March 1911
Cincinnati Orchestra
Schubert Symphony No 8
Ippolitov-Ivanov Caucasian Sketches
Tchaikovsky Symphony No 6

Cincinnati, 12 March 1911
Cincinnati Orchestra
Auber Fra Diavolo Overture
Vieuxtemps Ballade et Polonaise
Bizet L'Arlśienne Suite
Mozart Nozze di Figaro Overture
Brahms 2 Hungarian Dances
Herbert American Fantasy

Cincinnati, 17-18 March 1911
Cincinnati Orchestra
Wagner Faust Overture
Dvorak Cello Concerto
Brahms Symphony No 1

Cincinnati, 31 March-1 April 1911
Cincinnati Orchestra
Dvorak Symphony No 9
Beethoven Piano Concerto No 5
Tchaikovsky 1812 Overture

154

Cincinnati, 19 April 1911
Cincinnati Orchestra
Sheffield Philharmonic Choir
Beethoven Symphony No 9

Cincinnati, 20 April 1911
Cincinnati Orchestra
Sheffield Philharmonic Choir
Verdi Requiem

In a concert on 18 April 1911 the
Cincinnati Orchestra and Sheffield
Philharmonic Choir had performed
Elgar's Dream of Gerontius under the
composer's direction; other works
which Stokowski may have directed
during the 1910-1911 Cincinnati
season are Bruch Violin Concerto,
Busoni Comedy Overture, Busoni
Konzertstück and Smetana Bartered
Bride Overture

Cincinnati, 17-18 November 1911
Cincinnati Orchestra
Brahms Symphony No 1
Strube Puck, Comedy Overture
Wagner Tannhäuser Overture
Vocal items by Weber and Wagner

Cincinnati, 24-25 November 1911
Cincinnati Orchestra
Elgar Symphony No 2
Strauss Dance of the 7 veils
Strauss Serenade for wind
Strauss Don Juan

Cincinnati, 8-9 December 1911
Cincinnati Orchestra
Tchaikovsky programme
Romeo and Juliet
Piano Concerto No 1
Symphony No 5

Cincinnati, 22-23 December 1911
Cincinnati Orchestra
Brahms Academic Festival Overture
Bruch Violin Concerto
Schumann Symphony No 4

Cincinnati, 5-6 January 1912
Cincinnati Orchestra
Franck Symphony in D minor
Debussy Prélude à l'après-midi
Saint Saens Piano Concerto No 2
Berlioz Damnation de Faust excerpts

Cincinnati, 19-20 January 1912
Cincinnati Orchestra
Beethoven Symphony No 2
Weber Euryanthe Overture
Wagner Entry of the Gods (Rheingold)

Cincinnati, 28 January 1912
Cincinnati Orchestra
Wagner Meistersinger Overture
Mozart Aria from Don Giovanni
Schubert Andante (Symphony No 9)
Délibes Sylvia Suite
J.Strauss Blue Danube Waltz

Cincinnati, 2-3 February 1912
Cincinnati Orchestra
Sibelius Symphony No 2
Glazunov Violin Concerto
Tchaikovsly Marche slave

Cincinnati, 11 February 1912
Cincinnati Orchestra
Mendelssohn Ruy Blas Overture
Saar Gonoliera & Chanson d'amour
Liszt Piano Concerto No 2
Mozart Minuet (Symphony No 39)
Chopin Nocturne and Polonaise
Wagner Entry of the Guests

Cincinnati, 16-17 February 1912
Cincinnati Orchestra
Haydn Symphony No 104
Beethoven Piano Concerto No 1
Borodin Steppes of Central Asia
Jaernefelt Praeludium
Strauss Till Eulenspiegel

Cincinnati, 25 February 1912
Cincinnati Orchestra
Wagner Fliegende Holländer Overture
Bruch Violin Concerto No 2, 1st mvt.
Tchaikovsky Capriccio italien
Mendelssohn Adagio (Symphony No 3)
Chabrier Espana

Cincinnati, 1-2 March 1912
Cincinnati Orchestra
Beethoven Egmont Overture
Mendelssohn Symphony No 3
Paganini Violin Concerto No 1
Liszt Mephisto Waltz

Cincinnati, 10 March 1912
Cincinnati Orchestra
Mozart Zauberflöte Overture
Bizet Carmen Suite No 1
Beethoven Andante (Symphony No 1)
Handel Aria from Acis and Galatea
Boccherini Minuet
Michiels Styrian Dance

Cincinnati, 15-16 March 1912
Cincinnati Orchestra
Stanford Irish Symphony
Suite by English composers
Elgar Enigma Variations
Sullivan Di Ballo Overture

Cincinnati, 24 March 1912
Cincinnati Orchestra
Wagner Rienzi Overture
Sarasate Zigeunerweisen
Offenbach Contes d'Hoffmann excerpts
Ponchielli Dance of the Hours
Haydn Finale (Symphony No 103)
Mendelssohn Violin Concerto, mvts.2-3
Brahms 2 Hungarian Dances
Rossini Guilleaume Tell Overture

Cincinnati, 29-30 March 1912
Cincinnati Orchestra
Brahms Symphony No 2
Schumann Piano Concerto
Wagner Wotan's Farewell (Walküre)

Cincinnati, 7 April 1912
Cincinnati Orchestra
Tchaikovsky Finale (Symphony No 5)
Handel Largo (Serse)
Bizet Carmen Suite No 2
Wunderle Swedish Paraphrase
Umlauf Mein Vaterland
Thomas Mignon Overture
Vocal items by Mozart, Sullivan and
Donizetti

Cincinnati, 12-13 April 1912
Cincinnati Orchestra
Goldmark Sakuntala Overture
Wagner Meistersinger excerpts
Beethoven Symphony No 5

London, 22 May 1912
London Symphony Orchestra
Zimbalist
Wagner Meistersinger Overture
Brahms Symphony No 1
Debussy Prélude à l'après-midi
Glazunov Violin Concerto
Tchaikovsky Marche slave

London, 14 June 1912
New Symphony Orchestra
Nordica
Wagner programme
Tannhäuser Overture
Ride of the Valkyries
Excerpts from Tristan & Götterdämmerung
Concert also included items from
Nordica not accompanied by Stokowski

Philadelphia, 11-12 October 1912
Philadelphia Orchestra
Beethoven Leonore No 3 Overture
Brahms Symphony No 1
Ippolitov-Ivanov Caucasian Sketches
Wagner Tannhäuser Overture

Philadelphia, 18-19 October 1912
Philadelphia Orchestra
Schumann-Heink
Weber Freischütz Overture
Beethoven Symphony No 5
Strauss Don Juan
Vocal items by Wagner

Philadelphia, 25-26 October 1912
Philadelphia Orchestra
Tchaikovsky programme
Symphony No 5
Romeo and Juliet
Marche slave

Philadelphia, 1-2 November 1912
Philadelphia Orchestra
Persinger
Schumann Symphony No 4
Bruch Violin Concerto
Davies Parthenia, Suite
Elgar Pomp and Circumstance March

Philadelphia, 8-9 November 1912
Philadelphia Orchestra
Sibelius Symphony No 2
Bizet L'Arlésienne Suite No 1
Liszt Les Préludes

Philadelphia, 15-16 November 1912
Philadelphia Orchestra
Namara-Toye
Beethoven Coriolan Overture
Haydn Symphony No 104
Rimsky-Korsakov Scheherazade
Vocal items by Mozart

Philadelphia, 20 November 1912
Philadelphia Orchestra
Rosenberg, Goldsmith
Nicolai Die lustigen Weiber Overture
Liszt Piano Concerto No 1
Délibes Sylvia Suite
Wagner Lohengrin Act 3 Prelude
Rossini Guilleaume Tell Overture
Vocal items by Bizet and Saint-Saens

Philadelphia, 22-23 November 1912
Philadelphia Orchestra
Elgar Symphony No 1
Wagner Rienzi Overture
Wagner Lohengrin Prelude
Wagner Kaisermarsch

Philadelphia, 29-30 November 1912
Philadelphia Orchestra
Godowsky
Franck Symphony in D minor
Beethoven Piano Concerto No 4
Strube Puck, Comedy Overture

Philadelphia, 4 December 1912
Philadelphia Orchestra
Harwood Baugher, Such
Auber Fra Diavolo Overture
Paganini Intro, theme & variations
Grieg Peer Gynt Suite No 1
Saint-Saens Danse macabre
Chabrier Espana
Vocal items by Verdi and Puccini

Philadelphia, 6-7 December 1912
Philadelphia Orchestra
Hinkle
Sanby Vikings at Hegeland,Act 4 Prelude
Beethoven Symphony No 1
Strauss Tod und Verklärung
Vocal items by Handel and Charpentier

Philadelphia, 20-21 December 1912
Philadelphia Orchestra
Elman
Schubert Symphony No 9
Saint-Saens Violin Concerto No 3
Berlioz Damnation de Faust excerpts

Philadelphia, 27-28 December 1912
Philadelphia Orchestra
Wagner programme
Meistersinger Overture & Act 3 Prelude
Tristan Liebesnacht
A Faust Overture
Siegfried Idyll
Fliegende Holländer Overture

Philadelphia, 3-4 January 1913
Philadelphia Orchestra
Ganz
Goldmark Sakantula Overture
Chopin Piano Concerto No 1
Mozart Symphony No 39
Rachmaninov Isle of the Dead

Philadelphia, 10-11 January 1913
Philadelphia Orchestra
Rich
Mendelssohn Symphony No 3
Lalo Violin Concerto
Berlioz Benvenuto Cellini Overture

Philadelphia, 15 January 1913
Philadelphia Orchestra
Tallarico, Maquarre
Sullivan Di Ballo Overture
Weber Konzertstück
Tchaikovsly Casse noisette Suite
Brahms 2 Hungarian Dances
Saint-Saens Adagio and Variations
Reinecke Lento
Enesco Presto
Ponchielli La Gioconda Ballet music

Philadelphia, 17-18 January 1913
Philadelphia Orchestra
Beethoven Egmont Overture
Bach Suite No 2
Martucci Symphony No 1
Dukas L'apprenti sorcier

Philadelphia, 24-25 January 1913
Philadelphia Orchestra
Gerhardt
Beethoven Symphony No 8
Loeffler La vilanelle du diable
Brahms Academic Festival Overture
Vocal items by Gluck, Marcello & Wolf

Philadelphia, 29 January 1913
Philadelphia Orchestra
Green, Lipschütz, Sandby
Mendelssohn Midsummer Night's Dream
  Suite
Elgar Salut d'amour
Boccherini Minuet
Tchaikovsky Rococo Variations
Michiels Czardas
Vocal duets by Verdi

Philadelphia,31January-1 February 1931
Philadelphia Orchestra
Mendelssohn Hebrides Overture
Liszt Tasso
Enesco Symphony in E flat

Philadelphia, 7-8 February 1931
Philadelphia Orchestra
Mero
Brahms Symphony No 3
Tchaikovsky Piano Concerto No 2
Moszkowski The Steppes

Springfield, Massachusetts
18 February 1913
Philadelphia Orchestra
Sembrich, Gilly
Wagner Meistersinger Overture
Liszt Tasso
Dalcroze L'oiseau bleu
Sibelius Valse triste
Jaernefelt Praeludium
Tchaikovsky Marche slave
Arias, duets and songs by Verdi,
Rossini, Rachmaninov, Wolf,
Strauss and Mozart

Philadelphia, 21-22 February 1913
Philadelphia Orchestra
Weber Euryanthe Overture
Schubert Symphony No 8
Glière Les sirènes
Jaernefelt Praeludium
Sibelius Valse triste
Wagner Huldigungsmarsch

Philadelphia, 26 February 1913
Philadelphia Orchestra
Hood, Horner
Thomas Mignon Overture
German 3 Dances from Henry VIII
Heckscher 5 Dances from the Pyrenees
Saint-Saens Bacchanale
Meyerbeer Coronation March
Vocal items by Massenet & Leoncavallo

Philadelphia, 28 February-1 March 1913
Philadelphia Orchestra
Ysaye
Mozart Zauberflöte Overture
Mozart Violin Concerto No 3
Elgar Enigma Variations
Beethoven Violin Concerto

Philadelphia, 7-8 March 1913
Philadelphia Orchestra
Gluck/Mottl Ballet Suite
Stanford Symphony No 3
Smetana The Moldau
Debussy Prélude à a'après-midi
Dvorak Carnival Overture

Philadelphia, 12 March 1913
Philadelphia Orchestra
Thullan, Rich
Rossini Guilleaume Tell Overture
Bizet Aria from Carmen
Brahms 2 Hungarian Dances
Townsend Serenade
Grieg Peer Gynt Suite No 1
Mendelssohn Midsummer Night's Dream
  Suite
Mueller Träume
Bazzini Ronde des lutins
Wagner Lohengrin Act 3 Prelude

MAYOR THOMAS D. TAGGART, Jr.

Presents

LEOPOLD STOKOWSKI

Conducting the

All-American Youth Orchestra

In Its World Premiere

★

BALLROOM — CONVENTION HALL

Atlantic City, N. J.

SUNDAY, MAY 11, 1941

★

Program

BACH-STOKOWSKI	Toccata and Fugue in D Minor
BEETHOVEN	Symphony in C Minor

    1. Allegro con brio
    2. Andante con moto
    3. Allegro. Scherzo
    4. Allegro. Presto

INTERMISSION

HENRY COWELL	Tales of Our Countryside
(California)	

    1. Deep Tides
    2. Exultation
    3. The Harp of Life
    4. Country Reel

WAGNER	Love Music from "Tristan and Isolde"
	(Repeated by request)

The Philadelphia Orchestra Association
(INCORPORATED 1903)

MAINTAINING

The Philadelphia Orchestra
(FOUNDED 1900)

LEOPOLD STOKOWSKI, Conductor

NINETEENTH PAIR OF SYMPHONY CONCERTS

Friday Afternoon at 3.00,   Saturday Evening at 8.15
February 28 and March 1, 1913

Soloist: **Eugene Ysaye**, Violinist

Program

1. **Wolfgang Amadeus Mozart**   *Overture, "The Magic Flute"*
   (1756-1791)

2. **Wolfgang Amadeus Mozart**   *Concerto No. 3, in G Major,*
   (1756-1791)   *for Violin and Orchestra*

   EUGENE YSAYE

   INTERMISSION
   Of ten minutes' duration, at evening concert only

3. **Edward Elgar**   *Variations, "Enigma"*
   (1857-   )   *(First Time at These Concerts)*

4. **Ludwig van Beethoven**   *Concerto in D Major,*
   (1770-1827)   *for Violin and Orchestra*

   EUGENE YSAYE

   Mr. Ysaye Uses the Chickering Piano

Since the afternoon concerts of the Orchestra start promptly on time and are relatively short, owing to the fact that there are no intermissions, patrons who desire to leave the auditorium before the concert is over are asked to withdraw before the last number begins, in order to avoid the inevitable annoyance that comes to those who wish to listen, from the movements of people leaving during the interpretation of any given number.

Philadelphia, 14-15 March 1913
Philadelphia Orchestra
Sandby
Schumann Symphony No 2
Dvorak Cello Concerto
Strauss Love Scene (Feuersnot)
Strauss Dance of the 7 veils

Philadelphia, 21-22 March 1913
Philadelphia Orchestra
Schelling
Tchaikovsky Symphony No 6
Liszt Piano Concerto No 1
Rimsky-Korsakov Russian Easter Overture

Philadelphia, 28-29 March 1913
Philadelphia Orchestra
Wagner programme
Entrance of the Gods (Rheingold)
Ride of the Valkyries (Walküre)
Wotan's Farewell (Walküre)
Forest murmurs (Siegfried)
Rhine Journey, Funeral March and
    Closing scene (Götterdämmerung)

Reading, Pennsylvania, 2 April 1913
Philadelphia Orchestra
MacNamee-Bentz, Zeckwer, Bawden
Van Den Beemt Introduction and Scene
Zeckwer Allegro (Piano Concerto)
Lang The Isle of the Blest
Leps Nirvana
Mueller Atlantis
Bawden Ballade
Pfitzner Scherzo
Gerstley Spanish Dance
Goepp Festal March

Philadelphia, 4-5 April 1913
Philadelphia Orchestra
Gerville-Reache
Beethoven Symphony No 7
Arensky Tchaikovsky Variations
Tchaikovsky 1812 Overture
Vocal items by Gluck and Bruneau

Philadelphia, 11-12 April 1913
Philadelphia Orchestra
Goldmark Sakantula Overture
Beethoven Symphony No 5
Liszt Les Préludes
Sibelius Valse triste
Wagner Meistersinger Overture

**Additional concerts in the Orchestra's
1912-1913 season took place in Akron,
Cleveland, Columbus, Toledo, Atlantic
City, Camden, Detroit, Germanstown,
Kensington and Wilmington, as well as
in Philadelphia's Stetson Auditorium
and Weightman Hall of the University
of Pennsylvania**

Philadelphia, 17-18 October 1913
Philadelphia Orchestra
Wagner Meistersinger Overture
Beethoven Symphony No 3
Hausegger Wieland der Schmied
Liszt Tasso

Princeton, 22 October 1913
Philadelphia Orchestra
Brahms Academic Festival Overture
Tchaikovsky Symphony No 5
Bach Air (Suite No 3)
Sibelius Valse triste
Liszt Tasso

Philadelphia, 24-25 October 1913
Philadelphia Orchestra
Kreisler
Smetana Bartered Bride Overture
Rabaud Symphony No 2
Tchaikovsky Violin Concerto
Berlioz Carnaval romain Overture

Philadelphia,31October-1 November 1913
Philadelphia Orchestra
Bach Brandenburg Concerto No 3
Schubert Rosamunde Overture & Entr'actes
Schelling Légende symphonique
Tchaikovsky Symphony No 4

Philadelphia, 5 November 1913
Philadelphia Orchestra
Kerns, Seydel
Wagner Tannhäuser Overture
Vieuxtemps Violin Concerto No 4
Bizet Carmen Suite No 1
Schubert Marche militaire
Weber Invitation to the Dance
Charpentier Aria from Louise
Liszt Hungarian Rhapsody No 1

Philadelphia, 7-8 November 1913
Philadelphia Orchestra
Homer
Beethoven Prometheus Overture
Schumann Genoveva Overture
Strauss Ein Heldenleben
Vocal items by Bach, Gluck and Verdi

Philadelphia, 14-15 November 1913
Philadelphia Orchestra
Pfitzner Käthchen von Heilbronn Ov.
Dvorak Symphony No 9
Rimsky-Korsakov Scheherazade

Philadelphia, 21-22 November 1913
Philadelphia Orchestra
Hofmann
Beethoven Coriolan Overture
Brahms Symphony No 1
Schumann Piano Concerto
Berlioz Benvenuto Cellini Overture

Philadelphia, 26 November 1913
Philadelphia Orchestra
Harvard, Knauss
Goldmark Sakantula Overture
Weber Rondo alla polacca
Grieg Sigurd Jorsalfar
Jaernefelt Praeludium
Sibelius Valse triste
Tchaikovsky Capriccio italien
Vocal items by Weber and Wagner

Philadelphia, 28-29 November 1913
Philadelphia Orchestra
Grimson
Cherubini Anacreon Overture
Bach Violin Concerto No 2
Franck Symphony in D minor
Violin solos by Arbor and Schmitt

Philadelphia, 5-6 December 1913
Philadelphia Orchestra
Wagner programme
Lohengrin Prelude & Procession to
    Minster
Tannhäuser Overture, Venusberg Music
    and Act 3 Prelude
Siegfried Idyll
Tristan Prelude, Act 3 Prelude and
    Liebestod

Philadelphia, 19-20 December 1913
Philadelphia Orchestra
Carreno
Mozart Nozze di Figaro Overture
Beethoven Symphony No 2
MacDowell Piano Concerto No 2
Strauss Tod und Verklärung

Philadelphia, 26-27 December 1913
Philadelphia Orchestra
Elman
Brahms Tragic Overture
Schubert Symphony No 8
Beethoven Violin Concerto
Wagner Fliegende Holländer Overture

Philadelphia, 31 December 1913
Philadelphia Orchestra
Young Peoples' Matinee
Arensky Tchaikovsky Variations
Tchaikovsky Christ Child Legend
Episodes in the life of a child
    (Narrator Kitty Cheathams)
J.Strauss Blue Danube Waltz
Tchaikovsky Casse noisette Suite

Philadelphia, 2-3 January 1914
Philadelphia Orchestra
Zeckwer
Mendelssohn Ruy Blas Overture
Roussel Evocation No 2
Zeckwer Piano Concerto in E minor
Tchaikovsky Symphony No 6

Philadelphia, 9-10 January 1914
Philadelphia Orchestra
Connell
Beethoven Marcia funebre (Symphony 3)
Hadley Symphony No 4
Dvorak Carnival Overture
Vocal items by Mozart, Schubert and
    Brahms

Philadelphia, 14 January 1914
Philadelphia Orchestra
Ware, Morris
Hérold Zampa Overture
Saint-Saens Piano Concerto No 2
Massenet Scènes napolitaines
Thomas Gavotte from Mignon
Tchaikovsky Sérénade mélancholique
Hubay Azt Mondjak
Tchaikovsky Marche slave

Philadelphia, 16-17 January 1914
Philadelphia Orchestra
Wagner programme
Parsifal Transformation and Good
    Friday Music
Entrance of the Gods (Rheingold)
Ride of the Valkyries (Walküre)
Wotan's Farewell (Walküre)
Forest murmurs (Siegfried)
Funeral March and Immolation
    (Götterdämmerung)

New York, 21 January 1914
Philadelphia Orchestra
Gluck
Mozart Nozze di Figaro Overture
Brahms Symphony No 1
Strauss Tod und Verklärung
Vocal items by Mozart & Charpentier

Philadelphia, 23-24 January 1914
Philadelphia Orchestra
Bauer
Weber Freischütz Overture
Brahms Piano Concerto No 1
Tchaikovsky Symphony No 5

Philadelphia, 30-31 January 1914
Philadelphia Orchestra
Mendelssohn Midsummer Night's Dream
    Suite
Brahms Haydn Variations
Schumann Symphony No 1
Strauss Till Eulenspiegel

Philadelphia, 6-7 February 1914
Philadelphia Orchestra
Rich
Korngold Schauspiel Overture
Sibelius Violin Concerto
Beethoven Symphony No 7

Boston, 15 February 1914
Philadelphia Orchestra
Elman
Brahms Symphony No 1
Korngold Schauspiel Overture
Saint-Saens Violin Concerto No 3
Wagner Tannhäuser Overture and
    Venusberg Music

Philadelphia, 20-21 February 1914
Philadelphia Orchestra
Backhaus
Mozart Don Giovanni Overture
Beethoven Piano Concerto No 5
Brahms Symphony No 2
Mueller Atlantis

Philadelphia, 27-28 February 1914
Philadelphia Orchestra
Culp
Gluck Iphigenie in Aulis Overture
Haydn Symphony No 100
Debussy Nuages & Fêtes (Nocturnes)
Liszt Les Préludes
Vocal items by Monteverdi, Brahms
    and Schubert

Philadelphia, 6-7 March 1914
Philadelphia Orchestra
Sandby
Weber Euryanthe Overture
Lang Phantasies of a Poet
Boellman Symphonic Variations
Strauss Serenade for wind
Strauss Dance of the 7 veils

Philadelphia, 13-14 March 1914
Philadelphia Orchestra
Hinkle, Stone-Langston, Douty,
Connell
Beethoven programme
Leonore No 3 Overture
Symphony No 9

Philadelphia, 18 March 1914
Philadelphia Orchestra
Braun, Rahmig
Thomas Raymonda Overture
Mozart Gavotte from Idomeneo
Wagner Entry of the Guests(Tannhäuser)
German 3 Dances from Henry VIII
Stein Konzertstück
Michiels Czardas
Vocal items by Haydn, Wagner, Heger
    and Othergraven

Philadelphia, 20-21 March 1914
Philadelphia Orchestra
Flesch
Schillings Symphonic Prologue(Oedipus)
Schumann Symphony No 2
Brahms Violin Concerto
Brahms Academic Festival Overture

Philadelphia, 27-28 March 1914
Philadelphia Orchestra
Goodson
Vivaldi Concerto in A minor
Grieg Piano Concerto
Berlioz Symphonie fantastique

Philadelphia, 1 April 1914
Philadelphia Orchestra
Paderewski
Gluck/Mottl Ballet Suite
Wagner Tristan Prelude and Liebestod
Beethoven Piano Concerto No 5

Philadelphia, 3-4 April 1914
Philadelphia Orchestra
Schumann-Heink
Beethoven Egmont Overture
Mozart Symphony No 40
Van Den Beemt Intro & Shepherd Scene
Strauss Don Juan
Vocal items by Mozart and Schubert

Philadelphia, 11-13 April 1914
Philadelphia Orchestra
Powell
Weber Oberon Overture
Brahms Symphony No 4
Mendelssohn Violin Concerto
Berlioz Damnation de Faust excerpts

Philadelphia, 15 April 1914
Philadelphia Orchestra
Conti, Liebling
Wagner Tannhäuser Overture
Weber Invitation to the Dance
Strauss Blue Danube Waltz
Goldmark Sakantula Overture
Sibelius Valse triste
Boellman Symphonic Variations
Liszt Hungarian Rhapsody No 1

Philadelphia, 17-18 April 1914
Philadelphia Orchestra
Beethoven Leonore No 3 Overture
Schubert Symphony No 8
Wagner Tannhäuser Overture and
    Venusberg Music
Liszt Les Préludes

Additional concerts in the Orchestra's
1913-1914 season took place in Easton,
Pittsburgh, Reading, Scranton, Detroit,
Ann Arbor, Akron, Cleveland, Oberlin,
Washington, Wilmington, Princeton,
Atlantic City, Bridgeport, Meriden,
Middlebury, Norwich, Waterbury and
North Adams, as well as in
Philadelphia's Stetson Auditorium,
the University of Pennsylvania and
Kensington

Philadelphia, 16-17 October 1914
Philadelphia Orchestra
Weber Freischütz Overture
Brahms Symphony No 2
Sibelius Swan of Tuonela
Rimsky-Korsakov Capriccio espagnol

Philadelphia, 23-24 October 1914
Philadelphia Orchestra
Gluck
Mozart Nozze di Figaro Overture
Schubert Rosamunde, excerpts
Tchaikovsky Symphony No 4
Vocal items by Mozart and Verdi

Philadelphia, 30-31 October 1914
Philadelphia Orchestra
Gittelson
Bruckner Symphony No 4
Lalo Violin Concerto
Liszt Hungarian Rhapsody No 1

Philadelphia, 6-7 November 1914
Philadelphia Orchestra
Zimbalist
Schumann Symphony No 3
Bruch Violin Concerto
Sibelius Finlandia
Zimbalist 2 Russian Dances
Tchaikovsky Marche slave

Philadelphia, 13-14 November 1914
Philadelphia Orchestra
Homer
Handel Arminius Overture
Beethoven Symphony No 8
Saint Saens Rouet d'Omphale
Svendsen Carnival in Paris
Vocal items by Bach and Meyerbeer

Philadelphia, 20-21 November 1914
Philadelphia Orchestra
Samaroff
Smetana Bartered Bride Overture
Mendelssohn Symphony No 4
Tchaikovsky Piano Concerto No 1
Wagner Lohengrin Prelude

Philadelphia, 27-28 November 1914
Cincinatti Orchestra
Wagner programme
Parsifal Prelude & Symphonic synthesis
A Faust Overture/Siegfried Idyll
Kaisermarsch

Philadelphia, 11-12 December 1914
Philadelphia Orchestra
Borwick
Mozart Zauberflöte Overture
Beethoven Piano Concerto No 3
Brahms Symphony No 4
Weber Oberon Overture

Philadelphia, 18-19 December 1914
Philadelphia Orchestra
Schumann-Heink
Schubert Symphony No 9
Berlioz Romeo et Juliette, excerpts
Wagner Rienzi Overture
Vocal items by Bruch and Meyerbeer

Philadelphia, 25-26 December 1914
Philadelphia Orchestra
Bauer
Bach Sinfonia (Christmas Oratorio)
Bach Concerto for piano, flute & violin
Mozart Symphony No 41
Franck Variations symphoniques
Grieg Sigurd Jorsalfar

Philadelphia, 1-2 January 1915
Philadelphia Orchestra
Dvorak Symphony No 9
Vivaldi Concerto in A minor
Smetana The Moldau

New York, 4 January 1915
Philadelphia Orchestra
Samaroff
Vivaldi Concerto in A minor
Beethoven Piano Concerto No 5
MacDowell Dirge (Indian Suite)
Tchaikovsky Symphony No 4

Philadelphia, 8-9 January 1915
Philadelphia Orchestra
Gerhardt
Beethoven Fidelio Overture
Beethoven Symphony No 4
Wagner Meistersinger Act 3 Prelude
Wagner Fliegende Holländer Overture
Vocal items by Goetz and Wagner

Philadelphia, 15-16 January 1915
Philadelphia Orchestra
Liszt Tasso
Paderewski Symphony in B minor

Philadelphia, 22-23 January 1915
Philadelphia Orchestra
Gabrilowitsch
Haydn Symphony No 94
Mozart Piano Concerto No 20
Weber Konzertstück
Strauss Till Eulenspiegel

Philadelphia, 29-30 January 1915
Philadelphia Orchestra
Kreisler
Schumann Manfred Overture
Brahms Violin Concerto
Beethoven Symphony No 5

Philadelphia, 5-8 February 1915
Philadelphia Orchestra
Sandby
Stock Symphony in C minor
Lalo Cello Concerto
Chabrier Espana

Philadelphia, 12-13 February 1915
Philadelphia Orchestra
Bloomfield-Zeisler
Lully Suite
Mozart Piano Concerto No 24
Kalinnikov Symphony No 1
Liszt Hungarian Fantasia

Philadelphia, 19-20 February 1915
Philadelphia Orchestra
Busoni
Sandby The Woman & the Fiddler, Suite
Brahms Symphony No 3
Busoni Indian Fantasy
Liszt/Busoni Spanish Fantasy

Philadelphia, 26-27 February 1915
Philadelphia Orchestra
Randolph
Mozart Don Giovanni Overture
Beethoven Piano Concerto No 4
Goldmark Rustic Wedding Symphony
Weber Invitation to the Dance

Philadelphia, 12-13 March 1915
Philadelphia Orchestra
Rich
Amy Beach Gaelic Symphony
Paganini Violin Concerto No 1
Strauss Tod und Verklärung

Philadelphia, 19-20 March 1915
Philadelphia Orchestra
Harrison
Bach Wachet auf
Wolf Italian Serenade
Tchaikovsky Symphony No 5
Vocal items by Mozart and Verdi

Philadelphia, 26-27 March 1915
Philadelphia Orchestra
Hofmann
Mendelssohn Hebrides Overture
Schumann Symphony No 4
Rubinstein Piano Concerto No 3
Dukas L'apprenti sorcier

Philadelphia, 3-5 April 1915
Philadelphia Orchestra
Wagner programme
Entry of the Gods (Rheingold)/Ride
of the Valkyries & Wotan's Farewell
(Walküre)/Forest murmurs (Siegfried)/
Rhine Journey, Funeral March and
Immolation (Götterdämmerung)

Philadelphia, 9-10 April 1915
Philadelphia Orchestra
Casals
Enesco Rumanian Rhapsody No 2
Dvorak Cello Concerto
Beethoven Symphony No 3

Richmond, 12 April 1915
Philadelphia Orchestra
Choirs
Destinn, Arndt-Ober, Sembach,
De Gogorza
Liszt Les Préludes
Verdi Requiem

Richmond, 13 April 1915 (afternoon)
Philadelphia Orchestra
Larrabes
Mozart Nozze di Figaro Overture
Beethoven Symphony No 5
Rubinstein Piano Concerto No 3
Weber Invitation to the Dance
Vocal items by Gluck and Massenet

Richmond, 13 April 1915 (evening)
Philadelphia Orchestra
Choirs
Destinn, Arndt-Ober, Sembach,
De Gogorza
Tchaikovsky Marche slave
Sibelius Valse triste
Sibelius Finlandia
Vocal solos and choruses by Wagner,
Verdi, Gounod, Liszt, Mendelssohn,
Donizetti and Handel

Philadelphia, 16-17 April 1915
Philadelphia Orchestra
Tchaikovsky programme
1812 Overture
Casse noisette Suite
Symphony No 6

**Additional concerts in the Orchestra's
1914-1915 season took place in Akron,
Atlantic City, Baltimore, Buffalo,
Cleveland, Detroit, Erie, Indianapolis,
Oberlin, Reading, Washington and
Wilmington as well as the Universities
of Michigan and Princeton**

Philadelphia, 15-16 October 1915
Philadelphia Orchestra
Beethoven Leonore No 3 Overture
Beethoven Symphony No 7
Mendelssohn Midsummer Night's Dream
 Suite
Wagner Rienzi Overture

Philadelphia, 22-23 October 1915
Philadelphia Orchestra
Hofmann
Brahms Tragic Overture
Beethoven Piano Concerto No 5
Tchaikovsky Symphony No 4

Philadelphia, 29-30 October 1915
Philadelphia Orchestra
Scott
Gluck Iphigenie in Aulis Overture
Brahms Symphony No 2
Strauss Don Juan
Vocal items by Mozart and Massenet

Philadelphia, 5-6 November 1915
Philadelphia Orchestra
Elman
Schoenberg Kammersinfonie
Goldmark Violin Concerto
Dvorak Carnival Overture

Philadelphia, 12-13 November 1915
Philadelphia Orchestra
Hutcheson
Rousseau Devin du village Overture
Schubert Symphony No 8
Grétry Cephale et Procris
Liszt Piano Concerto No 1
Ippolitov-Ivanov Caucasian Sketches

Philadelphia, 19-20 November 1915
Philadelphia Orchestra
Breslau
Smetana Bartered Bride Overture
Scriabin Divine Poem
Tchaikovsky Romeo and Juliet
Vocal items by Gluck and Saint-Saens

Philadelphia, 26-27 November 1915
Philadelphia Orchestra
Wagner programme
Entrance of the Gods & Alberich's
Curse (Rheingold)/Ride of the
Valkyries & Wotan's Farewell(Walküre)/
Forest murmurs (Siegfried)/ Rhine
Journey, Funeral March & Immolation
(Götterdämmerung)

Philadelphia, 10-11 December 1915
Philadelphia Orchestra
Schelling
Mozart Nozze di Figaro Overture
Beethoven Symphony No 6
Schelling Symphonic Variations
Liszt Les Préludes

Philadelphia, 17-18 December 1915
Philadelphia Orchestra
De Gogorza
Bach Suite No 2
Haydn Symphony No 104
Debussy Prélude à l'après-midi
Dukas L'apprenti sorcier
Vocal items by Gluck and Berlioz

Philadelphia, 31 December 1915-
1 January 1916
Philadelphia Orchestra
Murphey
Weber Oberon Overture
Schumann Symphony No 1
Strube Variations
(conducted by the composer)
Svendsen Carnival in Paris
Vocal items by Mozart and Wagner

Philadelphia, 7-8 January 1916
Philadelphia Orchestra
Gabrilowitsch
Schumann Genoveva Overture
Chopin Piano Concerto No 1
Sibelius Symphony No 1

Philadelphia, 14-15 January 1916
Philadelphia Orchestra
Culp
Gluck Alceste Overture
Brahms Haydn Variations
Dvorak Symphony No 9
Vocal items by Beethoven, Kreisler,
Strauss and Schubert

Philadelphia, 21-22 January 1916
Philadelphia Orchestra
Parlow
Mozart Don Giovanni Overture
Beethoven Violin Concerto
Strauss Ein Heldenleben

Philadelphia, 28-29 January 1916
Philadelphia Orchestra
Grainger
Berlioz Corsair Overture
Rabaud Symphony No 2
Grieg Piano Concerto
Grainger Molly on the shore
Elgar Pomp and Circumstance March

Philadelphia, 4-5 February 1916
Philadelphia Orchestra
Sandby
Cherubini Anacreon Overture
Sandby Cello Concerto
Zeckwer Sohrab and Rustum
(conducted by the composer)
Mozart Symphony No 39
Sibelius Finlandia

Philadelphia, 11-12 February 1916
Philadelphia Orchestra
Bauer
Mendelssohn Symphony No 3
Brahms Piano Concerto No 2
Berlioz Carnaval romain Overture

Philadelphia, 18-19 February 1916
Philadelphia Orchestra
Spalding
Beethoven Prometheus Overture
Brahms Violin Concerto
Mason Symphony in C minor
Wagner Huldigungsmarsch

Philadelphia, 25-26 February 1916
Philadelphia Orchestra
Mero
Schumann Symphony No 2
Debussy Nuages et fêtes (Nocturnes)
Liszt Piano Concerto No 2
Goldmark Sakantula Overture

Philadelphia, 2-4 March 1916
Philadelphia Orchestra
Choirs
Hinkle, Barbour, Fischer, Keyes,
Dercum, Murphey, Werrenrath,
Whitehill
Mahler Symphony No 8

Philadelphia, 10-11 March 1916
Philadelphia Orchestra
Beserkirsky
Beethoven Coriolan Overture
Brahms Symphony No 3
Tchaikovsky Violin Concerto
Granados Intermezzo & Epilogue
 (Goyescas)

Philadelphia, 17-18 March 1916
Philadelphia Orchestra
Wagner programme
Fliegende Holländer Overture
Lohengrin Prelude & Procession to
Minster/Tannhäuser Overture and
Venusberg Music/Meistersinger
Overture & Act 3 Prelude/Siegfried
Idyll/Tristan Prelude and Liebestod

Philadelphia, 24 March 1916
Philadelphia Orchestra
Rich, Kindler
Mendelssohn Hebrides Overture
Brahms Double Concerto
Franck Symphony in D minor

Philadelphia, 25 March 1916
Philadelphia Orchestra
Rich
Mendelssohn Hebrides Overture
Wieniawski Violin Concerto No 2
Franck Symphony in D minor

Philadelphia, 27-29 March 1916
Details as for 2-4 March

Philadelphia, 3-5 April 1916
Details as for 2-4 March

Philadelphia, 7-8 April 1916
Philadelphia Orchestra
Craft
Mozart Zauberflöte Overture
Beethoven Symphony No 5
Strauss Tod und Verklärung
Vocal items by Stradella & Strauss

New York, 9 April 1916
Details as for 2-4 March

Philadelphia, 14-15 April 1916
Philadelphia Orchestra
Godowsky
Beethoven Fidelio Overture
Brahms Symphony No 1
D'Indy Istar
Tchaikovsky Piano Concerto No 1

Philadelphia, 28-29 April 1916
Philadelphia Orchestra
Strauss programme
Eine Alpensinfonie
Tod und Verklärung

Additional concerts in the Orchestra's 1915-1916 season took place in Atlantic City, Baltimore, Bryn Mawr, Buffalo, Cleveland, Columbus, Dayton, Detroit, Easton, New York, Oberlin, Wilmington and Ypsilanti as well as the University of Princeton and the Philadelphia Metropolitan Opera. Visits to local schools and colleges replaced the Wednesday series of popular concerts for the first time

Philadelphia, 13-14 October 1916
Philadelphia Orchestra
Beethoven Coriolan Overture
Brahms Symphony No 3
Reger Hiller Variations
Sibelius Finlandia

Philadelphia, 17 October 1916
Philadelphia Orchestra
Multer
Beethoven Coriolan Overture
Brahms Symphony No 3
Bizet L'Arlésienne Suite
Sibelius Finlandia
Vocal items by Verdi and Leoncavallo

Philadelphia, 20-21 October 1916
Philadelphia Orchestra
Schumann-Heink
Mozart Don Giovanni Overture
Beethoven Symphony No 2
Bizet L'Arlésienne Suite
Tchaikovsky Marche slave
Vocal items by Bruch and Wagner

Philadelphia, 27-28 October 1916
Philadelphia Orchestra
Gittelson
Cherubini Anacreon Overture
Brahms Violin Concerto
Rimsky-Korsakov Scheherazade

Philadelphia, 3-4 November 1916
Philadelphia Orchestra
Samaroff
Wagner Meistersinger Overture
Brahms Piano Concerto No 1
Beethoven Allegretto (Symphony No 7)
Schumann Symphony No 4

Philadelphia, 6 November 1916
Philadelphia Orchestra
Radcliffe-Miller
Wagner Meistersinger Overture
Rimsky-Korsakov Scheherazade
Liszt Hungarian Fantasia
Wagner Entry of the Gods (Rheingold)

Philadelphia, 10-11 November 1916
Philadelphia Orchestra
Wagner programme
Entry of the Gods & Alberich's Curse (Rheingold)/Ride of the Valkyries and Wotan's Farewell (Walküre)/Forest murmurs (Siegfried)/Rhine Journey, Funeral March & Immolation (Götterdämmerung)

Philadelphia, 17-18 November 1916
Philadelphia Orchestra
Gluck
Haydn Symphony No 88
Arensky Tchaikovsky Variations
Tchaikovsky Francesca da Rimini
Vocal items by Mozart and Glinka

Philadelphia, 5 December 1916
Philadelphia Orchestra
Farringdon-Smith, Kindler
Wagner Ride of the Valkyries
Wagner Forest murmurs (Siegfried)
Wagner Wotan's Farewell (Walküre)
Boellmann Symphonic Poem
Tchaikovsky Marche slave
Vocal items by Massenet, Charpentier and Puccini

Philadelphia, 8-9 December 1916
Philadelphia Orchestra
Zimbalist
Weber Euryanthe Overture
Schumann Symphony No 3
Stock Violin Concerto in D minor
Oldberg June
(Conducted by the composer)
Liszt Hungarian Rhapsody No 2

Philadelphia, 15-16 December 1916
Philadelphia Orchestra
Koenen, Sembach
Beethoven Egmont Overture
Strauss Don Juan
Mahler Das Lied von der Erde

Philadelphia, 22-23 December 1916
Philadelphia Orchestra
Gabrilowitsch
Wagner Funeral March (Götterdämmerung)
Brahms Piano Concerto No 2
Strauss Sinfonia domestica

Philadelphia, 29-30 December 1916
Philadelphia Orchestra
R.Sutro, O.Sutro
Weber Freischütz Overture
Beethoven Symphony No 4
Bruch Concerto for 2 pianos
Wagner Rienzi Overture

Philadelphia, 2 January 1917
Philadelphia Orchestra
Zeckwer-Holt, McGuigan
Weber Freischütz Overture
Haydn Minuet & Finale (Symphony No 88)
Saint-Saens Violin Concerto No 3
Wagner Rienzi Overture
Vocal items by Weber and Puccini

Philadelphia, 5-6 January 1917
Philadelphia Orchestra
Elman
Brahms Haydn Variations
Vogrich Unidentified composition
Saint-Saens Intro & Rondo capriccioso
Scriabin Divine Poem

New York, 11 January 1917
Philadelphia Orchestra
Hofmann, Kreisler
Brahms Haydn Variations
Dvorsky Chromaticon
Schelling Violin Concerto
Scriabin Divine Poem

Philadelphia, 12-13 January 1917
Philadelphia Orchestra
Hofmann
Franck Symphony in D minor
Saint-Saens Piano Concerto No 4
Dvorsky Chromaticon
Weber Invitation to the Dance

Philadelphia, 19-20 January 1917
Philadelphia Orchestra
Connell
Beethoven Prometheus Overture
Mozart Symphony No 40
Elgar Enigma Variations
Vocal items by Handel, Mahler
and Schubert

Philadelphia, 26-27 January 1917
Philadelphia Orchestra
Garrison
Rabaud Symphony No 2
Debussy La demoiselle élue
Debussy Prélude à l' après-midi

Philadelphia, 2-3 February 1917
Philadelphia Orchestra
Schelling
Schumann Manfred Overture
Mendelssohn Symphony No 4
Schelling Impressions from an Artist's
Life
Strauss Tod und Verklärung

Philadelphia, 9-10 February 1917
Philadelphia Orchestra
Werrenrath
Gluck Alceste Overture
Beethoven Symphony No 8
Sibelius Swan of Tuonela
Liszt Tasso
Vocal items by Mozart and Chadwick

Philadelphia, 23-24 February 1917
Philadelphia Orchestra
Glinka Ruslan and Ludmila Overture
Borodin Symphony No 2
Glière Les sirènes
Tchaikovsky Intermezzo (Suite No 1)
Rimsky-Korsakov Capriccio espagnol

Philadelphia, 2-3 March 1917
Philadelphia Orchestra
Murphey, Spiering
Mozart Nozze di Figaro Overture
Beethoven Violin Concerto
Liszt Faust Symphony

Philadelphia, 6 March 1917
Philadelphia Orchestra
Meiskey, Abbas
Mozart Nozze di Figaro Overture
Mendelssohn March (Symphony No 4)
Lalo Cello Concerto
Rimsky-Korsakov Capriccio espagnol
Liszt Hungarian Rhapsody No 2
Vocal items by Mozart and Wagner

Philadelphia, 9-10 March 1917
Philadelphia Orchestra
Gerhardt
Bach Brandenburg Concerto No 3
Mahler Kindertotenlieder
Brahms Symphony No 1
Wagner Huldigungsmarsch
Other vocal items by Beethoven

Philadelphia, 15-17 March 1917
Philadelphia Orchestra
Kindler
Gluck/Mottl Ballet Suite
D'Albert Cello Concerto
Strauss Ein Heldenleben

Philadelphia, 23-24 March 1917
Philadelphia Orchestra
Wagner programme
Fliegende Holländer Overture/Lohengrin
Prelude/Tannhäuser Overture and
Venusberg Music/Meistersinger Overture
& Act 3 Prelude/Siegfried Idyll/
Tristan Prelude & Liebestod

Philadelphia, 29-31 March 1917
Philadelphia Orchestra
Chorus
Hinkle, Keyes, Kingston,
Werrenrath, Witherspoon
Bach Saint Matthew Passion

Philadelphia, 6-7 April 1917
Philadelphia Orchestra
Rich
Mozart Zauberflöte Overture
Beethoven Symphony No 3
Vieuxtemps Violin Concerto No 4
Rimsky-Korsakov Russian Easter Overture

Philadelphia, 13-14 April 1917
Philadelphia Orchestra
Bauer
Lully Suite
Bach Piano Concerto in D minor
D'Indy Symphony on a French mountain
    song
Berlioz Carnaval romain Overture

Philadelphia, 18 April 1917
Philadelphia Orchestra
Lyons-Cook, Feinman
Lully Suite
Liszt Piano Concerto No 1
Tchaikovsky Casse noisette Suite
Berlioz Carnaval romain Overture
Vocal items by Puccini and Bizet

Philadelphia, 20-21 April 1917
Philadelphia Orchestra
Tchaikovsky programme
Symphony No 6
Casse noisette Suite
1812 Overture

**Additional concerts in the orchestra's
1916-1917 season took place in Albany,
Atlantic City, Baltimore, Buffalo,
Cleveland, Dayton, Detroit, Grand
Rapids, Jamestown, Lebanon, Lima,
Manchester NJ, Oberlin, Pittsburgh,
Portland, Reading PA, Richmond,
Springfield, Wilmington and
Ypsilanti as well as Princeton
University and the Philadelphia
Metropolitan Opera House**

Philadelphia, 12-13 October 1917
Philadelphia Orchestra
R.Goldmark Samson
Kelley New England Symphony
Foote 4 Character pieces
Goepp Heroic March

Philadelphia, 19-20 October 1917
Philadelphia Orchestra
Friedberg
Dvorak Symphony No 9
Franck Variations symphoniques
Liszt Piano Concerto No 1
Charpentier Impressions italiens

Philadelphia, 25 October 1917
Philadelphia Orchestra
Mendelssohn Symphony No 5
Bach Suite No 2
Mathews The City of God
(conducted by the composer)

Philadelphia, 26-27 October 1917
Philadelphia Orchestra
Borodin Polovtsian Dances
Kalinnikov Symphony No 1
Scriabin Poème de l'extase
Tchaikovsky Marche slave

Philadelphia, 2-3 November 1917
Philadelphia Orchestra
Matzenauer
Cherubini Anacreon Overture
Schubert Symphony No 8
Stravinsky L'oiseau de feu
Vocal items by Mozart and Wagner

Philadelphia, 9-10 November 1917
Philadelphia Orchestra
Beethoven programme
Coriolan Overture/3 Equali/
Symphony No 2/Symphony No 5

Philadelphia, 16-17 November 1917
Philadelphia Orchestra
Elman
Nicolai Die lustigen Weiber Overture
Goldmark Rustic Wedding Symphony
Wieniawski Violin Concerto No 2
Amani/Elman Orientale
Chabrier Espana

Philadelphia, 30 November-
1 December 1917
Philadelphia Orchestra
Samaroff, Bauer, Gabrilowitsch
Haydn Symphony No 99
Bach Concerto for 3 pianos
Mozart Concerto for 2 pianos
Beethoven Leonore No 3 Overture

Philadelphia, 7-8 December 1917
Philadelphia Orchestra
Thibaud
Dvorak In Nature's Realm Overture
Brahms Symphony No 4
Lalo Violin Concerto
Ravel Rapsodie espagnole

Philadelphia, 14-15 December 1917
Philadelphia Orchestra
Tchaikovsky programme
Symphony No 6
Casse noisette Suite
1812 Overture

Philadelphia, 21-22 December 1917
Philadelphia Orchestra
Svendsen Norwegian Rhapsody No 2
Sinding Symphony in D minor
Grieg Symphonic Dance No 2
Grieg Aftenstemming (Lyric Suite)
Jaernefelt Praeludium
Sibelius Valse triste
Sibelius En Saga

Philadelphia, 28-29 December 1917
Philadelphia Orchestra
Novaes
Weber Euryanthe Overture
Beethoven Piano Concerto No 4
Schubert Symphony No 9

Philadelphia, 4-5 January 1918
Philadelphia Orchestra
Douty
Mozart Zauberflöte Overture
Schumann Symphony No 1
Saint-Saens Danse macabre
Wagner Tannhäuser Overture
Vocal items by Handel, Debussy,
Duparc and Lalo

Philadelphia, 11-12 January 1918
Philadelphia Orchestra
Rich
Brahms Symphony No 2
Chausson Poeme
Berlioz Damnation de Faust excerpts

Concert on 18-19 January 1918 devoted
to the works of **Bloch** and conducted
by the composer

Philadelphia, 21 January 1918
Philadelphia Orchestra
Bizet L'Arlesienne Suite
Saint-Saens Piano Concerto No 2
(Duo-Art Piano)
Dvorak Symphony No 9

Philadelphia, 25-26 January 1918
Philadelphia Orchestra
Claussen
Gluck Alceste Overture
Mozart Symphony No 41
Liszt Tasso
Vocal items by Gluck & Tchaikovsky

Philadelphia, 1-2 February 1918
Philadelphia Orchestra
Hofmann
Franck Symphony in D minor
Rubinstein Piano Concerto No 4
Wagner Tristan Prelude & Liebestod

Philadelphia, 8-9 February 1918
Philadelphia Orchestra
Rosen
Wagner Meistersinger Overture
Brahms Violin Concerto
Tchaikovsky Symphony No 4

Toronto, 18 February 1918
Philadelphia Orchestra
Beethoven Leonore No 3 Overture
Dvorak Symphony No 9
Concert for Toronto Mendelssohn Choir

Toronto, 19 February 1918
Philadelphia Orchestra
Berlioz Carnaval romain Overture
Debussy Prélude à l'après-midi
Sibelius Valse triste
Borodin Polovtsian Dances
Concert for Toronto Mendelssohn Choir

Toronto, 20 February 1918
Philadelphia Orchestra
Programme included
Smetana Bartered Bride Overture
Concert for Toronto Mendelssohn Choir

Philadelphia, 22-23 February 1918
Philadelphia Orchestra
Salzedo
Saint-Saens Symphony No 2
Grétry Cephale et Procris
Debussy Danse sacre et danse profane
Ravel Introduction and Allegro
Berlioz Carnaval romain Overture

Philadelphia, 1-2 March 1918
Philadelphia Orchestra
Casals
Wagner Fliegende Holländer Overture
Dorlay Concert passione
Rimsky-Korsakov Scheherazade

Philadelphia, 8-9 March 1918
Philadelphia Orchestra
Fremstad
Brahms Symphony No 1
Wagner Rienzi Overture
Vocal items by Mendelssohn & Liszt

Philadelphia, 15-16 March 1918
Philadelphia Orchestra
Tchaikovsky Romeo and Juliet
Arensky Tchaikovsky Variations
Borodin Polovtsian Dances
Scriabin Poème de l'extase
Rimsky-Korsakov Capriccio espagnol

Philadelphia, 22-23 March 1918
Philadelphia Orchestra
Zimbalist
Rimsky-Korsakov Russian Easter Overture
Wagner Parsifal Good Friday Music
Bach Suite No 2
Beethoven Violin Concerto

New York, 27 March 1918
Philadelphia Orchestra
Samaroff, Bauer, Gabrilowitsch
Bach Suite No 2
Mozart Concerto for 2 pianos
Lully Suite
Bach Concerto for 3 pianos

Philadelphia, 29-30 March 1918
Philadelphia Orchestra
Shattuck
Lully Suite
Beethoven Symphony No 8
Palmgren Piano Concerto No 2
Debussy Nuages et fêtes (Nocturnes)

Philadelphia, 6-7 April 1918
Philadelphia Orchestra
Jacobinoff
Mozart Symphony No 40
Brahms Haydn Variations
Tchaikovsky Violin Concerto
Svendsen Carnival in Paris

Philadelphia, 13-14 April 1918
Philadelphia Orchestra
Mendelssohn Midsummer Night's Dream
    Suite
Liszt Les Préludes
Tchaikovsky Symphony No 5

Philadelphia, October 1918
Philadelphia Orchestra
Liten
Elgar Prelude & Farewell (Gerontius)
Elgar Carillon
Elgar Le drapeau belge
Tchaikovsky Symphony No 4

Philadelphia, November 1918
Philadelphia Orchestra
Matzenauer
Chabrier Gwendoline Overture
Chausson Poème de l'amour et de la mer
Skilton 2 Indian Dances
Rimsky-Korsakov Scheherazade
Tchaikovsky group of songs

Baltimore, 11 November 1918
Philadelphia Orchestra
Seidl
Chabrier Gwendoline Overture
Brahms Violin Concerto
Tchaikovsky Symphony No 4

Philadelphia, November 1918
Philadelphia Orchestra
Programme included
MacDowell Dirge (Indian Suite)
Concert to celebrate end of World
War I

New York, 19 November 1918
Philadelphia Orchestra
Matzenauer
Tchaikovsky Symphony No 4
Tchaikovsky group of songs
Chausson Poème de l'amour et de la mer
Svendsen Carnival in Paris

Philadelphia, November 1918
Philadelphia Orchestra
Seidel
Svendsen Carnival in Paris
MacDowell Indian Suite
Brahms Violin Concerto

Philadelphia, November 1918
Philadelphia Orchestra
Kindler
Beethoven Coriolan Overture
Tchaikovsky Symphony No 6
Saint-Saens Cello Concerto
Brahms Haydn Variations

Philadelphia, December 1918
Philadelphia Orchestra
Ferir
Dvorsky Haunted Castle
Liszt Les Préludes
Berlioz Harold en Italie

Philadelphia, December 1918
Philadelphia Orchestra
Dresser
Saint-Saens Rouet d'Omphale
Brahms Symphony No 3
Chabrier Espana
Vocal items by Mozart and Duparc

Philadelphia, December 1918
Philadelphia Orchestra
Cortot
Beethoven programme
Egmont Overture/Piano Concerto No 1/
Symphony No 7

New York, 17 December 1918
Philadelphia Orchestra
Gabrilowitsch
Brahms Symphony No 3
Rachmaninov Piano Concerto No 2
Rimsky-Korsakov Capriccio espagnol

Philadelphia, December 1918
Philadelphia Orchestra
Pollain
Hadley Lucifer, symphonic poem
Lalo Cello Concerto
Dvorak Symphony No 9

Philadelphia, December 1918
Philadelphia Orchestra
Teyte
Gluck Alceste Overture
Berlioz Damnation de Faust suite
Mendelssohn Symphony No 3
Vocal items by Mozart and Debussy

Philadelphia, January 1919
Philadelphia Orchestra
Thibaud
Beethoven Symphony No 8
Mozart Violin Concerto
Chausson Poème
Debussy 3 Nocturnes

Philadelphia, January 1919
Philadelphia Orchestra
Bauer
Wagner Tristan Prelude and Liebestod
Beethoven Piano Concerto No 5
Amy Beach Symphony in E minor

New York, 21 January 1919
Philadelphia Orchestra
Zimbalist
Beethoven Symphony No 8
Mozart Violin Concerto No 5
Debussy 3 Nocturnes

Philadelphia, January 1919
Philadelphia Orchestra
Samaroff
Beethoven Leonore No 3 Overture
Scriabin Poème de l'extase
Brahms Piano Concerto No 2

Philadelphia, February 1919
Philadelphia Orchestra
Stanford Irish Rhapsody
Rachmaninov Air
Glière Sirènes
Beethoven Symphony No 5

Philadelphia, February 1919
Philadelphia Orchestra
Evans
Weber Freischütz Overture
Debussy Prélude à l'après-midi
Schubert Symphony No 8
Wagner Meistersinger Overture
Vocal items by Carpenter, Converse,
    Clough-Leighter and Forsyth

New York, 11 February 1919
Philadelphia Orchestra
Samaroff
Beethoven Leonore No 3 Overture
Scriabin Poème de l'extase
Brahms Piano Concerto No 2

Philadelphia, February 1919
Philadelphia Orchestra
Ornstein
Beethoven Prometheus Overture
Mozart Symphony No 40
MacDowell Piano Concerto in D minor
Tchaikovsky Marche slave
Piano solos by Ornstein

Toronto, 21 February 1919
Philadelphia Orchestra

Philadelphia, February 1919
Philadelphia Orchestra
Rich
Lully Suite
Sibelius Violin Concerto
Beethoven Symphony No 1
Wagner Holländer Overture

Philadelphia, March 1919
Philadelphia Orchestra
Hofmann
Berlioz Carnaval romain Overture
Liszt Piano Concerto No 1
Brahms Symphony No 2

New York, 11 March 1919
Philadelphia Orchestra
Macquarre, Thibaud, Bauer
Bach Concerto for flute, violin & piano
Mozart Symphony No 40
Chausson Concerto for violin and piano
Wagner Tristan Prelude and Liebestod

Philadelphia, March 1919
Philadelphia Orchestra
Rachmaninov
Lalo Norwegian Rhapsody
Rachmaninov Piano Concerto No 1
Rabaud Symphony No 2

Philadelphia, March 1919
Philadelphia Orchestra
Zimbalist
Rimsky-Korsakov Russian Easter Overture
Brahms Violin Concerto
Tchaikovsky Symphony No 6

Philadelphia, March 1919
Philadelphia Orchestra
Smetana Bartered Bride Overture
Bloch Symphony No 1
Rimsky-Korsakov Scheherazade

Philadelphia, 27 March 1919
Philadelphia Orchestra
Courboin
Beethoven Leonore No 3 Overture
Debussy Prélude à l'après-midi
Wagner Tristan Prelude and Liebestod
Widor Organ Symphony No 6
Organ solos by Bach, Franck and
  Ravanello
Concert in Wanamakers department store

Philadelphia, April 1919
Philadelphia Orchestra
Gabrilowitsch
Beethoven Fidelio Overture
Mozart Piano Concerto No 20
Weber Konzertstück
Pizzetti Fedra Prelude
Ysaye Exile
Schumann Symphony No 4

Philadelphia, 15-16 April 1919
Philadelphia Orchestra
Maquarre, Salzedo
Beethoven Leonore No 3 Overture
Mozart Flute and Harp Concerto
Glazunov Symphony No 7

Philadelphia, April 1919
Philadelphia Orchestra
Frijsh
Chadwick Tam O'Shanter Overture
Garnier Vision for orchestra
Mussorgsky Gopak
Franck Symphony in D minor
Vocal items by Duparc, Franck and
  Georges

Philadelphia, 29 April 1919
Philadelphia Orchestra
Thibaud, Samaroff
Bizet L'Arlésienne Suite
Liszt Piano Concerto No 1
Debussy Prélude à l'après-midi
Saint-Saens Violin Concerto No 3
Tchaikovsky Marche slave
French War Relief concert

Philadelphia, 2-3 May 1919
Philadelphia Orchestra
Tchaikovsky Symphony No 5
Schubert Rosamunde excerpta
Wagner Tannhäuser Overture

Philadelphia, 17-18 October 1919
Philadelphia Orchestra
Weber Oberon Overture
Hill Stevensoniana
Beethoven Symphony No 5
Mendelssohn Midsummer Night's Dream
  Suite

Philadelphia, 24-25 October 1919
Philadelphia Orchestra
Gardner
Bizet L'Arlésienne Suite
Gardner New Russia, tone poem
Mendelssohn Violin Concerto
Dvorak Symphony No 9

Philadelphia, 31 October-
1 November 1919
Philadelphia Orchestra
Samaroff
Tchaikovsky Romeo and Juliet
Liszt Piano Concerto No 2
Mozart Symphony No 39
Beethoven Choral Fantasy

Philadelphia, 7-8 November 1919
Philadelphia Orchestra
Weber Freischütz Overture
Beethoven Symphony No 7
Dvorsky Haunted Castle
Wagner Rienzi Overture

New York, 11 November 1919
Philadelphia Orchestra
Programme as for 7-8 November

Philadelphia, 14-15 November 1919
Philadelphia Orchestra
Matzenauer
Beethoven Prometheus Overture
Malipiero 7 espressioni sinfoniche
Haydn Symphony No 88
Vocal items by Schubert, Schumann,
    Brahms and Wagner

Philadelphia, 28-29 November 1919
Philadelphia Orchestra
Rich, Kindler
Mozart Don Giovanni Overture
Brahms Double Concerto
Rimsky-Korsakov Scheherazade

New York, 2 December 1919
Philadelphia Orchestra
Rich, Kindler
Programme as for 28-29 November

Philadelphia, 5-6 December 1919
Philadelphia Orchestra
Bauer
Beethoven Leonore No 3 Overture
Schubert Symphony No 8
Mozart Piano Concerto No 23
Loeffler Pagan Poem
Wagner Holländer Overture

Philadelphia, 19-20 December 1919
Philadelphia Orchestra
Bach Sinfonia (Christmas Oratorio)
Griffes Notturno, White Peacock,
    Clouds and Bacchanale
Liszt Hungarian Rhapsody No 2
Brahms Symphony No 4

Philadelphia, 26-27 December 1919
Philadelphia Orchestra
Moiseiwitsch
Hadley Othello Overture
Liszt Piano Concerto No 1
Beethoven Symphony No 6

Philadelphia, 2-3 January 1920
Philadelphia Orchestra
Cortot
Smetana Bartered Bride Overture
Rachmaninov Piano Concerto No 3
Tchaikovsky Symphony No 5

New York, 6 January 1920
Philadelphia Orchestra
Cortot
Programme as for 2-3 January

Philadelphia, 9-10 January 1920
Philadelphia Orchestra
Kreisler
Beethoven Fidelio Overture
Schumann Symphony No 2
Brahms Violin Concerto

Philadelphia, 23-24 January 1920
Philadelphia Orchestra
Werrenrath
Gluck Iphigenie in Aulis Overture
Mozart Symphony No 41
Wagner Siegfried's Funeral March
Vocal items by Bach and Mason

Philadelphia, 30-31 January 1920
Philadelphia Orchestra
Wagner Meistersinger Overture
Beethoven Symphony No 8
Herbert Natoma, Act 3 Prelude
Gilbert Riders to the Sea
Wagner Siegfried Idyll

Philadelphia, 6-7 February 1920
Philadelphia Orchestra
Rachmaninov, Hinkle, Hackett, Patton
Rachmaninov programme
Piano Concerto No 3
The Bells

New York, 10 February 1920
Philadelphia Orchestra
Samaroff, Hinkle, Hackett, Patton
Beethoven Leonore No 3 Overture
Beethoven Choral Fantasy
Rachmaninov The Bells

Philadelphia, 13-14 February 1920
Philadelphia Orchestra
Teyte
Walford Davies Solemn Melody
Elgar Enigma Variations
Wagner Tannhäuser Overture & Venusberg
Vocal items by Chausson and Duparc

Toronto, 23 February 1920
Philadelphia Orchestra
Toronto Mendelssohn Choir
Wagner Meistersinger Overture
Debussy Prélude à l'après-midi
Wagner Tannhäuser Overture & Venusberg
Choral works by Rachmaninov, Brahms,
    Schindler, Taylor, Cornelius and
    Elgar

Toronto, 24 February 1920
Philadelphia Orchestra
Toronto Mendelssohn Choir
Verdi Requiem

Toronto, 25 February 1920 (afternoon)
Philadelphia Orchestra
Samaroff
Tchaikovsky Symphony No 5
Liszt Piano Concerto No 2
Wagner Rienzi Overture

Toronto, 25 February 1920 (evening)
Philadelphia Orchestra
Toronto Mendelssohn Choir
Weber Freischütz Overture
Elgar Enigma Variations
Tchaikovsky Marche slave
Choral works by Elgar, Bossi, Bridge,
    Verdi and traditional

Philadelphia, 27-28 February 1920
Philadelphia Orchestra
Rich, Torello
Dvorak Symphony No 9
Lorenziti Concerto for viola d'amore
    and double bass
Weber Oberon Overture

Philadelphia, 5-6 March 1920
Philadelphia Orchestra
Given
Schubert Rosamunde excerpts
Paganini Violin Concerto No 1
Brahms Symphony No 1

New York, 9 March 1920
Philadelphia Orchestra
Schubert Rosamunde excerpts
Hadley Othello Overture
    (conducted by the composer)
Brahms Symphony No 1

Philadelphia, 12-13 March 1920
Philadelphia Orchestra
Goodson
Franck Symphony in D minor
Wagner Lohengrin Prelude
Wagner Entry of the Gods (Rheingold)
Wagner Ride of the Valkyries
Liapounov Piano Concerto in E major

Philadelphia, 24 March 1920
Philadelphia Orchestra
Yon, Courboin
Yon Concerto gregoriano
Wagner Entry of the Gods (Rheingold)
Bach Brandenburg Concerto No 2
Wagner Lohengrin Prelude
Saint-Saens Largo (Organ Symphony)
Also organ works by Bach, Widor,
    Russell, Gigout, Franck & Saint-Saens
Concert in Wanamakers department store

Philadelphia, 25 March 1920
Philadelphia Orchestra and Chorus
Beethoven Leonore No 3 Overture
Bach Opening Chorus (Christmas Oratorio)
Schubert Rosamunde excerpts
Parker Ballad for chorus and orchestra
Wagner Ride of the Valkyries
Elgar March and Choral Epilogue
Unaccompanied choral works by Dett,
    Gretchaninov, MacDowell & Lutkin

Philadelphia, 26-27 March 1920
Philadelphia Orchestra
Roberts
Beethoven Coriolan Overture
Mozart Symphony No 40
Sachnovski The Clock
Rimsky-Korsakov Russian Easter Overture
Vocal items by Gluck, Aubert
    & Rachmaninov

Philadelphia, 9-10 April 1920
Philadelphia Orchestra
Krueger
Brahms Symphony No 2
Maquarre Au clair de lune/Chanson
d'amour
Weber Bassoon Concertino
Berlioz Damnation de Faust excerpts

Philadelphia, 16-17 April 1920
Philadelphia Orchestra
Brown
Schubert Symphony No 9
Bruch Scottish Fantasy
Wagner Siegfried's Rhine Journey

Philadelphia, 23-24 April 1920
Philadelphia Orchestra
Ganz
Sibelius Swan of Tuonela
Saint-Saens Piano Concerto No 5
Tchaikovsky Symphony No 4

Philadelphia, 30 April-1 May 1920
Philadelphia Orchestra
Hughes, Tabuteau
Rossini Barbiere di Siviglia Overture
Mozart Oboe Concerto
Wagner Forest murmurs (Siegfried)
Wagner Wotan's Farewell (Walküre)
Vocal items by Rossini & Donizetti

Philadelphia, 7-8 May 1920
Philadelphia Orchestra and Chorus
Hanbury, Fidler, Quait, McInnes
Beethoven programme
Leonore No 3 Overture
Symphony No 9

Philadelphia, 15-16 October 1920
Philadelphia Orchestra
Sowerby Comes Autumn Time Overture
Weber Euryanthe Overture
Wagner Lohengrin Prelude
Wagner Tannhäuser Overture
Beethoven Symphony No 3

Philadelphia, 22-23 October 1920
Philadelphia Orchestra
Schubert Symphony No 9
Casella Italia
Sibelius Swan of Tuonela
Sibelius Finlandia

New York, 26 October 1920
Philadelphia Orchestra
Programme as for 22-23 October

Philadelphia, 29-30 October 1920
Philadelphia Orchestra
Matzenauer
Berlioz Carnaval romain Overture
Ropartz Symphony No 4
Vocal items by Chausson, Duparc,
Debussy and Tchaikovsky

Philadelphia, 5-6 November 1920
Philadelphia Orchestra
Scott
Bach Brandenburg 3, 1st movement
Brahms Symphony No 4
Scott 2 Passacaglias for orchestra
(conducted by the composer)
Scott Piano Concerto in C

New York, 9 November 1920
Philadelphia Orchestra
Scott
Programme as for 5-6 November

Philadelphia, 19-20 November 1920
Philadelphia Orchestra
Schmitz
Goldmark In Spring Overture
Tchaikovsky Piano Concerto No 1
Beethoven Symphony No 5
Weber Aufforderung zum Tanz
Wagner Entry of the Gods (Rheingold)
Philadelphia Orchestra's 20th
birthday concert: replica of the
1st programme in 1900

Philadelphia, 26-27 November 1920
Philadelphia Orchestra
Dvorak Symphony No 9
Brahms Haydn Variations
Carpenter A Pilgrim Vision
Wagner Tannhäuser Overture & Venusberg

New York, 30 November 1920
Philadelphia Orchestra
Dvorak Symphony No 9
Brahms Haydn Variations
Wagner Tannhäuser Overture & Venusberg

Philadelphia, 3-4 December 1920
Philadelphia Orchestra and Chorus
Baker, Rumsey, Murphy, Dadman
Beethoven programme
Leonore No 3 Overture
Symphony No 9

Philadelphia, 17-18 December 1920
Philadelphia Orchestra
Rich, Penha
Mozart Symphony No 41
Strauss Tod und Verklärung
Brahms Double Concerto

New York, 21 December 1920
Philadelphia Orchestra
Flonzaley String Quartet
Mozart Symphony No 41
Moor Concerto for quartet & orchestra
Strauss Tod und Verklärung

Philadelphia, 31 December 1920-
1 January 1921
Philadelphia Orchestra
Beethoven Symphony No 6
Wagner Rienzi Overture
Debussy Nuages et fêtes (Nocturnes)
Liszt Hungarian Rhapsody No 2

New York, 4 January 1921
Philadelphia Orchestra
Programme as for 31 December-1 January

New York, 5 January 1921
Philadelphia Orchestra
Novaes
Rimsky-Korsakov Scheherazade
Saint-Saens Piano Concerto No 2
Wagner Rienzi Overture

Philadelphia, 7-8 January 1921
Philadelphia Orchestra
Kreisler
Mozart Don Giovanni Overture
Beethoven Violin Concerto
Rimsky-Korsakov Scheherazade

Philadelphia, 21-22 January 1921
Philadelphia Orchestra
Weber Oberon Overture
Brahms Symphony No 1
Mendelssohn Midsummer Night's Dream
     Overture
Strauss Don Juan

Philadelphia, 4-5 February 1921
Philadelphia Orchestra
Kindler
Weber Freischütz Overture
Schubert Symphony No 8
Lalo Cello Concerto
Wagner Meistersinger Overture
Same programme was repeated on 11-12
February with Mengelberg conducting

New York, 8 February 1921
Philadelphia Orchestra
Matzenauer
Berlioz Carnaval romain Overture
Chausson Symphony in B flat
Wagner Siegfried's Funeral March
Vocal items by Debussy, Duparc & Wagner

Philadelphia, 25-26 February 1921
Philadelphia Orchestra
Tchaikovsky programme
Symphony No 6
Casse noisette Suite
1812 Overture

Philadelphia, 4-5 March 1921
Philadelphia Orchestra
Levitski
Bach Brandenburg Concerto No 1
Beethoven Piano Concerto No 3
Brahms Symphony No 3

New York, 8 March 1921
Philadelphia Orchestra and Chorus
Hinkle, Werrenrath
Brahms Ein deutsches Requiem

Philadelphia, 11-12 March 1921
Programme as for 8 March

Philadelphia, 18-19 March 1921
Philadelphia Orchestra
Bispham
Beethoven Symphony No 4
Mozart Per questo bella mano
Schillings Hexenlied
Schoenberg Pelleas und Melisande

Philadelphia, 25-26 March 1921
Philadelphia Orchestra
Lashanka
Weber Oberon Overture
Liszt Les Préludes
Strauss Ein Heldenleben
Vocal items by Massenet and Faccio

Philadelphia, 1-2 April 1921
Philadelphia Orchestra
Thibaud
Quilter Childrens' Overture
Lalo Symphonie espagnole
Turina La procession del rocio
Wagner Parsifal Prelude and
    Good Friday Music
Rimsky-Korsakov Russian Easter Overture

New York, 5 April 1921
Philadelphia Orchestra
Tchaikovsky programme
Symphony No 6
Casse noisette Suite
1812 Overture

Toronto, 11 April 1921
Philadelphia Orchestra
Toronto Mendelssohn Choir
Wagner Parsifal Prelude
Arcadelt Ave Maria
Palestrina Surge illuminare
Sibelius Swan of Tuonela
Vaughan Williams A Sea Symphony

Toronto, 12 April 1921
Philadelphia Orchestra
Toronto Mendelssohn Choir
Macmillan England
Rimsky-Korsakov Russian Easter Overture
Debussy La demoiselle élue
Fanning How sweet the Moonlight sleeps
Stanford Songs of the Sea
Wagner Entry of the Gods (Rheingold)

Toronto, 13 April 1921 (afternoon)
Philadelphia Orchestra
Programme as for 5 April

Toronto, 13 April (evening)
Philadelphia Orchestra
Toronto Mendelssohn Choir
Beethoven Leonore No 3 Overture
Liszt Hungarian Rhapsody No 2
Vaughan Williams Scherzo
    (A Sea Symphony)
Choral pieces by Rachmaninov, Brahms,
    Wagner, Sibelius, Host, Storch,
    and traditional

Philadelphia, 15-16 April 1921
Philadelphia Orchestra
Rachmaninov
Mozart Symphony No 40
Wagner Ride of the Valkyries
Stravinsky Fireworks
Rachmaninov Piano Concerto No 2

Philadelphia, 22-23 April 1921
Philadelphia Orchestra
Cooley
Franck Symphony in D minor
Wieniawski Violin Concerto No 2
Tchaikovsky Marche slave

Philadelphia, 29-30 April 1921
Philadelphia Orchestra
Wagner programme
Entry of Gods & Alberich's Curse
    (Rheingold)
Ride of Valkyries & Wotan's Farewell
    (Walküre)
Forest murmurs (Siegfried)
Funeral March and Immolation
    (Götterdämmerung)

Philadelphia, 6-7 May 1921
Philadelphia Orchestra
Samaroff
Tchaikovsky Symphony No 4
Schumann Piano Concerto
Gilchrist Symphonic Poem
Malipiero Ditirambo tragico

Philadelphia, 13-14 May 1921
Philadelphia Orchestra and Chorus
Peterson, Alcock
Mahler Symphony No 2

Philadelphia, 7-8 October 1921
Philadelphia Orchestra
Wagner Wotan's Farewell (Walküre)
Elgar Enigma Variations
Franck Symphony in D minor

Philadelphia, 14-15 October 1921
Philadelphia Orchestra
Telmanyi
Brahms Symphony No 2
Debussy Prélude à l'après-midi
Lalo Symphonie espagnole
Braunfels Variations on a theme of
    Berlioz

New York, 18 October 1921
Philadelphia Orchestra
Brahms Symphony No 2
Debussy Prélude à l'après-midi
Braunfels Variations on a theme of
    Berlioz

Philadelphia, 21-22 October 1921
Philadelphia Orchestra
Dvorak Carnival Overture
Satie Gymnopédies
Tchaikovsky Francesca da Rimini
Sibelius Symphony No 5

Philadelphia, 28-29 October 1921
Philadelphia Orchestra
Casella
Beethoven Symphony No 7
Casella Pages of War
Mozart Piano Concerto No 20
Berlioz Damnation de Faust excerpts

On 31 October 1921 in New York the
Philadelphia Orchestra played a
programme of Richard Strauss under
the composer's direction

New York, 1 November 1921
Philadelphia Orchestra
Casella
Beethoven Symphony No 7
Casella Pages of War
Franck Variations symphoniques
Berlioz Damnation de Faust excerpts

Philadelphia, 4-5 November 1921
Philadelphia Orchestra
Bailly
Fitelberg Polish Rhapsody
Bloch Suite for viola and orchestra
Brahms Symphony No 4

Philadelphia, 18-19 November 1921
Philadelphia Orchestra
Wagner programme
Faust Overture/Lohengrin Prelude/
Tannhäuser Overture and Venusberg/
Meistersinger Overture & Act 3
Prelude/Tristan Prelude & Liebestod

Philadelphia, 25-26 November 1921
Philadelphia Orchestra
Beethoven Coriolan Overture
Schubert Symphony No 8
Schoenberg 5 Orchestral pieces
Sibelius Finlandia

New York, 29 November 1921
Philadelphia Orchestra
Beethoven Coriolan Overture
Schubert Symphony No 8
Schoenberg 5 Orchestral pieces
Sibelius Finlandia
Wagner Wotan's Farewell (Walküre)

Philadelphia, 2-3 December 1921
Philadelphia Orchestra
Serato
Mozart Symphony No 40
Liszt Les Préludes
Beethoven Violin Concerto

Philadelphia, 14 December 1921
Philadelphia Orchestra
Verney, Penha, Torello
Childrens' concert
Bizet Carmen Prelude
Bach Air (Suite No 3)
Sitt Andante (Violin Concerto)
J.Strauss An der schonen blauen Donau
Dvorak Waldesruhe
Torello Introduction, Adagio & Fantasy
Wagner Ride of the Valkyries

Philadelphia, 16-17 December 1921
Philadelphia Orchestra
Bach Brandenburg Concerto No 2
Haydn Symphony No 88
Rimsky-Korsakov Scheherazade

New York, 20 December 1921
Philadelphia Orchestra
Programme as for 16-17 December

Philadelphia, 23-24 December 1921
Philadelphia Orchestra
Kochanski
Strauss Bourgeois gentilhomme Suite
Vivaldi Violin Concerto in A minor
Strauss Ein Heldenleben

Philadelphia, 30-31 December 1921
Philadelphia Orchestra
Gerhardt
Brahms Symphony No 3
Stravinsky Firebird Suite
Vocal items by Mahler and Wagner

New York, 3 January 1922
Philadelphia Orchestra
Gerhardt
Programme as for 30-31 December 1921

Philadelphia, 20-21 January 1922
Philadelphia Orchestra
Hess
Goldmark Sakantula Overture
Dvorak Symphony No 9
Schumann Piano Concerto
Strauss Tod und Verklärung

Philadelphia, 27-28 January 1922
Philadelphia Orchestra
Tchaikovsky Symphony No 4
Mussorgsky Night on Bare Mountain
Borodin Polovtsian Dances

Philadelphia, 1 February 1922
Philadelphia Orchestra
Tabuteau, L.Raho, Henkelman, E.Raho
Childrens' concert
Grieg In the Hall of the Mountain King
Ropartz Pastoral Dance
Beethoven Moonlight Sonata, 1st mvt.
Brahms Hungarian Dance No 6
Saint-Saens The Swan
Bartaletto Il sogno
Wagner Lohengrin Act 3 Prelude

Philadelphia, 3-4 February 1922
Philadelphia Orchestra
Vecsey
Beethoven Leonore No 3 Overture
Schumann Symphony No 4
Sibelius Violin Concerto
Strauss Dance of the 7 veils(Salome)

New York, 7 February 1922
Philadelphia Orchestra
Ivogün
Beethoven Leonore No 3 Overture
Schumann Symphony No 4
Strauss Dance of the 7 veils(Salome)
Vocal items by Mozart and Strauss

Philadelphia, 10-11 February 1922
Philadelphia Orchestra
Bach Passacaglia & Fugue in C minor
Handel Concerto grosso
Beethoven Symphony No 5

Toronto, 20 February 1922
Philadelphia Orchestra
Toronto Mendelssohn Choir
Holst Festival Te Deum
Schubert Moment musical No 3
Bach Sing ye to the Lord
Rimsky-Korsakov Scheherazade
Parry Blest Pair of Sirens

Toronto, 21 February 1922
Philadelphia Orchestra
Toronto Mendelssohn Choir
Hinkle, Burke, Barclay, Clapperton
Berlioz La damnation de Faust

Toronto, 22 February 1922 (afternoon)
Philadelphia Orchestra
Brahms Symphony No 3
Handel Concerto grosso
Bach Passacaglia and Fugue in C minor

Toronto, 22 February 1922 (evening)
Philadelphia Orchestra
Toronto Mendelssohn Choir
Wagner Lohengrin Act 3 Prelude
Vaughan Williams Sea Symphony,pts.1&2
Strauss Dance of the 7 veils(Salome)
Choral works by Stanford, Ferrari,
    Ippolitov-Ivanov, O'Hara, Wagner
    and Gartenveld-Schindler

Philadelphia, 24-25 February 1922
Philadelphia Orchestra
Rich, Verney
Schubert Rosamunde Overture
Mozart Sinfonia concertante K364
Tchaikovsky Symphony No 6

New York, 28 February 1922
Philadelphia Orchestra
Beethoven Symphony No 5
Handel Concerto grosso
Bach Passacaglia and Fugue in C minor

Philadelphia, 3-4 March 1922
Philadelphia Orchestra
Schelling
Wagner Entry of the Gods (Rheingold)
Wagner Forest murmurs (Siegfried)
Wagner Rhine Journey(Götterdämmerung)
Schelling Fantastic Suite
Stravinsky Le sacre du printemps

Philadelphia, 8 March 1922
Philadelphia Orchestra
Kincaid, Fischer, La Monaca
<u>Childrens' concert</u>
Beethoven Turkish March
Widor Romance for flute & orchestra
Bizet Danse (L'Arlésienne)
Damm Concert Polka
Schubert Moment musical No 3
La Monaca Primavera Melody
Ippolitov-Ivanov Procession of the
 Sardar (Caucasian Sketches)

Philadelphia, 10-11 March 1922
Philadelphia Orchestra
Hofmann
Carpenter Pilgrim Vision
Beethoven Piano Concerto No 5
Mozart Symphony No 41
Liszt Hungarian Rhapsody No 1

New York, 14 March 1922
Philadelphia Orchestra
Gabrilowitsch
Wagner Entry of the Gods (Rheingold)
Wagner Forest murmurs (Siegfried)
Wagner Rhine Journey (Götterdämmerung)
Brahms Piano Concerto No 2
Carpenter Pilgrim Vision
Liszt Hungarian Rhapsody No 1

Philadelphia, 17-18 March 1922
Philadelphia Orchestra
Penha
Brahms Symphony No 1
Dvorak Cello Concerto
Tchaikovsky Marche slave

Philadelphia, 24-25 March 1922
Philadelphia Orchestra
Ivogün
Wagner Holländer Overture
Mendelssohn Symphony No 3
Strauss Tod und Verklärung
Vocal items by Mozart and Strauss

New York, 28 March 1922
Philadelphia Orchestra
Kindler
Wagner Holländer Overture
Mendelssohn Symphony No 3
D'Albert Cello Concerto
Strauss Tod und Verklärung

Philadelphia, 7-8 April 1922
Philadelphia Orchestra
Bauer
Beethoven Egmont Overture
Strauss Burleske
Brahms Haydn Variations
Sibelius Swan of Tuonela
Scriabin Prometheus

Philadelphia, 14-15 April 1922
Philadelphia Orchestra
Bach Passacaglia and Fugue in C minor
Mozart Symphony No 39
Falla El amor brujo
Rimsky-Korsakov Russian Easter Overture

New York, 18 April 1922
Philadelphia Orchestra
Bauer
Rimsky-Korsakov Russian Easter Overture
Scriabin Prometheus
Mozart Symphony No 39
Bach Passacaglia and Fugue in C minor

Philadelphia, 21-22 April 1922
Philadelphia Orchestra
Lane
Mueller Schlaraffiada
 (conducted by the composer)
Liszt Piano Concerto No 1
Tchaikovsky Symphony No 5

Philadelphia, 28-29 April 1922
Philadelphia Orchestra
Beethoven Leonore No 3 Overture
Franck Symphony in D minor
Rimsky-Korsakov Scheherazade

Philadelphia, October 1922
Philadelphia Orchestra
Wagner Meistersinger Overture
Beethoven Symphony No 4
Bach Suite No 2
Debussy Cour de Lys
Ravel La valse

New York, 17 October 1922
Philadelphia Orchestra
Wagner Meistersinger Overture
Beethoven Symphony No 4
Strauss Ein Heldenleben

Philadelphia, October 1922
Philadelphia Orchestra
Dux
Schubert Ländler
Strauss Ein Heldenleben
Vocal items by Halévy, Reger and
  Korngold

Philadelphia, October 1922
Philadelphia Orchestra
Lully Suite
Vivaldi Concerto grosso in D minor
Rossini Guilleaume Tell Overture
Dvorak Symphony No 9

New York, 31 October 1922
Philadelphia Orchestra
Onegin
Schubert Rosamunde Overture
Schumann Symphony No 2
Mussorgsky Khovanschina Entr'acte
Stravinsky Fireworks
Vocal items by Bruch and Strauss

Philadelphia, November 1922
Philadelphia Orchestra
Kindler
Schubert Rosamunde Overture
Schumann Symphony No 2
Mussorgsky Khovanschina Entr'acte
Bloch Schelomo
Stravinsky Fireworks

Philadelphia, November 1922
Philadelphia Orchestra
Samaroff
Beethoven Coriolan Overture
Mozart Symphony No 40
Tchaikovsky Piano Concerto No 1
Strauss Dance of 7 veils (Salome)

Philadelphia, November 1922
Philadelphia Orchestra
Huberman
Liszt Hungarian Rhapsody No 1
Beethoven Violin Concerto
Brahms Symphony No 4

New York, 21 November 1922
Philadelphia Orchestra
Gerardy
Brahms Symphony No 4
Elgar Cello Concerto
Liszt Hungarian Rhapsody No 1

Philadelphia, November 1922
Philadelphia Orchestra
Franck Symphony in D minor
Dukas L'apprenti sorcier
Debussy Prélude à l'après-midi
Chabrier Espana
Saint-Saens Danse macabre

Philadelphia, December 1922
Philadelphia Orchestra
Siloti
Bach Brandenburg Concerto No 4
Haydn Symphony No 104
Zeckwer Jade Butterflies
  (conducted by the composer)
Liszt Totentanz

Philadelphia, December 1922
Philadelphia Orchestra
Tchaikovsky programme
Symphony No 6
Casse noisette Suite
1812 Overture

Philadelphia, December 1922
Philadelphia Orchestra
Gauthier
Brahms 2 Hungarian Dances
Chausson Symphony in B flat
Debussy Cour de Lys
Borodin Polovtsian Dances
Vocal items by Stravinsky, Delage
  and Ravel

New York, 19 December 1922
Philadelphia Orchestra
Samaroff
Debussy Cour de Lys
Chausson Symphony in B flat
Tchaikovsky Piano Concerto No 1
Wagner Immolation (Götterdämmerung)

Philadelphia, December 1922
Philadelphia Orchestra
Thibaud
Bach Passacaglia and Fugue in C minor
Bach Sinfonia (Christmas Oratorio)
Bach Violin Concerto in G minor
Lalo Symphonie espagnole
Wagner Wotan's Farewell (Walküre)

Philadelphia, December 1922
Philadelphia Orchestra
Cortot
Beethoven Symphony No 7
Saint-Saens Piano Concerto No 4
Strauss Don Juan

Philadelphia, January 1923
Philadelphia Orchestra
Enesco
Enesco Roumanian Rhapsody No 2
Enesco Symphony in E flat
   (both Enesco works conducted by
   the composer)
Brahms Violin Concerto

Philadelphia, January 1923
Philadelphia Orchestra
Brahms Symphony No 1
Mussorgsky Night on Bare Mountain
Satie Gymnopédies
Sibelius Finlandia

New York, 6 February 1923
Philadelphia Orchestra
Brahms Symphony No 1
Mussorgsky Night on Bare Mountain
Satie Gymnopédies
Sibelius Finlandia

Philadelphia, February 1923
Philadelphia Orchestra
Wagner programme
Tannhäuser Act 3 Prelude, Overture
& Venusberg/Siegfried Idyll/
Siegfried's Funeral March/Parsifal
Prelude & Good Friday Music/Tristan
Act 3 Prelude, Prelude and Liebestod

Toronto, 15 February 1923
Philadelphia Orchestra
Toronto Mendelssohn Choir
Bach Wachet auf
Brahms Symphony No 1
Holst Choral Hymns from Rig-Veda
Mussorgsky Khovanschina Entr'acte
Satie Gymnopédies
Sibelius Finlandia

Toronto, 16 February 1923
Philadelphia Orchestra
Toronto Mendelssohn Choir
Lully Suite
Brahms Hungarian Dance No 5
Brahms Ein deutsches Requiem
Also choral works by Palestrina,
   Purcell and Stanford

Toronto, 17 February 1923 (afternoon)
Philadelphia Orchestra
Wagner programme
Tannhäuser Act 3 Prelude, Overture
& Venusberg/Siegfried Idyll/
Siegfried's Funeral March/Parsifal
Prelude & Good Friday Music/Tristan
Act 3 Prelude, Prelude & Liebestod

Toronto, 17 February 1923 (evening)
Philadelphia Orchestra
Toronto Mendelssohn Choir
Boito Prologue to Mefistofele
Debussy Prélude à l'après-midi
Holst Choral Hymns from Rig-Veda
Borodin Polovtsian Dances
Also choral works by Saint-Saens,
   Stanford and Rimsky-Korsakov

Philadelphia, 19-21 February 1923
Philadelphia Orchestra
Grisez, Serpentini, Alemann
Childrens' concert
Rossini Guilleaume Tell Overture
Pierne Canzonetta
Boccherini Minuetto
Cavallini Andante tarantelle
Grieg Anitra's Dance (Peer Gynt)
Massenet Elégie
J.Strauss An der schönen blauen Donau

Philadelphia, February 1923
Philadelphia Orchestra
Montague
Berlioz Hungarian March (Faust)
Schelling Victory Ball
Rimsky-Korsakov Scheherazade
Vocal items by Debussy & Tchaikovsky

New York, 27 February 1923
Philadelphia Orchestra
Moiseiwitsch
Lully Suite
Vivaldi Concerto grosso in D minor
Bach Passacaglia & Fugue in C minor
Schelling Victory Ball
Tcherepnin Piano Concerto

Philadelphia, March 1923
Philadelphia Orchestra
Backhaus
Wagner Lohengrin Prelude
Pick-Mangianelli Sortileggi
Beethoven Piano Concerto No 4
Schubert Symphony No 9

Philhadelphia, March 1923
Philadelphia Orchestra
Powell
Eichheim Chinese Sketch
Eichheim Japanese Nocturne
Powell Negro Rhapsody
Mason Prelude and Fugue
Sibelius Swan of Tuonela
Strauss Till Eulenspiegel

New York, 13 March 1923
Philadelphia Orchestra
Schubert Symphony No 9
Eichheim Chinese Sketch
Eichheim Japanese Nocturne
Strauss Till Eulenspiegel

Philadelphia, March 1923
Philadelphia Orchestra
Koshetz
Glinka Ruslan and Ludmila Overture
Rimsky-Korsakov Dance (Snow Maiden)
Tchaikovsky Symphony No 5
Vocal items by Rimsky-Korsakov and
    Mussorgsky

Philadelphia, 26-28 March 1923
Philadelphia Orchestra
Guetter, Del Megro
Childrens' concert
Quilter Childrens' Overture
Weissenborn Capriccio for bassoon
Brahms Hungarian Dance No 5
Del Negro Down in the Deep Cellar
Tchaikovsky 1812 Overture

New York, 3 April 1923
Philadelphia Orchestra
Schoenberg Chamber Symphony
Debussy Nuages et fêtes (Nocturnes)
Mozart Symphony No 41

Philadelphia, April 1923
Philadelphia Orchestra
Schnabel
Mendelssohn Hebrides Overture
Brahms Piano Concerto No 1
Schubert Symphony No 8
Strauss Tod und Verklärung

Philadelphia, 9-11 April 1923
Philadelphia Orchestra
A.Horner, J.Horner, Henneberg, Riese
Childrens' concert
Gounod Waltz (Faust)
Saint-Saens Romance
Saint-Saens Carnaval des animaux
Mohring Forest Song
Rossini Guilleaume Tell Overture

Philadelphia, April 1923
Philadelphia Orchestra
Hackett
Tchaikovsky Romeo and Juliet
Liszt A Faust Symphony

New York, 17 April 1923
Philadelphia Orchestra
Hackett
Tchaikovsky Romeo and Juliet
Liszt A Faust Symphony

Philadelphia, April 1923
Philadelphia Orchestra
Wagner programme
Entry of the Gods & Alberich's Curse
    (Rheingold)
Ride of the Valkyries & Wotan's
    Farewell (Walküre)
Forest murmurs & Siegfried approaches
    Brünnhilde (Siegfried)
Rhine Journey, Funeral March and
    Immolation (Götterdämmerung)

Philadelphia, May 1923
Philadelphia Orchestra
Beethoven Symphony No 5
Wagner Tannhäuser Overture & Venusberg
Tchaikovsky 1812 Overture

During the 1922-1923 season
Stokowski also guest-conducted in
France and Italy. A concert with
the Pasdeloup Orchestra in Paris
included works by Lully

Philadelphia, 5-6 October 1923
Philadelphia Orchestra
Wagner Rienzi Overture
Beethoven Symphony No 7
Sibelius Swan of Tuonela
Tchaikovsky Capriccio italien

Philadelphia, 12-13 October 1923
Philadelphia Orchestra
Kochanski
Schubert Rosamunde excerpts
Bach Suite No 2
Brahms Violin Concerto

New York, 16 October 1923
Philadelphia Orchestra
Schubert Rosamunde excerpts
Bach Suite No 2
Beethoven Symphony No 7

Philadelphia, 19-20 October 1923
Philadelphia Orchestra
Beethoven Leonore No 3 Overture
Haydn Symphony No 95
Stravinsky Le chant du rossignol
Tchaikovsky Casse noisette Suite

Philadelphia, 22 October 1923
Philadelphia Orchestra
Beethoven Symphony No 7
Tchaikovsky Casse noisette Suite
Wagner Rienzi Overture

Philadelphia, 26-27 October 1923
Philadelphia Orchestra
Wagner Holländer Overture
Brahms Symphony No 3
Rimsky-Korsakov City of Kitesh excpts.
Strauss Tod und Verklärung

New York, 30 October 1923
Philadelphia Orchestra
Programme as for 26-27 October

Philadelphia, 2-5 November 1923
Philadelphia Orchestra
Wagner programme
Huldigungsmarsch/Tristan Act 3
Prelude/Wotan's Farewell (Walküre)/
Forest murmurs & Siegfried approaches
Brünnhilde (Siegfried)/Rhine Journey,
Funeral March & Immolation (Götter-
dämmerung)

Philadelphia, 10 November 1923
Philadelphia Orchestra
Kincaid
Lecture concert
Wagner Lohengrin Prelude
Hue Fantasy for flute and orchestra
Mussorgsky Khovanschina Entr'acte
Tchaikovsky Danse des mirlitons
    (Casse noisette)
Wagner Entry of the Gods (Rheingold)

Philadelphia, 12-14 November 1923
Philadelphia Orchestra
Cohen, Donatelli, J.Fischer
Childrens' concert
Chabrier Espana
Arban Fantasie brilliante
Kling The Elephant and the Mosquito
Tchaikovsky Casse noisette Suite

Philadelphia, 16-17 November 1923
Philadelphia Orchestra
Landowska
Gluck Alceste Overture
Handel Harpsichord Concerto B minor
Bach Italian Concerto
Mozart Piano Concerto No 9
Schubert Symphony No 8

New York, 20 November 1923
Philadelphia Orchestra
Landowska
Programme as for 16-17 November

Philadelphia, 23-24 November 1923
Philadelphia Orchestra
Rich
Sibelius Finlandia
Bruch Violin Concerto No 1
Stravinsky Symphonies of wind
Strauss Till Eulenspiegel
Weber Aufforderung zum Tanz

Philadelphia, 26-28 November 1923
Philadelphia Orchestra
Fanelli, Nicoletta, Schwar
Childrens' concert
Jaernefelt Praeludium
Hasselmans La gitana
Nicoletta Fantasy on Irish airs
Ippolitov-Ivanov Shepherd in the
  Valley
Schreiner Concerto grosso
Rimsky-Korsakov Dance (Snow Maiden)

Philadelphia, 30 November-
1 December 1923
Philadelphia Orchestra
Bonner
Bach Suite No 3
Beethoven Allegretto (Symphony No 7)
Beethoven Symphony No 2
Wagner Entry of the Gods (Rheingold)
Vocal items by Handel and Wagner

Philadelphia, 7-10 December 1923
Philadelphia Orchestra
Siloti
Weber Freischütz Overture
Beethoven Piano Concerto No 5
Tchaikovsky Symphony No 6

Philadelphia, 12 December 1923
Philadelphia Orchestra
Tabuteau
Lecture concert
Sibelius Finlandia
Handel Oboe Concerto
Bach Air (Suite No 3)
Tchaikovsky Symphony No 6, 2nd and
  3rd movements

Philadelphia, 14-15 December 1923
Philadelphia Orchestra
Flesch
Mozart Le nozze di Figaro Overture
Mozart Symphony No 40
Beethoven Violin Concerto
Wagner Tristan Prelude & Liebestod

New York, 18 December 1923
Philadelphia Orchestra
Flesch
Mozart Le nozze di Figaro Overture
Mozart Symphony No 40
Brahms Violin Concerto
Wagner Tristan Prelude & Liebestod

Philadelphia, 21-22 December 1923
Philadelphia Orchestra
Penha
Bloch Poème juif
Berlioz Queen Mab Scherzo
Schumann Cello Concerto
Dvorak Symphony No 9

Philadelphia, 27 December 1923
Philadelphia Orchestra
Sibelius Finlandia
Bloch Poème juif
Berlioz Queen Mab Scherzo
Wagner Tristan Prelude & Liebestod
Dvorak Symphony No 9

Philadelphia, 28-29 December 1923
Philadelphia Orchestra
Hofmann
Programme included piano solos

New York, 2 January 1924
Philadelphia Orchestra
Hofmann
Programme included piano solos

Philadelphia, 4-5 January 1924
Philadelphia Orchestra
M.Nikisch
Beethoven Coriolan Overture
Brahms Piano Concerto No 1
Debussy Nuages et fêtes (Nocturnes)
Strauss Dance of 7 veils (Salome)

Philadelphia, 25-26 January 1924
Philadelphia Orchestra
Kindler
Strauss Don Juan
Dvorak Cello Concerto
Rimsky-Korsakov Scheherazade

Philadelphia, 26 January 1924
(afternoon)
Philadelphia Orchestra
Arey
Lecture concert
Rimsky-Korsakov Scheherazade,4th mvt.
Debussy Fêtes (Nocturnes)
Mozart Clarinet Concerto, 1st mvt.
Wagner Rienzi Overture

Philadelphia, 28-30 January 1924
Philadelphia Orchestra
Simons, Beemt
Childrens' concert
Bizet Danse bohème (Carmen)
Simons Atlantic Zephyrs
Beemt Grandma's Music Box
Rimsky-Korsakov Scheherazade,4th mvt.

Philadelphia, 1-2 February 1924
Philadelphia Orchestra
Enesco
Wagner Funeral March (Götterdämmerung)
Paganini Violin Concerto No 1
Stravinsky Firebird Suite
Tchaikovsky Symphony No 4

New York, 5 February 1924
Philadelphia Orchestra
Kindler
Bloch Schelomo
Stravinsky Symphonies of wind
Rimsky-Korsakov Scheherazade

Philadelphia, 8-9 February 1924
Philadelphia Orchestra
Mero
Respighi Sinfonia drammatica
Tchaikovsky Piano Concerto No 2
Borodin Polovtsian Dances

Philadelphia, 11 February 1924
Philadelphia Orchestra
Enesco
Programme as for 1-2 February

Philadelphia, 15-16 February 1924
Philadelphia Orchestra
Monasevitch
Glinka Ruslan and Ludmila Overture
Rimsky-Korsakov Dance (Snow Maiden)
Glazunov Violin Concerto
Tchaikovsky Symphony No 5

Philadelphia, 16 February 1924
(afternoon)
Philadelphia Orchestra
Del Negro
Lecture concert
Rimsky-Korsakov Dance (Snow Maiden)
Stravinsky Firebird, excerpts
Weber Adagio & Rondo (Bassoon Concerto)
Tchaikovsky Pizzicato (Symphony No 4)

Philadelphia, 25 February 1924
Philadelphia Orchestra
Rimsky-Korsakov Scheherazade,4th mvt.
Debussy Prélude à l'après-midi
Music played during the Philadelphia
Award ceremony

Philadelphia, 1-2 March 1924
Philadelphia Orchestra
Lashanska
Herbert Irish Rhapsody
Stanford Irish Symphony
Lalo Le roi d'Ys Overture
Vocal items by Mozart & Charpentier

New York, 4 March 1924
Philadelphia Orchestra
Toronto Mendelssohn Choir
Garrison, Alcock, Althouse, Dadmun
Beethoven Symphony No 9
Choral works by Palestrina, Byrd
    and Bach

New York, 5 March 1924
Philadelphia Orchestra
Toronto Mendelssohn Choir
Choral works by Palestrina, Bach,
    Purcell, Bennett, Stanford, Holst,
    Dvorak, Ravel and Borodin

Philadelphia, 6 March 1924
Philadelphia Orchestra
Toronto Mendelssohn Choir
Garrison, Alcock, Althouse, Dadmun
Programme as for 4 March

Philadelphia, 8-9 March 1924
Philadelphia Orchestra
Deems Taylor Through the Looking Glass
Stravinsky Firebird Suite
Beethoven Symphony No 5

New York, 11 March 1924
Philadelphia Orchestra
Koshetz
Glinka Ruslan & Ludmila Overture
Rimsky-Korsakov Dance (Snow Maiden)
Tchaikovsky Symphony No 5
Vocal items by Mussorgsky and
    Rimsky-Korsakov

Philadelphia, 13 March 1924
Philadelphia Orchestra
Kincaid
<u>Schools' concert</u>
Wagner Tannhäuser Overture
Grieg Anitra's Dance (Peer Gynt)
Widor Romance
Boccherini Minuetto
Wagner Ride of the Valkyries(Walküre)

Philadelphia, 15-16 March 1924
Philadelphia Orchestra
Lamond
Bach Aus der Tiefe & Wir glauben all
Beethoven Piano Concerto No 4
Brahms Symphony No 2

Philadelphia, 17 March 1924
Philadelphia Orchestra
Lashanska
Programme as for 1-2 March

Philadelphia, 22-23 March 1924
Philadelphia Orchestra
Wagner Meistersinger Overture
Debussy Prélude à l'après-midi
Ducasse Nocturne de printemps
Krasa March
Magnard Hymne à la justice
Wagner Meistersinger Act 3 Prelude
Wagner Wotan's Farewell (Walküre)

New York, 25 March 1924
Philadelphia Orchestra
Programme as for 8-9 March

Philadelphia, 27 March 1924
Philadelphia Orchestra
Tabuteau
<u>Schools' concert</u>
Rimsky-Korsakov Scheherazade,4th mvt.
Mozart Minuet
Schubert Moment musical No 3
Ippolitov-Ivanov March of Caucasian
    Chief (Caucasian Sketches)
Godard Légende pastorale
Wagner Lohengrin Act 3 Prelude

Philadelphia, 29-30 March 1924
Philadelphia Orchestra
Delaquerierre, Hansen, Barclay,
Linscott, Salzedo
Rimsky-Korsakov Russian Easter Overture
Mussorgsky Khovanschina Entr'acte
Stravinsky Renard
Schumann Symphony No 4
Bach Passacaglia & Fugue in C minor

New York, 1 April 1924
Philadelphia Orchestra
Lamond
Programme as for 15-16 March

Philadelphia, 3 April 1924
Philadelphia Orchestra
Arey
<u>Schools' concert</u>
Bizet Carmen Prelude/Mendelssohn
Scherzo/Pierne Canzonetta
Tchaikovsky Danse des mirlitons
Wagner Wotan's Farewell (Walküre)

Philadelphia, 6-7 April 1924
Philadelphia Orchestra
Wagner Tannhäuser Overture & Venusberg
Wagner Parsifal Prelude & Good Friday
    Music
Mozart Symphony No 41

Philadelphia, 7-9 April 1924
Philadelphia Orchestra
<u>Childrens' concert</u>
Rossini Guilleaume Tell Overture
Tchaikovsky Pizzicato (Symphony No 4)
J.Strauss An der schönen blauen Donau

Philadelphia, 13-14 April 1924
Philadelphia Orchestra
Sibelius Finlandia
Franck Symphony in D minor
Rimsky-Korsakov Scheherazade

New York, 15 April 1924
Philadelphia Orchestra
Programme as for 29-30 March

Philadelphia, 10-11 October 1924
Philadelphia Orchestra
Weber Euryanthe Overture
Beethoven Symphony No 5
Bizet L'Arlésienne Suite
Casella Heroic Elegy
Wagner Rienzi Overture

Philadelphia, 15-16 October 1924
Philadelphia Orchestra
Childrens' concert
Borodin Polovtsian Dances
Beethoven Allegretto (Symphony No 7)
Sibelius Finlandia
Programme also included piano solos
and audience singing

Philadelphia, 17-18 October 1928
Philadelphia Orchestra
Brahms Symphony No 1
Stravinsky Fireworks
Stravinsky Song of the Volga Boatmen
Stravinsky Firebird Suite

Philadelphia, 24-25 October 1924
Philadelphia Orchestra
Press
Tchaikovsky programme
Symphony No 4
Violin Concerto
Marche slave

Philadelphia, 31 October-
1 November 1924
Philadelphia Orchestra
Medtner
Beethoven Leonore No 3 Overture
Mozart Symphony No 39
Medtner Piano Concerto in C minor
Borodin Polovtsian Dances

Philadelphia, 7-8 November 1924
Philadelphia Orchestra
Dvorak Symphony No 9
Loeffler Pagan Poem
Varèse Hyperprism
Brahms Haydn Variations

Philadelphia, 14-15 November 1924
Philadelphia Orchestra
Bach Wir glauben all an einen Gott
Beethoven Symphony No 4
Hindemith Dances from Nusch-Nuschi
Strauss Tod und Verklärung

Philadelphia, 21-22 November 1924
Philadelphia Orchestra
Wagner programme
Holländer Overture/Lohengrin Acts 1
& 3 Preludes/Tannhäuser Overture/
Siegfried Idyll/Walküre Ride of the
Valkyries & Wotan's Farewell

Philadelphia, 28-29 November 1924
Philadelphia Orchestra
Kochanski
Weber Freischütz Overture
Haydn Symphony No 88
Szymanowski Violin Concerto

Philadelphia, 5-6 December 1924
Philadelphia Orchestra
Alwyne
Debussy Nuages et fêtes (Nocturnes)
Atterberg Symphony No 2
Strauss Burleske
Franck Variations symphoniques

Philadelphia, 10-11 December 1924
Philadelphia Orchestra
Shumsky
Childrens'concert
Chopin Polonaise in A
Tchaikovsky Symphony No 5, 3rd mvt.
Mozart Violin Concerto No 5,1st mvt.
Berlioz Marche hongroise
Programme also included audience
singing

Philadelphia, 12-13 December 1924
Philadelphia Orchestra
Franck Symphony in D minor
Sekles Fantastische Miniaturen
Berlioz Damnation de Faust excerpts

Philadelphia, 19-20 December 1924
Philadelphia Orchestra
Penha
Vaughan Williams Symphony No 3
Lalo Cello Concerto
Saint-Saens Danse macabre

Philadelphia, 26-27 December 1924
Philadelphia Orchestra
Landowska
Purcell Trumpet Prelude
Bach Harpsichord Concerto in F minor
Handel Pastoral Symphony (Messiah)
Haydn 18th century Dance
Mozart Piano Concerto No 20
Beethoven Egmont Overture

Philadelphia, 2-3 January 1925
Philadelphia Orchestra
Bruckner Symphony No 7
Joslyn War Dance
Eichheim Japanese Nocturne
Pierne Sur la route de Poggio-Bustone

Philadelphia, 9-10 January 1925
Philadelphia Orchestra
Schubert Symphony No 9
Tchaikovsky Romeo and Juliet
Unidentified work by Brahms

Philadelphia, 4-5 February 1925
Philadelphia Orchestra
Childrens' concert
Mozart Le nozze di Figaro Overture
Schubert Symphony No 8, 1st movement
Carl Hahn Cello Romance
J.Strauss Radetzky March
Programme also included audience
singing

Philadelphia, 6-7 February 1925
Philadelphia Orchestra
Wagner programme
Parsifal Prelude & Good Friday Music/
Rheingold Alberich's Curse & Entry
of the Gods/Siegfried Forest murmurs
& Siegfried approaches Brünnhilde/
Götterdämmerung Rhine Journey,
Funeral March and Immolation

Philadelphia, 13-14 February 1925
Philadelphia Orchestra
Ornstein
Schumann Symphony No 2
Ornstein Piano Concerto
Tchaikovsky Romeo and Juliet

Philadelphia, 20-21 February 1925
Philadelphia Orchestra
Tchaikovsky Symphony No 5
Mussorgsky Khovanschina Entr'acte
Prokofiev Scythian Suite

Philadelphia, 27-28 February 1925
Philadelphia Orchestra
Beethoven Coriolan Overture
Brahms Symphony No 3
Bliss Melee fantastique
Strauss Don Juan

Philadelphia, 6-7 March 1925
Philadelphia Orchestra
Purcell Trumpet Prelude
Bach Suite No 2
Gluck Ballet Suite
Rimsky-Korsakov Scheherazade

Toronto, 12 March 1925
Philadelphia Orchestra
Toronto Mendelssohn Choir
Bach Suite No 2
Wagner Götterdämmerung Rhine Journey
and Funeral March
Choral works by Bach, Wesley, Willan,
Cornelius and Wagner

Toronto, 13 March 1925
Philadelphia Orchestra
Toronto Mendelssohn Choir
Van der Veer, Crooks, Clapperton
Elgar The Dream of Gerontius

Toronto, 14 March 1925 (afternoon)
Philadelphia Orchestra
Franck Symphony in D minor
Gluck Ballet Suite
Bach Passacaglia & Fugue in C minor

Toronto, 14 March 1925 (evening)
Philadelphia Orchestra
Toronto Mendelssohn Choir
Purcell Trumpet Prelude
Wagner Rheingold Song of the Rhine
Maidens
Tchaikovsky Romeo and Juliet
Choral works by Handel, Berlioz,
Fletcher, Dunhill, Roger-Ducasse,
Elgar, Schindler, Brahms and
Sullivan

Philadelphia, 18 March 1925
Philadelphia Orchestra
Guetter
Schools' concert
Purcell Trumpet Prelude
Weissenborn Bassoon Capriccio
Rimsky-Korsakov Scheherazade

Philadelphia, 20-21 March 1925
Philadelphia Orchestra
Cortot
Berlioz Carnaval romain Overture
Chausson Symphony in B flat
Schumann Piano Concerto
Albeniz Fête-Dieu à Seville

Philadelphia, 25 March 1925
Philadelphia Orchestra
Purcell Trumpet Prelude
Albeniz Fête-Dieu à Seville
Music played during the Philadelphia
Award ceremony

Philadelphia, 27-28 March 1925
Philadelphia Orchestra
Flesch
Weber Euryanthe Overture
Mozart Violin Concerto No 4
Suk Fantasy for violin & orchestra
Bizet Scherzo (Roma)
Liszt Hungarian Rhapsody No 2

Philadelphia, 3-4 April 1925
Philadelphia Orchestra
Maier, Pattison
Beethoven Symphony No 3
Rachmaninov Isle of the Dead
Rimsky-Korsakov Russian Easter Overture
Schubert Symphony No 8
Bach Passacaglia & Fugue in C minor

Philadelphia, 8 April 1925
Philadelphia Orchestra
Horner
Schools' concert
Wagner Meistersinger Overture
Saint-Saens Horn Romance
Debussy Prélude à l'après-midi
Tchaikovsky Marche slave

Philadelphia, 11-13 April 1925
Philadelphia Orchestra
Balakirev Islamay
Rachmaninov Isle of the Dead
Rimsky-Korsakov Russian Easter Overture
Schubert Symphony No 8
Bach Passacaglia & Fugue in C minor

Philadelphia, 17-18 April 1925
Philadelphia Orchestra
Wagner programme
Faust Overture/Tannhäuser Overture &
Venusberg/Meistersinger Overture &
Act 3 Prelude/Tristan Prelude, Act
3 Prelude and Liebestod
Programme may have also included a
Bach transcription

Philadelphia, 22-23 April 1925
Philadelphia Orchestra
Kincaid, La Monaca, J.Fischer,
Schlegel
Childrens' concert
Stravinsky Song of the Volga Boatmen
La Monaca Scherzo for 4 flutes
Schubert Symphony No 8, 2nd movement
J.Strauss An der schönen blauen Donau
Programme also included audience
singing

Philadelphia, 24-25 April 1925
Philadelphia Orchestra
Tchaikovsky Symphony No 6
Debussy Prélude à l'après-midi
Bizet L'Arlésienne excerpts

Philadelphia, 28 April 1925
Philadelphia Orchestra
Caston
Schools' concert
Tchaikovsky Symphony No 6, 2nd mvt.
Arban Fantasie brilliante
Wagner Tristan Prelude & Liebestod

Philadelphia, 1-2 May 1925
Philadelphia Orchestra
Franck Symphony in D minor
Rimsky-Korsakov Scheherazade

1924-1925 season also included ten
Philadelphia Orchestra concerts in
New York, which were direct repeats
or permutations of programmes also
performed in Philadelphia

Philadelphia, 9-10 October 1925
Philadelphia Orchestra
Mendelssohn Midsummer Night's Dream
    Suite
Wagner Tristan Prelude & Liebestod
Beethoven Symphony No 7

Philadelphia, 14-15 October 1925
Philadelphia Orchestra
Pick
Childrens' concert
Bach Wir glauben all an einen Gott
Arensky Chant triste
Stitt Cello Serenade
Dvorak Largo (Symphony No 9)
Mendelssohn Scherzo (Midsummer
    Night's Dream)
Programme also included audience
singing

Philadelphia, 16-17 October 1925
Philadelphia Orchestra
Bach Wir glauben all an einen Gott
Brahms Symphony No 3
Holst Japanese Suite
Liszt Les Préludes

Philadelphia, 23-24 October 1925
Philadelphia Orchestra
Pick
Mozart Zauberflöte Overture
Haydn Cello Concerto in C
Schubert Symphony No 8
Debussy Nuages et fêtes (Nocturnes)
Strauss Dance of 7 veils (Salome)

Philadelphia, 30-31 October 1925
Philadelphia Orchestra
Donahue
Balakirev Islamay
Rachmaninov Piano Concerto No 2
Dvorak Symphony No 9

Philadelphia, 6-7 November 1925
Philadelphia Orchestra
Rich
Berlioz Damnation de Faust excerpts
Loeffler La mort de Tintagiles
Tchaikovsky Symphony No 4

Philadelphia, 13-14 November 1925
Philadelphia Orchestra
Gabrilowitsch
Orchestra's 25th birthday concert,
with same soloist and programme as
on 16 November 1900
Goldmark Overture Im Frühling
Beethoven Symphony No 5
Tchaikovsky Piano Concerto No 1
Weber Aufforderung zum Tanz
Wagner Rheingold Entry of the Gods

Philadelphia, 20-21 November 1925
Philadelphia Orchestra
Rich
Wagner Lohengrin Act 3 Prelude
Brahms Violin Concerto
Salzedo The Enchanted Isle
Stravinsky Firebird Suite

Philadelphia, 27-28 November 1925
Philadelphia Orchestra
Jaernefelt Praeludium
Sibelius Symphony No 5
Debussy Prélude à l'après-midi
Strauss Tod und Verklärung

Philadelphia, 4-5 December 1925
Philadelphia Orchestra
Szigeti
Jarecki Chimere
Bloch Concerto grosso
Beethoven Violin Concerto

Philadelphia, 9-10 December 1925
Philadelphia Orchestra
Childrens' concert
Wagner Lohengrin Act 3 Prelude
Franck Symphony, 2nd movement
Brahms Hungarian Dance No 1
Programme also included harp solos
and audience singing

Philadelphia, 11-12 December 1925
Philadelphia Orchestra
Handel Overture in D minor
Rimsky-Korsakov Scheherazade
Mussorgsky Khovanschina Prelude
    and Entr'acte
Stravinsky Firebird Suite

Philadelphia, 18-19 December 1925
Philadelphia Orchestra
Leps Loretto
Gilchrist Symphony in C
Brahms Haydn Variations
Schubert German Dances
J.Strauss G'schichten aus dem
   Wienerwald

Philadelphia, 22 December 1925
Philadelphia Orchestra
Kincaid, Tabuteau
Childrens' concert
Bach Wir glauben all an einen Gott
Widor Flute Romance and Scherzo
Tchaikovsky Symphony No 4, 3rd mvt.
Handel Oboe Concerto in G
J.Strauss An der schönen blauen Donau

Philadelphia, 26-28 December 1925
Philadelphia Orchestra
Hayes
Handel Pastoral Symphony (Messiah)
Mozart Symphony No 40
Rimsky-Korsakov Christmas Eve
Vocal items by Mozart and spirituals

Philadelphia, 2-4 January 1926
Philadelphia Orchestra
Frijsh
Miaskovsky Symphony No 5
Loeffler Canticum fratris solis
Rimsky-Korsakov Scheherazade
Rimsky work accompanied by
demonstration by Thomas Wilfred of
sound and light (Clavilux)

Philadelphia, 8-9 January 1926
Philadelphia Orchestra
Wagner programme
Lohengrin Prelude/Siegfried Idyll/
Parsifal Prelude/Tannhäuser Overture
& Venusberg/Götterdämmerung Rhine
Journey, Funeral March & Immolation

Philadelphia, 3-4 February 1925
Philadelphia Orchestra
Belov, Geoffrion
Childrens' concert
Debussy Children's Corner
Wiedoeft Saxarella
Mozart Symphony No 40, 3rd movement
Programme also included traditional
dances and audience singing

Philadelphia, 5-6 February 1925
Philadelphia Orchestra
Franck Symphony in D minor
Albeniz Fête-Dieu à Seville
Saint-Saens Danse macabre
Debussy La cathédrale engloutie
Dukas L'apprenti sorcier

Philadelphia, 10 February 1926
Philadelphia Orchestra
Bach Toccata and Fugue in D minor
Debussy La cathédrale engloutie
J.Strauss G'schichten aus dem
   Wienerwald
The Star-spangled Banner
Music played during the Philadelphia
Award ceremony

Philadelphia, 12-13 February 1926
Philadelphia Orchestra
Samuel
Beethoven Leonore No 3 Overture
Beethoven Piano Concerto No 5
Bach Piano Concerto in D minor
Bach Toccata and Fugue in D minor

Philadelphia, 19-20 February 1926
Philadelphia Orchestra
Enesco
Enesco Orchestral Suite No 2
Mozart Violin Concerto No 4
Chausson Poème
Dopper Ciaconna gotica

Pittsburgh, 22 February 1926
Philadelphia Orchestra
Donahue
Rachmaninov Piano Concerto No 2
Albeniz Fête-Dieu à Seville
Debussy La cathédrale engloutie
Stravinsky Firebird Suite
Bach Passacaglia & Fugue in C minor

Dayton, 23 February 1926
Philadelphia Orchestra
Donahue
Programme as for 22 February

Chicago, 24 February 1926
Philadelphia Orchestra
Donahue
Programme as for 22 February

Toledo, 25 February 1926
Philadelphia Orchestra
Donahue
Programme as for 22 February

Cleveland, 26 February 1926
Philadelphia Orchestra
Donahue
Programme as for 22 February

Detroit, 27 February 1926
Philadelphia Orchestra
Donahue
Programme as for 22 February

Philadelphia, 5-6 March 1926
Philadelphia Orchestra
Bizet L'Arlésienne Suite
Ravel Alborada del gracioso
Debussy La cathédrale engloutie
Beethoven Symphony No 6

Philadelphia, 12-13 March 1926
Philadelphia Orchestra
Tchaikovsky programme
Symphony No 6
Casse noisette Suite
1812 Overture

Philadelphia, 19-20 March 1926
Philadelphia Orchestra
Schubert Rosamunde excerpts
J.Strauss G'schichten aus dem
    Wienerwald
Sibelius Symphony No 5

Philadelphia, 26-27 March 1926
Philadelphia Orchestra
Sapperton, Rich, Kindler
Bach Toccata and Fugue in D minor
Beethoven Triple Concerto
Strauss Don Quixote
Sibelius Finlandia

Philadelphia, 3-5 April 1926
Philadelphia Orchestra
Bauer
Bach Wachet auf
Brahms Piano Concerto No 1
Sibelius Symphony No 7
Rimsky-Korsakov Russian Easter Overture

Philadelphia, 9-10 April 1926
Philadelphia Orchestra
Lifschey
Varèse Amériques
Hue Thème varié
Sibelius Swan of Tuonela
Mozart Symphony No 41
Bach Passacaglia & Fugue in C minor

Philadelphia, 16-17 April 1926
Philadelphia Orchestra
Werrenrath
Lekeu Fantaisie contrapuntique
Wagner Ride of the Valkyries
Haydn Symphony No 45
Vocal items by Brahms and Wagner

Philadelphia, 21-22 April 1926
Philadelphia Orchestra
Childrens' concert
Rossini Guilleaume Tell Overture
Wagner Forest murmurs (Siegfried)
M.Haydn Toy Symphony
Programme also included audience
singing

Philadelphia, 23-24 April 1926
Philadelphia Orchestra
Wagner Holländer Overture
Sibelius Symphony No 6
Tchaikovsky Romeo and Juliet
Rimsky-Korsakov May Night Overture
Borodin Polovtsian Dances

Philadelphia, 28 April 1926
Philadelphia Orchestra
Zimbalist
Tchaikovsky 1812 Overture
Mendelssohn Violin Concerto
Mendelssohn Octet
Bach Toccata and Fugue in D minor
Concert given in Wanamaker's
department store

197

Philadelphia, 30 April-1 May 1926
Philadelphia Orchestra
Wagner Meistersinger Overture
Franck Symphony in D minor
Bach Passacaglia & Fugue in C minor
Tchaikovsky 1812 Overture

**1925-1926 season also included ten
Philadelphia Orchestra concerts in
New York, which were direct repeats
or permutations of programmes also
performed in Philadelphia**

Philadelphia, 8-9 October 1926
Philadelphia Orchestra
Mozart Symphony No 33
Beethoven Symphony No 7
Schroeder Pan
Dukas L'apprenti sorcier

Philadelphia, 13-14 October 1926
Philadelphia Orchestra
Gusikoff
Childrens' concert
Dukas L'apprenti sorcier
Mendelssohn Andante (Violin Concerto)
J.Strauss G'schichten aus dem
    Wienerwald
Programme also included audience
singing
Philadelphia, 15-16 October 1926
Philadelphia Orchestra
Bach Wachet auf
Brahms Symphony No 2
Vaughan Williams Tallis Fantasia
Pingoud The Prophet

Philadelphia, 22-23 October 1926
Philadelphia Orchestra
Traubel
Berlioz Symphonie fantastique
Franck Prelude, chorale et fugue
Vocal items by Duparc and Ravel

Philadelphia, 29-30 October 1926
Philadelphia Orchestra
Marachel
Handel Overture in D
C.P.E.Bach Cello Concerto No 3
Mozart Symphony No 40
Caplet Cello Rhapsody
Ravel Rapsodie espagnole

Philadelphia, 5-6 November 1926
Philadelphia Orchestra
Zimbalist
Mendelssohn Symphony No 3
Brahms Violin Concerto
Wagner Tristan Prelude & Liebestod

Philadelphia, 12-13 November 1926
Philadelphia Orchestra
Bach programme
Brandenburg Concerti Nos 1, 2 & 3/
Aus der Tiefe/Toccata & Fugue in D minor

Philadelphia, 19-20 November 1926
Philadelphia Orchestra
Crooks, Gusikoff
Berners Fantaisie espagnole
Saint-Saens Violin Concerto No 3
Szymanowski Symphony No 3

Philadelphia, 26-27 November 1926
Philadelphia Orchestra
Miaskowsky Symphony No 6
Prokofiev Scythian Suite

Philadelphia, 3-4 December 1926
Philadelphia Orchestra
Weber Freischütz Overture
Mendelssohn Midsummer Night's Dream
    excerpts
Wagner Forest murmurs (Siegfried)
Wagner Funeral March(Götterdämmerung)
Strauss Tod und Verklärung

Philadelphia, 8-9 December 1926
Philadelphia Orchestra
Lifschey
Childrens' concert
Brahms Symphony No 1, 4th movement
Bach Komm süsser Tod
Borodin Viola Serenade
Mendelssohn Spring Song and
    Wedding March
Programme also included audience
singing

Philadelphia, 10-11 December 1926
Philadelphia Orchestra
Lifschey, Van den Burgh
Kaminsky Concerto grosso
Handel Viola Concerto in B minor
Lalo Cello Concerto
Chabrier Espana

Philadelphia, 17-18 December 1926
Philadelphia Orchestra
Breton
Smetana Bartered Bride Overture
Goldmark Violin Concerto
Beethoven Symphony No 5

Philadelphia, 23-24 December 1926
Philadelphia Orchestra
Haskil
Franck Symphony in D minor
Schumann Piano Concerto
Handel Pastoral Symphony (Messiah)
Bach Ich ruf' zu dir

Philadelphia, 30-31 December 1926
Philadelphia Orchestra
Bach programme
Brandenburg Concerti Nos 4, 5 & 6/
Fantasia and Fugue in G minor

Philadelphia, 7-8 January 1927
Philadelphia Orchestra
Landowska
Haydn Symphony No 88
Mozart Piano Concerto No 20
Falla Harpsichord Concerto
Albeniz Fête-Dieu à Seville

Philadelphia, 14-15 January 1927
Philadelphia Orchestra
Glinka Ruslan and Ludmila Overture
Glazunov Symphony No 4
Ravel Daphnis et Chloé Suite
Stravinsky Petrushka Suite

Philadelphia, 11-12 February 1927
Philadelphia Orchestra
Kreisler
Beethoven programme
Symphony No 2/3 Equali/Violin Concerto

Philadelphia, 18-19 February 1927
Philadelphia Orchestra
Handel Overture in D minor
Handel Water Music Suite
Debussy Nuages et fêtes (Nocturnes)
Bach Toccata and Fugue in D minor

Indianapolis, 21 February 1927
Philadelphia Orchestra
Handel Overture in D minor
Handel Water Music Suite
Bach Ich ruf' zu dir
Bach Toccata and Fugue in D minor
Debussy Nuages et fetes (Nocturnes)
Ravel Rapsodie espagnole

St Louis, 22 February 1927
Philadelphia Orchestra
Programme as for 21 February

Chicago, 23 February 1927
Philadelphia Orchestra
Programme as for 21 February

Milwaukee, 24 February 1927
Philadelphia Orchestra
Programme as for 21 February

Cleveland, 25 February 1927
Philadelphia Orchestra
Programme as for 21 February

Detroit, 26 February 1927
Philadelphia Orchestra
Programme as for 21 February

Philadelphia, 4-5 March 1927
Philadelphia Orchestra
Webern Passacaglia
Caprillo Concertino
Debussy Prélude à l'après-midi
Wagner Tannhäuser Overture & Venusberg

Philadelphia, 11-12 March 1927
Philadelphia Orchestra
Atterberg Symphony No 4
Alfven Midsommarvaka
Stenhammar Midwinter
Peterson-Berger Symphony No 3

Philadelphia, 18-19 March 1927
Philadelphia Orchestra
Rachmaninov
Toronto Mendelssohn Choir
Rachmaninov Piano Concerto No 4
Rachmaninov 3 Russian Songs
Tchaikovsky Romeo and Juliet

Philadelphia, 25-26 March 1927
Philadelphia Orchestra
Beethoven programme
Egmont/Symphony No 8/Symphony No 3

Baltimore, 30 March 1927
Philadelphia Orchestra
Rachmaninov
Toronto Mendelssohn Choir
Programme as for 18-19 March

Philadelphia, 1-2 April 1927
Philadelphia Orchestra
Gieseking
Malipiero Sui fiume del tempo
Falla Noches en los jardines de Espana
Hindemith Kammermusik No 2
Koutzen Solitude
     (conducted by the composer)

Philadelphia, 8-9 April 1927
Philadelphia Orchestra
Loeffler Memories of Childhood
Varèse Arcanes
Ravel Rapsodie espagnole
Handel Water Music Suite
Bach Preludes in E flat minor & B minor
Bach Passacaglia and Fugue in C minor

Philadelphia, 16-18 April 1927
Philadelphia Orchestra
Wagner Parsifal Prelude and synthesis
Mengelberg Scherzo sinfonico
Illashenko Suite of Ancient Dances
Rimsky-Korsakov Russian Easter Overture

Philadelphia, 22-23 April 1927
Philadelphia Orchestra
Rosenthal, Parme
Mendelssohn Hebrides Overture
J.P.Beach New Orleans Street Cries
Debussy Saxophone Rhapsody
Chopin Piano Concerto No 2
Eichheim Burma

Philadelphia, 29-30 April 1927
Philadelphia Orchestra
Beethoven Leonore No 3 Overture
Beethoven Symphony No 5
Wagner Meistersinger Overture
Bach Toccata and Fugue in D minor

**1926-1927 season also included ten
Philadelphia Orchestra concerts in
New York, which were direct repeats
or permutations of programmes also
performed in Philadelphia**

1927-1928 season
Stokowski did not conduct during this
season. Apart from recording sessions
in October 1927, it appears that he
probably took a complete sabbatical
from conducting.

Philadelphia, 4 October 1928
Philadelphia Orchestra
Bach Wir glauben all an einen Gott
Beethoven Symphony No 5
Sibelius Finlandia
Wagner Entry of the Gods (Rheingold)

Philadelphia, 5-6 October 1928
Philadelphia Orchestra
Bach Wir glauben all an einen Gott
Beethoven Symphony No 5
Roussel Concerto pour petit orchestre
Sibelius Finlandia

Philadelphia, 12-13 October 1928
Philadelphia Orchestra
Mozart Nozze di Figaro Overture
Brahms Symphony No 3
Knipper Märchen eines Gyps-Gottes
Bliss Introduction and Allegro
Wagner Tannhäuser Overture & Venusberg

Philadelphia, 19-20 October 1928
Philadelphia Orchestra
Mischakoff
Bliss Introduction & Allegro
Schelling Violin Concerto
Tchaikovsky Symphony No 5

Philadelphia, 26-27 October 1928
Philadelphia Orchestra
Koshetz
Prokofiev March (Love of 3 Oranges)
Tchaikovsky Romeo and Juliet
Falla La vida breve excerpts
Albeniz Fête-Dieu à Seville
Nin Andalusian Dances
Vocal items by Gretchaninov and
     Mussorgsky & Spanish songs

Philadelphia, 2-3 November 1928
Philadelphia Orchestra
Gluck Alceste Overture
Bach Brandenburg Concerto No 2
Handel Overture in D minor
Shostakovich Symphony No 1

Philadelphia, 9-10 November 1928
Philadelphia Orchestra
Wagner programme
Meistersinger Overture & Act3 Prelude/
Tristan Prelude & Liebestod/Siegfried
Forest murmurs/Götterdämmerung Rhine
Journey, Funeral March & Immolation

Philadelphia, 16-17 November 1928
Philadelphia Orchestra
Caffaret
Wagner Lohengrin Prelude
Schubert Symphony No 8
Roussel Piano Concerto
Strauss Tod und Verklärung

Philadelphia, 23-24 November 1928
Philadelphia Orchestra
Bach Suite No 2
Bach Prelude in E flat minor
Bach Toccata and Fugue in D minor
Villa-Lobos African Dances
Casinière Hercule et les centaures

Bryn Mawr College, 4 December 1928
Philadelphia Orchestra
Alwyne
Wagner Lohengrin Prelude
Liszt Piano Concerto No 1
Wagner Tristan Prelude & Liebestod
Bach Christmas Oratorio excerpts
Bach Toccata and Fugue in D minor

Philadelphia, 30 March-1 April 1929
Philadelphia Orchestra
Harmati Prelude to a drama
Riegger Study in Sonority
Jacobi Indian Dances
Mozart Symphony No 40
Beethoven Leonore No 3 Overture

Philadelphia, 5-6 April 1929
Philadelphia Orchestra
Borodin Polovtsian Dances
Mussorgsky Khovanschina Entr'acte
Stravinsky Firebird Suite
Tchaikovsky Symphony No 6

Philadelphia, 12-13 April 1929
Philadelphia Orchestra
Van Barentzen, Kaufman
Tansman Ouverture symphonique
Eichheim Japanese Nocturne
Villa-Lobos Choros No 8
Bach Ich ruf' zu dir
Bach Fantasia and Fugue in G minor
Bach Passacaglia & Fugue in C minor

Philadelphia, 19-20 April 1929
Philadelphia Orchestra
Bizet L'Arlésienne Suite
Febvre-Longeray Stele pour le
    percheur de lune
Debussy La cathédrale engloutie
Franck Symphony in D minor

Philadelphia, 26-27 April 1929
Philadelphia Orchestra
Wagner Meistersinger Overture
Beethoven Symphony No 5
Rimsky-Korsakov Scheherazade

**1928-1929 season also included five
Philadelphia Orchestra concerts in
New York, which were direct repeats
or slight variations of programmes
also performed in Philadelphia**

Philadelphia, 4-5 October 1929
Philadelphia Orchestra
Brahms Symphony No 1
Wagner Ride of the Valyries(Walküre)
Wagner Rhine Journey(Götterdämmerung)
Wagner Entry of the Gods (Rheingold)

Philadelphia, 6 October 1929
Philadelphia Orchestra
Sunday afternoon radio broadcast
Bach Wir glauben all an einen Gott
Mozart Symphony No 40
Wagner Tannhäuser Overture & Venusberg

Philadelphia, 11-12 October 1929
Philadelphia Orchestra
Iturbi
Mozart Nozze di Figaro Overture
Beethoven Piano Concerto No 4
Prokofiev Symphony No 2
Bach Wir glauben all an einen Gott

Philadelphia, 18-19 October 1929
Philadelphia Orchestra
Schubert Symphony No 9
Schoenberg Orchestral Variations
Wagner Meistersinger Overture
This concert repeated in New York

Philadelphia, 25-26 October 1929
Philadelphia Orchestra
Yalkovsky
Krehn Ode to the memory of Lenin
Rachmaninov Piano Concerto No 2
Rimsky-Korsakov Flight of bumble bee
Rimsky-Korsakov Dance (Snow Maiden)
Tchaikovsky 1812 Overture

Philadelphia, 1-2 November 1929
Philadelphia Orchestra
Gramatte
Berlioz Carnaval romain Overture
Debussy Nuages et fêtes (Nocturnes)
Gramatte Elegy, Danse moracaine and
    Konzertstück
Wagner Wotan's Farewell (Walküre)

Philadelphia, 3 November 1929
Philadelphia Orchestra
Sunday afternoon radio broadcast
Borodin Polovtsian Dances
Stravinsky Le sacre du printemps
Rimsky-Korsakov Russian Easter Overture

Philadelphia, 8-9 November 1929
Philadelphia Orchestra
Piatigorsky
Eichheim Java (cond.by the composer)
Dvorak Cello Concerto
Tchaikovsky Symphony No 4

Philadelphia, 13 November 1929
Philadelphia Orchestra
Pension Fund concert
J.Strauss An der schönen blauen Donau
Chabrier Espana
Debussy Fêtes (Nocturnes)
Debussy Danse sacrée et danse profane
Mozart Zauberflöte Overture
Gluck Air gai (Ballet Suite)
Mussorgsky Night on Bare Mountain
Other works not conducted by Stokowski

Philadelphia, 15-16 November 1929
Philadelphia Orchestra
Beethoven Symphony No 3
Taylor Jurgen
Elgar Enigma Variations
This concert repeated in New York

Philadelphia, 22-23 November 1929
Philadelphia Orchestra
Molie
Handel Overture in D minor
Gluck/Mottl Ballet Suite
Bach Piano Concerto in G minor
Debussy Fantaisie pour piano et orch.
Mussorgsky/Ravel Pictures from an
    exhibition

Philadelphia, 29-30 November 1929
Philadelphia Orchestra
Mendelssohn Club Chorus
Braslau, Crooks, Baklanov, Patton,
Gould
Mussorgsky Boris Godunov

Philadelphia, 6-7 December 1929
Philadelphia Orchestra
Milstein
Dvorak Symphony No 9
Glazunov Violin Concerto
Tchaikovsky Marche slave

Philadelphia, 8 December 1929
Philadelphia Orchestra
Sunday afternoon radio broadcast
Berlioz Hungarian March (Faust)
Franck Symphony in D minor
Debussy Fêtes (Nocturnes)

Philadelphia, 13-14 December 1929
Philadelphia Orchestra
Brahms Symphony No 2
Bach Brandenburg Concerto No 6
Bach Prelude in B minor
Bach Toccata and Fugue in D minor
This concert repeated in New York

Philadelphia, 20-21 December 1929
Philadelphia Orchestra
Wagner programme
Lohengrin Prelude/Meistersinger Act 3
Prelude/Tristan Prelude & Liebestod/
Parsifal Prelude/Tannhäuser Overture
& Venusberg Music/Rienzi Overture
Ravel Bolero played after this concert

Philadelphia, 10 January 1930
Philadelphia Orchestra
Chopin Funeral March
Played in memory of Edward Bok
(No other works conducted by
Stokowski in this concert)

Philadelphia, 28-29 March 1930
Philadelphia Orchestra
Barth
Weber Freischütz Overture
Beethoven Symphony No 8
Barth Concerto
Sibelius Valse triste
Sibelius Swan of Tuonela
Sibelius Finlandia

Philadelphia, 4-5 April 1930
Philadelphia Orchestra
Chopin Funeral March
Played in memory of James C. Brown
Glinka Kamarinskaya
Rimsky-Korsakov Russian Easter Overture
Mussorgsky Khovanschina Entr'acte
Tchaikovsky Romeo and Juliet
Prokofiev Overture in B flat
Krehn Ode to the memory of Lenin
Miaskowsky Symphony No 10
This concert repeated in New York

Philadelphia, 11-14 April 1930
Philadelphia Orchestra and Chorus
Humphrey, Ivantzoff, Howland,
Weidman, M.Graham Ballet company
Schoenberg Die glückliche Hand
Stravinsky Le sacre du printemps
First US stage performance of
Stravinsky's ballet; programme
performed in the Metropolitan Opera
House, Philadelphia

Philadelphia, 19-21 April 1930
Philadelphia Orchestra
Mendelssohn Club Chorus
Gridley, Monasevitch, Zenker,
Simkin, Weinberg
Bach Wachet auf
Bach Concerto in D minor 2 violins
Bach Passacaglia & Fugue in C minor
Roussel Psalm 80
Wagner Parsifal Good Friday Music

New York, 23 April 1930
Philadelphia Orchestra
Programme and soloists as for 11-14
April in Philadelphia
This performance given in the
Metropolitan Opera House

Philadelphia, 25-26 April 1930
Philadelphia Orchestra
Franck Symphony in D minor
Wagner Meistersinger Act 3 Prelude
Coppola Burlesque
Ravel Bolero

Philadelphia, 3-4 October 1930
Philadelphia Orchestra
Bauer
Tchaikovsky Symphony No 5
Scriabin Prometheus
Stravinsky Firebird Suite

Philadelphia, 10-11 October 1930
Philadelphia Orchestra
Bampton, Copeland
Falla El amor brujo
Falla Noches en los jardines Espana
Debussy Danse sacrée et danse profane
Ravel Bolero

Philadelphia, 12 October 1930
Philadelphia Orchestra
Sunday afternoon radio broadcast
Albeniz Fête-Dieu à Seville
Falla El amor brujo
Debussy La cathédrale engloutie
Ravel Bolero

Philadelphia, 17-18 October 1930
Philadelphia Orchestra
Franck Symphony in D minor
Debussy Nuages et fêtes (Nocturnes)
Debussy La cathédrale engloutie

Philadelphia, 24-25 October 1930
Philadelphia Orchestra
Gabrilowitsch
Beethoven Egmont Overture
Mozart Piano Concerto No 20
Brahms Symphony No 4

Philadelphia, 31 Oct-1 November 1930
Philadelphia Orchestra
Stravinsky Le sacre du printemps
Rimsky-Korsakov Scheherazade

Philadelphia, 7-8 November 1930
Philadelphia Orchestra
Reiner, Wallenstein
Sibelius Symphony No 1
Ibert Concerto for cello and wind
Bloch Schelomo
Berg Wozzeck fragments
This performance of the Wozzeck
fragments preceded Stokowski's
performance of the complete score
(see November 1931)

Philadelphia, 14-15 November 1930
Philadelphia Orchestra
Wagner programme
Rheingold Entry of Gods & Alberich's
Curse/Walküre Wotan's Farewell/
Siegfried Forest murmurs/Götterdämm-
erung Rhine Journey, Funeral March
and Immolation

Philadelphia, 16 November 1930
Philadelphia Orchestra
Sunday afternoon radio broadcast
Programme as for 14-15 November

Philadelphia, 21-22 November 1930
Philadelphia Orchestra
Brahms Academic Festival Overture
Beethoven Symphony No 5
Debussy Ibéria
Zemachson Chorale and Fugue

New York, 27-28 November 1930
NYPSO
Brahms Symphony No 4
Bach Wir glauben all an einen Gott
Bach Ich ruf' zu dir
Bach Toccata and Fugue in D minor
Stokowski's first appearance with
the New York Philharmonic

New York, 30 November 1930
NYPSO
Guidi, Wallenstein
Brahms Academic Festival Overture
Brahms Double Concerto
Bach Wir glauben all an einen Gott
Bach Ich ruf' zu dir
Bach Toccata and Fugue in D minor

New York, 4-5 December 1930
NYPSO
Sibelius Symphony No 1
Stravinsky Le sacre du printemps

New York, 6-7 December 1930
NYPSO
Zimbalist
Sibelius Finlandia
Sibelius Violin Concerto
Stravinsky Le sacre du printemps

During the period of Stokowski
guest-conducting the New York
Philharmonic, Toscanini conducted
several concerts with the
Philadelphia Orchestra

Philadelphia, 19-20 December 1930
Philadelphia Orchestra
Martenot
Bach Fugue in G minor
Buxtehude Sarabande and Courante
Mozart Larghetto
Beethoven Leonore No 3 Overture
Levidis Poem for electrical instrument
Strauss Tod und Verklärung

Philadelphia, 25 December 1930
Philadelphia Orchestra
Christmas Day radio broadcast
Handel Pastoral Symphony (Messiah)
Handel Overture in D minor
Bach Sinfonia (Christmas Oratorio)
Bach Chaconne in D minor
Bach Prelude in E flat minor
Bach Toccata and Fugue in D minor

Philadelphia, 26-27 December 1930
Philadelphia Orchestra
Bach programme
Brandenburg Concerti Nos 2 and 5/
Chaconne/Prelude in E flat minor/
Toccata and Fugue in D minor

Mexico City, 2 January 1931
Programme included
Carrillo Sonido 13

Philadelphia, 23 February 1931
Philadelphia Orchestra
Tchaikovsky Marche slave
Wagner Entry of the Gods (Rheingold)
Wagner Tristan Prelude & Liebestod
Music played during the Philadelphia
Award ceremony

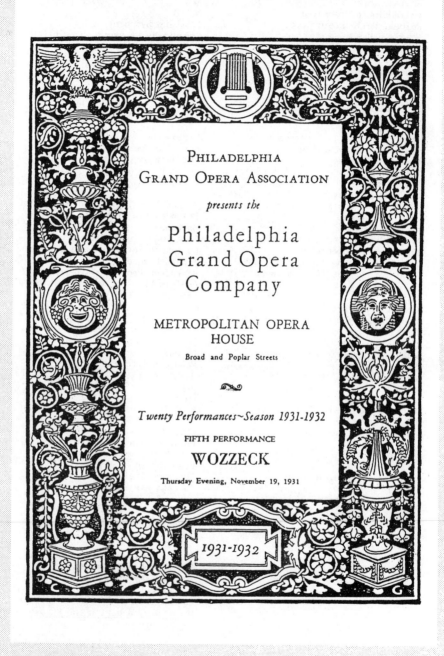

Philadelphia
Grand Opera Association

presents the

Philadelphia
Grand Opera
Company

METROPOLITAN OPERA
HOUSE

Broad and Poplar Streets

Twenty Performances~Season 1931-1932

FIFTH PERFORMANCE

WOZZECK

Thursday Evening, November 19, 1931

1931-1932

PHILADELPHIA GRAND OPERA COMPANY

WILLIAM C. HAMMER, General Manager

WOZZECK

From the Drama by GEORG BÜCHNER

(In German)

The Music by ALBAN BERG

MARIE ....ANNE ROSELLE
WOZZECK ....IVAN IVANTZOFF
THE CAPTAIN ....BRUNO KORELL
THE DOCTOR ....IVAN STESCHENKO
ANDRES ....SERGEI RADAMSKY
THE DRUM-MAJOR ....NELSON EDDY
FIRST ARTISAN ....ABRASHA ROBOFSKY
SECOND ARTISAN ....BENJAMIN DE LOACHE
THE IDIOT ....ALBERT MAHLER
A SOLDIER ....GEORGE GERHARDI
MARGRET ....EDWINA EUSTIS
MARIE'S CHILD ....DORIS WILSON

Soldiers—Artisans—Youths—Girls—Children

CONDUCTOR ....LEOPOLD STOKOWSKI
STAGE DIRECTOR ....WILHELM von WYMETAL, Jr.
ASSISTANT CONDUCTOR ....SYLVAN LEVIN
CHORUS MASTER ....ANDREAS FUGMANN

The orchestra comprises the entire personnel of one hundred and sixteen members of the
Philadelphia Orchestra: the stage band of twenty-five is composed
of musicians selected from The Curtis Symphony Orchestra

Scenery and Costumes Designed by

ROBERT EDMOND JONES

Scenery by A. Jarin Scenic Studios
Costumes by Van Horn & Son

SYNOPSIS OF SCENES

ACT I

Scene 1—The Captain's Room
Scene 2—Open Country
Scene 3—Marie's Room.
Scene 4—The Doctor's Study
Scene 5—A Street in Front of Marie's House

ACT II

Scene 1—Marie's Room
Scene 2—A Street in the City
Scene 3—A Street in Front of Marie's House
Scene 4—An Inn Garden
Scene 5—The Guard-room of the Barracks

ACT III

Scene 1—Marie's Room
Scene 2—A Wood-path Near a Pond
Scene 3—A Tavern
Scene 4—A Wood-path Near a Pond
Scene 5—A Street in Front of Marie's House.

SPECIAL NOTICE

As there will be no pauses in the music by the orchestra during changes of scene, it
is earnestly requested that there be no applause during the orchestral interludes.
There will be short intermissions between the acts.

In order to preserve intact the visual and aural impression of Wozzeck as an art-
work, there will be no curtain calls after the performance.

Philadelphia, March 1931
Philadelphia Orchestra
Zecchi
Brahms Piano Concerto No 1
Wagner Holländer Overture
Wagner Lohengrin Prelude
Wagner Tannhäuser Overture & Venusberg

New York, March 1931
Philadelphia Orchestra
Brahms Symphony No 4
Wagner Holländer Overture
Wagner Lohengrin Prelude
Wagner Tannhäuser Overture & Venusberg

Philadelphia, April 1930
Philadelphia Orchestra
Mendelssohn Club Chorus
Althouse, Davies, Simmons
Deyo Diadem of Stars Overture
Weill Lindbergh's Flight
Wagner Parsifal Good Friday Music
Rimsky-Korsakov Russian Easter Overture

Philadelphia, 5 April 1931
Philadelphia Orchestra
Mendelssohn Club Chorus
Althouse, Davies, Simmons
Sunday afternoon radio broadcast
Weill Lindbergh's Flight
Wagner Parsifal Good Friday Music
Rimsky-Korsakov Russian Easter Overture

Philadelphia, 10-11 April 1931
Philadelphia Orchestra
Chorus and soloists
Stravinsky Oedipus Rex
Prokofiev Le pas d'acier

Philadelphia, 15 April 1931
Philadelphia Orchestra
Benefit concert for unemployed
musicians
Bach Fugue in G minor
Bach Christ lag in Todesbanden
Bach Passacaglia & Fugue in C minor
Copland Dance Symphony
Wagner Entry of the Gods (Rheingold)
Wagner Tristan Prelude & Liebestod

Philadelphia, 16-17 April 1931
Philadelphia Orchestra
Hofmann
Berlioz Carnaval romain Overture
Chopin Piano Concerto No 1
Hofmann Chromaticon
Lourie Sinfonia dialectica

New York, 21 April 1931
Philadelphia Orchestra
Chorus and soloists
Stravinsky Oedipus Rex
Prokofiev Le pas d'acier
Concert given in Metropolitan Opera
House, where the Prokofiev work was
receiving its first USA stage
performance

Philadelphia, 23-24 April 1931
Philadelphia Orchestra
Brahms Symphony No 1
Wagner Meistersinger Overture
Bach Passacaglia & Fugue in C minor

**Apart from the March 1931 programme,
four other Philadelphia Orchestra
concerts of the 1930-1931 season
were repeated in New York**

Philadelphia, 9-10 October 1931
Philadelphia Orchestra
Monteverdi Orfeo excerpts
Lully Suite
Purcell Trumpet Voluntary
Vivaldi Concerto grosso in G minor
Rameau Castor et Pollux Overture
Bach Fugue in G minor
Bach Prelude in E flat minor
Bach Wir glauben all an einen Gott
Bach Nun komm der Heiden Heiland
Bach Toccata and Fugue in D minor
Handel Water Music Suite

Philadelphia, 16-17 October 1931
Philadelphia Orchestra
Weber Euryanthe Overture
Schubert Symphony No 8
Wagner Siegfried Idyll
Strauss Tod und Verklärung

Philadelphia, 23 October 1931
Philadelphia Orchestra
Stravinsky 4 Etudes
Sanjuan Castilla
Colestan Rumanian Rhapsody
Ferroud Symphony

Philadelphia, 24 October 1931
Philadelphia Orchestra
Tansman Toccata
Mossolov Iron Foundry
Vogel 2 Etudes
Bennett Abraham Lincoln Symphony
Webern Symphony

Philadelphia, 19 November 1931
Philadelphia Orchestra
Roselle, Eustis, Korell, Steschenko,
Ivantzoff, Eddy
Berg Wozzeck
Staged in the Metropolitan Opera
House, Philadelphia

Philadelphia, 21-22 November 1931
Philadelphia Orchestra
Berlioz Carnaval romain Overture
Schumann Symphony No 2
Schubert Rosamunde excerpts
Mendelssohn Scherzo (MND)
Weber Aufforderung zum Tanz

New York, 24 November 1931
Philadelphia Orchestra
Work and soloists as for 19 November

Philadelphia, 4-5 December 1931
Philadelphia Orchestra
Gluck Alceste Overture
Haydn Symphony No 88
Beethoven Symphony No 5

Philadelphia, 18-19 December 1931
Philadelphia Orchestra
Brahms Symphony No 1
Franck Symphony in D minor
Wagner Tristan Prelude & Liebestod

Philadelphia, 26-28 December 1931
Philadelphia Orchestra
Brahms Symphony No 3
Wagner Götterdämmerung Rhine Journey,
    Funeral March and Immolation

Philadelphia, 1-2 January 1932
Philadelphia Orchestra
Cartula 2 Cuban Dances
Zimbalist Daphnis and Chloe
Milhaud Percussion Concerto
Sibelius Swanh of Tuonela
Sibelius Finlandia
Mussorgsky/Ravel Pictures from an
    exhibition

Philadelphia, 8 January 1932
Philadelphia Orchestra
Dushkin
Fitelberg Polish Rhapsody
Stravinsky Violin Concerto
Lopatnikoff Symphony No 1
Tchaikovsky Francesca da Rimini

Philadelphia, 9 January 1932
Philadelphia Orchestra
Dushkin
Prokofiev Symphony No 3
Stravinsky Violin Concerto
Tchaikovsky Francesca da Rimini

Philadelphia, 15-16 January 1932
Philadelphia Orchestra
Alsen, Bampton, Carhart, Davies,
Diamond, Eustis, Gordon, Petina,
Robofsky, Althouse, Loache,
Horle, Mahler
Wagner programme
Tristan Liebesnacht/Rheingold Entry
of the Gods/Walküre Ride of the
Valkyries/Siegfried greets Brünnhilde/
Götterdämmerung Siegfried and the
Rhinemaidens & Immolation Scene

Philadelphia, 11-12 March 1932
Philadelphia Orchestra
Curtis Institute Choir
Levin
Illiashenko Dyptique mongol
Wassilenko Nocturnes
Scriabin Prometheus
Stravinsky Symphony of Psalms
Mussorgsky/Ravel Pictures from an
    exhibition

Philadelphia, 18-19 March 1932
Philadelphia Orchestra
Beethoven Symphony No 5
Rimsky-Korsakov Scheherazade

Philadelphia, 31 March 1932
Philadelphia Orchestra
Chavez Horsepower
Staged performance

Philadelphia, 1-2 April 1932
Philadelphia Orchestra
Piston Suite
Grunberg Moods
Cowell Synchrony
Powell 3 Virginia Country Dances
Copland Music for the theatre
Dubensky Fugue
Bennett Abraham Lincoln Symphony
Griffes Pleasure Dome of Kubla Khan

Philadelphia, 8-9 April 1932
Philadelphia Orchestra and Choruses
Bampton, Althouse, Vreeland,
Betts, De Loache, Robofsky
Schoenberg Gurrelieder

Philadelphia, 15-16 April 1932
Philadelphia Orchestra
Wagner Tristan Prelude, Liebesnacht
and Liebestod
Tchaikovsky Symphony No 6

New York, 20 April 1932
Philadelphia Orchestra
Work and soloists as for 8-9 April

Philadelphia, 22-23 April 1932
Philadelphia Orchestra
Levin
Sibelius Symphony No 4
Ravel Piano Concerto in G
Bach Chaconne
Bach Passacaglia & Fugue in C minor

Philadelphia, 29-30 April 1932
Philadelphia Orchestra
Wagner programme
Rheingold Entry of the Gods &
Alberich's Curse/Walküre Wotan's
Farewell & Ride of the Valkyries/
Siegfried Forest murmurs and Siegfried
greets Brünnhilde/Götterdämmerung
Rhine Journey, Funeral March and
Immolation

Four of the 1931-1932 concerts were
repeated in New York; eight radio
broadcast concerts also took place
during the season

Philadelphia, 7-8 October 1932
Philadelphia Orchestra
Bach Fugue in C minor
Debussy Prélude à l'après-midi
Josten The Jungle
Beethoven Symphony No 7

Philadelphia, 14-15 October 1932
Philadelphia Orchestra
Brahms Symphony No 1
Wagner Tristan Prelude, Liebesnacht
and Liebestod

Philadelphia, 28-29 October 1932
Philadelphia Orchestra
Shumsky
Wagner Lohengrin Prelude
Brooks 3 Units
Brahms Violin Concerto
Tchaikovsky Symphony No 5

Philadelphia, 4-5 November 1932
Philadelphia Orchestra
Levin
Ravel Piano Concerto in G
Sibelius Symphony No 4
Stravinsky Firebird Suite
Debussy La cathédrale engloutie
Ravel Daphnis et Chloé, 2nd suite

Philadelphia, 18-19 November 1932
Philadelphia Orchestra
Hofmann
Liadov 8 Russian Folksongs
Rubinstein Piano Concerto No 4
Rimsky-Korsakov Scheherazade

Philadelphia, 25-26 November 1932
Philadelphia Orchestra
Luboshutz, Salmond
Handel Overture in D minor
Brahms Double Concerto
Enesco Prélude à l'unisson
Gluck Ballet Suite
Beethoven Leonore No 3 Overture

Philadelphia, 9-10 December 1932
Philadelphia Orchestra
De Loache
MacDowell In Wartime
MacDowell Dirge
Halffter 2 Esquisses symphoniques
Dubensky The Raven
Debussy Nuages et fêtes (Nocturnes)
Sibelius Storm & Berceuse (Tempest)
Sibelius Finlandia

Philadelphia, 16-17 December 1932
Philadelphia Orchestra
Norton
Wagner Siegfried Symphonic synthesis
Hindemith Piano Concerto
Strauss Tod und Verklärung

Philadelphia, 30-31 December 1932
Philadelphia Orchestra
Vivaldi Concerto grosso in D minor
Schubert Symphony No 8
Dubensky Fugue
Shostakovich Symphony No 3

Philadelphia, 6-7 January 1933
Philadelphia Orchestra
Franck Symphony in D minor
Brahms Symphony No 1

Philadelphia, 23 February 1933
Philadelphia Orchestra
Benefit concert for unemployed
musicians
Bach Toccata and Fugue in D minor
Wagner Meistersinger Overture
Other works with other conductors

Philadelphia, 3-4 March 1933
Philadelphia Orchestra
Chasins
Wagner Rheingold Symphonic synthesis
Chasins Piano Concerto No 2
Schumann Symphony No 4

Philadelphia, 9 March 1933
Philadelphia Orchestra
Temple University Chorus
Youth concert
Bach Fugue in G minor
Beethoven Leonore No 3 Overture
Bach Wachet auf
Wagner Lohengrin Prelude
Debussy Fêtes (Nocturnes)
Stravinsky Firebird excerpts
Programme also included audience
singing

Philadelphia, 10-11 March 1933
Philadelphia Orchestra
Brahms Symphony No 4
Bach Chaconne
Bach Christ lag in Todesbanden
Bach Komm süsser Tod
Bach Toccata and Fugue in D minor

Philadelphia, 17-18 March 1933
Philadelphia Orchestra
Davies
Mussorgsky Khovanschina Prelude
La Monaca Festival of Gauri
Rachmaninov Isle of the Dead
Wagner Götterdämmerung Rhine
    Journey, Funeral March and
    Immolation

Philadelphia, 31 March 1933
Philadelphia Orchestra and Chorus
Bampton, Davies, Eustis, Eddy, Steel,
Marwick, Tcherkassky, Treash, Healy,
De Loache, Lowenthal
Wagner Parsifal Act 1

Philadelphia, 1 April 1933
Philadelphia Orchestra
Soloists as for 31 March
Wagner Parsifal Act 2

Philadelphia, 3 April 1933
Philadelphia Orchestra
Soloists as for 31 March
Wagner Parsifal Act 3

Philadelphia, 7-8 April 1933
Philadelphia Orchestra
Zimbalist
Rimsky-Korsakov Russian Easter Overture
Sibelius Violin Concerto
Stravinsky Le sacre du printemps

Philadelphia, 20 April 1933
Philadelphia Orchestra
Wittington Chorus
Baird Palmer
Youth concert
Wagner Meistersinger Overture and
    Opening and final choruses
Rimsky-Korsakov Russian Easter Overture
Mozart Queen of Night aria
    (Zauberflöte)
Brooks 3 Units
Eichheim Bali
Ravel Bolero
Tchaikovsky March (Symphony No 6)
Programme also included audience
singing

Philadelphia, 21-22 April 1933
Philadelphia Orchestra
Beethoven Symphony No 5
Tchaikovsky Symphony No 6

Philadelphia, 28-29 April 1933
Philadelphia Orchestra
Mendelssohn Club Chorus
Bampton
Brahms Haydn Variations
Brahms Alto Rhapsody
Brahms Song of Destiny
Wagner Walküre Symphonic synthesis

**Seventeen radio broadcast concerts
were also given during the 1932-1933
season**

London, 29 May 1933
RCM Jubilee Students' Orchestra
Wagner Meistersinger Overture
This was an unscheduled appearance

**Programmes for most of the final
Philadelphia seasons, from 1933-1934
onwards, were found by the Stokowski
Society's archivist to be missing
from the Orchestra's files; however,
programmes for a limited number of
the concerts could be traced from
other sources**

Philadelphia, 12 October 1933
Philadelphia Orchestra
Handel Overture in D minor
Bach Komm süsser Tod
Beethoven Symphony No 5
Griffes Poem for flute
La Monaca Saltarello
Wagner Pilgrims' Chorus (Tannhäuser)
Goldmark Sakantula Overture

Philadelphia, 28 December 1933
Philadelphia Orchestra
Handel Pastoral Symphony (Messiah)
Brahms Symphony No 2
Debussy Clarinet Rhapsody
Hahn Sarabande et thème varié
Wagner Tristan Liebesnacht

Philadelphia, 12-13 January 1934
Philadelphia Orchestra & Chorus
Mendelssohn Club Chorus
Marwick
Rimsky-Korsakov Scheherazade
Walton Belshazzar's Feast

Philadelphia, 15 January 1934
Philadelphia Orchestra & Chorus
Mendelssohn Club Chorus
Marwick, Horowitz
Brahms Piano Concerto No 2
Walton Belshazzar's Feast

Philadelphia, 31 March-2 April 1934
Philadelphia Orchestra
Horowitz
Beethoven Egmont Overture
Beethoven Piano Concerto No 5
Bach Brandenburg Concerto No 5
Bach Air (Suite No 3)
Bach Siciliano
Bach Fugue in C minor

Philadelphia, 26 April 1934
Philadelphia Orchestra
Vivaldi Concerto grosso in D minor
Beethoven 3 Equali
Schubert Symphony No 8
Debussy Saxophone Rhapsody
McDonald Workers' Festival
Wagner Tristan Liebesnacht

Philadelphia, 7 November 1934
Philadelphia Orchestra
Rachmaninov
Programme included
Rachmaninov Paganini Rhapsody

Philadelphia, 14 November 1934
Philadelphia Orchestra
Borodin Prince Igor Overture
Debussy Danse sacré et danse profane
Dawson Negro Folk Symphony
Ravel Bolero
Tchaikovsky 1812 Overture

Philadelphia, 12 December 1934
Philadelphia Orchestra
List
Grieg Peer Gynt Suite
Fredericksen Saga of Leif Ericson
Wyeth Christmas Fantasy
Tchaikovsky Casse noisette Suite
Shostakovich Piano Concerto No 1
Wagner Götterdämmerung Immolation

Philadelphia, 10 October 1935
Philadelphia Orchestra
Berlioz Carnaval romain Overture
Wagner Tristan Act 3 Prelude
Brahms Symphony No 4
Chopin Piano Concerto No 1
Stravinsky Firebird Suite

Philadelphia, 16 November 1935
Philadelphia Orchestra
Programme included
Ponce Chapultepec

Philadelphia, 29 November 1935
Philadelphia Orchestra
Programme included
Dubensky Tom Sawyer Overture

Philadelphia, 5 December 1935
Philadelphia Orchestra
McDonald Rhumba Symphony
Schreiner The Worried Drummer
Liszt Les Préludes

Philadelphia, 21 December 1935
Philadelphia Orchestra
McDonald Rhumba Symphony
Mozart Allegro (Concerto in E flat)
Rimsky-Korsakov Flight of Bumble Bee
Saint-Saens Carnaval des animaux

Philadelphia, 2 January 1936
Philadelphia Orchestra
Programme included
Gould Chorale and Fugue in Jazz

Concerts in Europe in summer of 1936

Los Angeles, 17 August 1936
Hollywood Bowl SO
Swarthout
Bach Ein' feste Burg
Bach Air (Suite No 3)
Bach Little Fugue
Bizet 3 arias from Carmen
Debussy Prélude à l'après-midi
Wagner Götterdämmerung Immolation

Philadelphia, 6 November 1936
Philadelphia Orchestra
Programme included
Rachmaninov Symphony No 3

Philadelphia, 18 November 1936
Philadelphia Orchestra
Wagner Rheingold excerpts
Mussorgsky Boris Godunov synthesis
Cowell Reel
Liszt Hungarian Rhapsody No 2

Philadelphia, 20 November 1936
Philadelphia Orchestra
Programme included
Khrennikov Symphony No 1

Philadelphia, 23 November 1936
Philadelphia Orchestra
Programme included
Barlow Babar

Philadelphia, 9 April 1937
Philadelphia Orchestra
Programme included
Nordoff Fugue

Philadelphia, 10 December 1937
Philadelphia Orchestra
Programme included
Still Symphony in G minor

Copenhagen, 8 April 1939
Royal Danish Orchestra
Bach Toccata and Fugue in D minor
Mussorgsky Night on Bare Mountain
Debussy Prélude à l'après-midi
Wagner Walküre Wotan's Farewell
Brahms Symphony No 1

Other concerts in Europe in summer of 1939

Los Angeles, 6 September 1939
Hollywood Bowl SO
Bach Fugue in G minor
Wagner Tristan Liebestod
Tchaikovsky Finale (Symphony No 4)
Programme also included Tchaikovsky
Marche slave conducted by the 9-year
old Lorin Maazel

Los Angeles, 25-26 January 1940
Los Angeles PO
Rachmaninov
Beethoven Symphony No 5
Rachmaninov Piano Concerto No 2
Stravinsky Firebird Suite

Los Angeles, 8-9 February 1940
Los Angeles PO
Kreisler
Shostakovich Prelude in E flat minor
Tchaikovsky Symphony No 6
Brahms Violin Concerto
Wagner Tristan Prelude & Liebestod

Los Angeles, 22-23 February 1940
Los Angeles PO
Bach Passacaglia & Fugue in C minor
Mussorgsky Pictures at an exhibition
Beethoven Leonore No 3 Overture
Schubert Symphony No 8
MacDonald The Mission

Santa Barbara, 27 February 1940
Los Angeles PO
Programme as for 22-23 February

Philadelphia, 28 March 1940
Philadelphia Orchestra
Mozart Minuet (Symphony No 39)
McDonald Legend
Prokofiev Peter and the Wolf
Also works composed by children

April-May 1941
All American Youth Orchestra
Pre-tour concerts in Washington,
New York and Boston

Atlantic City, 11 May 1941
All American Youth Orchestra
Bach Toccata and Fugue in D minor
Beethoven Symphony No 5
Cowell Tales of our Countryside
Wagner Tristan Liebesnacht

Baltimore, 13 May 1941
All American Youth Orchestra

New Brunswick, 18 May 1941
All American Youth Orchestra

Rhode Island, 21 May 1941
All American Youth Orchestra

Albany, 22 May 1941
All American Youth Orchestra

Springfield Massachusetts,23 May 1941
All American Youth Orchestra

Buffalo, 24 May 1941
All American Youth Orchestra

Toronto, 26 May 1941
All American Youth Orchestra

Philadelphia, 29 November 1940
Philadelphia Orchestra
Programme included
Shostakovich Symphony No 6

Philadelphia, 6 December 1940
Philadelphia Orchestra
Krasner
Programme included
Schoenberg Violin Concerto

Pittsburgh, 27 May 1941
All American Youth Orchestra
Bach Toccata and Fugue in D minor
Beethoven Symphony No 5
Cowell Ancient Desert Drone
Weber Invitation to the Dance
Wagner Tristan Liebesnacht

Toledo, 28 May 1941
All American Youth Orchestra

Detroit, 29 May 1941
All American Youth Orchestra

Chicago, 2 June 1941
All American Youth Orchestra

Milwaukee, 4 June 1941
All American Youth Orchestra
Bach Little Fugue
Brahms Symphony No 1
Wagner Tristan Liebesnacht
Bender San Luis Rey
Encores by Bach, Schubert & J.Strauss

St Paul Minnesota, 5 June 1941
All American Youth Orchestra
Brahms Symphony No 3
Wagner Tristan Liebesnacht
Wagner Walküre Ride of the Valkyries
Cowell Ancient Desert Drone

Omaha, 6 June 1941
All American Youth Orchestra
Handel Overture in D minor
Beethoven Symphony No 7
Young Shadows and Sunshine
Wagner Tristan Liebesnacht
Encores by Bach, Schubert & J.Strauss

St Louis, 9 June 1941
All American Youth Orchestra
Brahms Symphony No 1
Wagner Tristan Liebesnacht
Bach Little Fugue
Bach Prelude (Partita in E)
Miller Appalachian Sketches

Indianapolis, 10 June 1941
All American Youth Orchestra
Bach Toccata and Fugue in D minor
Brahms Symphony No 3
Wagner Tristan Liebesnacht
Harris Interlude (Folk Song Symphony)
Encores by Bach, Tchaikovsky and
J.Strauss

Louisville, 11 June 1941
All American Youth Orchestra
Novacek Perpetuum mobile
Tchaikovsky Symphony No 4
Creston Symphony
Wagner Tristan Liebesnacht
The Star-spangled Banner

Nashville, 13 June 1941
All American Youth Orchestra
Debussy Fêtes (Nocturnes)
Franck Symphony in D minor
Gould Guaracho
Wagner Tristan Liebesnacht
The Star-spangled Banner
Bach Air (Suite No 3)
Weber Invitation to the Dance

Memphis, 14 June 1941
All American Youth Orchestra
Bach Passacaglia & Fugue in C minor
Schubert Symphony No 8
Gould Guaracho
Strauss Tod und Verklärung

Kansas City, 16 June 1941
All American Youth Orchestra
Bach Little Fugue
Brahms Symphony No 3
Creston Symphony
Wagner Tristan Liebesnacht

Wichita, 17 June 1941
All American Youth Orchestra
Handel Overture in D minor
Brahms Symphony No 1
Bender San Luis Rey
Wagner Tristan Liebesnacht
The Star-spangled Banner
Debussy Prélude à l'après-midi

Colorado Springs, 19 June 1941
All American Youth Orchestra
Bach Little Fugue
Brahms Symphony No 3
Harris Interlude
Sessions Largo (Violin Concerto)
Strauss Tod und Verklärung

Denver, 20 June 1941
All American Youth Orchestra

Salt Lake City, 21 June 1941
All American Youth Orchestra
Bach Toccata and Fugue in D minor
Brahms Symphony No 3
Gould Guaracho
Strauss Tod und Verklärung

Seattle, 23 June 1941
All American Youth Orchestra
Debussy Fêtes (Nocturnes)
Franck Symphony in D minor
Bender San Luis Rey
Wagner Tristan Liebesnacht
Encores by Bach, Tchaikovsky and
J.Strauss

Portland, 24 June 1941
All American Youth Orchestra
Programme included
Bach Little Fugue
Brahms Symphony No 3

Sacramento, 26 June 1941
All American Youth Orchestra
Bach Toccata and Fugue in D minor
Beethoven Symphony No 5
Gould Guaracho
Wagner Tristan Liebesnacht

San Francisco, 27 June 1941
All American Youth Orchestra
Novacek Perpetuum mobile
Primsky-Korsakov Scheherazade
Gould Guaracho
Wagner Tristan Liebesnacht

Los Angeles, 29 June 1941
All American Youth Orchestra
Bach Little Fugue
Brahms Symphony No 1
Gould Guaracho
Wagner Tristan Liebesnacht

Tijuana, 4 July 1941
All American Youth Orchestra

New York, 9-10 October 1941
NYPSO
Bach Toccata and Fugue in D minor
Bach Andante sostenuto
Beethoven Symphony No 5
Cowell Tales of our Countryside
Wagner Tristan Prelude & Liebestod

New York, 11-12 October 1941
NYPSO
Bach Andante sostenuto
Beethoven Symphony No 7
Harris Folk Dance
Wagner Tristan Prelude & Liebestod

New York, 16-17 October 1941
NYPSO
Bach Ein feste Burg
Brahms Symphony No 1
Creston Scherzo
Mussorgsky Pictures from an
    exhibition

New York, 4 November 1941
NBC Symphony Orchestra
Bach Prelude in E flat
Warner Sinfonietta
Brahms Symphony No 3

New York, 11 November 1941
NBC Symphony Orchestra
Chorus and soloists
Beethoven Symphony No 9

New York, 18 November 1941
NBC Symphony Orchestra
Prokofiev Love of 3 Oranges excerpts
Kelly Sunset Reflections (Adirondack
    Suite)
Brahms Symphony No 4

New York, 21 November 1941
NBC Symphony Orchestra
Childrens' choir
Concert of short orchestral excerpts
and choral works

New York, 25 November 1941
NBC Symphony Orchestra
Bach Arioso (Cantata No 156)
Haufrecht 2 Fantastic Marches
Tchaikovsky Symphony No 4

New York, 24 March 1942
NBC Symphony Orchestra
Cooley Promenade
Beethoven Symphony No 6

New York, 31 March 1942
NBC Symphony Orchestra
Collegiate Chorale
Bach Final Chorus (St Matthew Passion)
Wagner Parsifal Good Friday Music and
    Symphonic synthesis
Rimsky-Korsakov Russian Easter Overture

New York, 7 April 1942
NBC Symphony Orchestra
Bach Ein feste Burg
MacDowell Piano Concerto No 2, 1st
    & 2nd movements
Stringfield Negro Parade
Stravinsky Firebird Suite

Pasadena, 13 July 1942
Los Angeles PO
Mussorgsky Night on Bare Mountain
Shostakovich Prelude in E flat minor
Stravinsky Firebird Suite
Tchaikovsky Symphony No 5

Los Angeles, 14 July 1942
Los Angeles PO
Programme as for 13 July

Los Angeles, 21-22 January 1943
Los Angeles PO
The Star-spangled Banner
Bach Wir glauben all an einen Gott
Brahms Symphony No 1
Wagner Tristan Prelude & Liebestod
Hovhaness Symphony No 1

Pasadena, 25 January 1943
Los Angeles PO
The Star-spangled Banner
Bach Wir glauben all an einen Gott
Brahms Symphony No 1
Wagner Tristan Prelude & Liebestod
Ravel Daphnis et Chloé, 2nd Suite
Debussy Clair de lune

Los Angeles, 26 January 1943
Los Angeles PO
Programme as for 25 January

San Diego, 30 June 1943 (matinee)
Los Angeles PO
Programme as for 25 January

San Diego, 30 June 1943 (evening)
Los Angeles PO
Bach Fugue
Wagner Lohengrin Act 3 Prelude
Haydn 18th century Dance
Boccherini Minuet
Debussy Saxophone Rhapsody
Debussy Clair de lune
Ravel Daphnis et Chloé, 2nd Suite

New York, 9 April 1943
Student orchestras
Shaw and Collegiate Chorales
Steber, Tourel, Darwin,
Metz, Pechner

Bach Saint Matthew Passion
This formed the musical accompaniment
to a staged enactment of the Passion

New York, 14 April 1942
NBC Symphony Orchestra
Collegiate Chorale
Milhaud 4 Dances (Saudades do Brasil)
Still And They Lynched Him on a Tree
Mussorgsky Boris Godunov excerpts

New York, 15 November 1942
NBC Symphony Orchestra
Triggs The Bright Land
Gould Spirituals

New York, 22 November 1942
NBC Symphony Orchestra
Beethoven Symphony No 7
Wagner Tristan Prelude & Liebestod

New York, 29 November 1942
NBC Symphony Orchestra
Tchaikovsky programme
The Storm/Symphony No 5

New York, 6 December 1942
NBC Symphony Orchestra
Bach Wir glauben all an einen Gott
Bach Adagio (Adagio, Toccata & Fugue)
Wagner Siegfried Idyll
Hovhaness Exile Symphony
Lavalle Symphonic Rumba

New York, 13 December 1942
NBC Symphony Orchestra
Shostakovich Symphony No 7

New York, 23 December 1942
NBC Symphony Orchestra
Childrens' concert

New York, 14 February 1943
NBC Symphony Orchestra
Womens' chorus
Holst The Planets

New York, 21 February 1943
NBC Symphony Orchestra
Stravinsky Symphony in C
Stravinsky Circus Polka
Debussy Soirée dans Grenade
Ravel Daphnis et Chloé, 2nd Suite

New York, 28 February 1943
NBC Symphony Orchestra
Hindemith Symphony in E flat
Wagner Tristan Liebesnacht

New York, 7 March 1943
NBC Symphony Orchestra
Westminster Choir
Tourel
Tchaikovsky The Storm
Prokofiev Alexander Nevsky

New York, 14 March 1943
NBC Symphony Orchestra
Vaughan Williams Symphony No 4
Gould New China March
Gould Red Cavalry March
Debussy Prélude à l'après-midi

Lakehurst, 17 March 1943
NBC Symphony Orchestra
Shostakovich Symphony No 7, 1st and
    4th movements
Debussy Soirée dans Grenade
Wagner Tristan Liebesnacht
Ravel Daphnis et Chloé, 2nd Suite
Tchaikovsky Symphony No 4
J.Strauss An der schönen blauen Donau
Programme also included audience
singing

New York, 21 March 1943
NBC Symphony Orchestra
Milhaud Symphony No 1
Mussorgsky Pictures from an
    exhibition

New York, 28 March 1943
NBC Symphony Orchestra
Bach Es ist vollbracht
Debussy Le martyre de St.Sébastien
Wagner Parifal Prelude and Symphonic
    synthesis

New York, 12 December 1943
NBC Symphony Orchestra
Bach Brandenburg Concerto No 2
Bach Christ lag in Todesbanden
Bach Toccata and Fugue in D minor
Schumann Prayer

New York, 19 December 1943
NBC Symphony Orchestra
Handel Pastoral Symphony (Messiah)
Vaughan Williams Fantasy on Christmas
    carols
Harris Folk Rhythms of Today
Mohaupt Concerto on Russian Army
    themes

New York, 26 December 1943
NBC Symphony Orchestra
Rossini Barbiere di Siviglia
    Overture
Beethoven Symphony No 5
Creston Chant
Deems Taylor Introduction and
    Ballet (Ramuntcho)

New York, 2 January 1944
NBC Symphony Orchestra
Wagner Tristan Liebesnacht
Hanson Symphony No 4

New York, 9 January 1944
NBC Symphony Orchestra
Albeniz Fête-Dieu à Seville
Debussy Prélude à l'après-midi
Fernandez Batuque
Guarnieri 3 pieces
Copland Short Symphony

New York, 16 January 1944
NBC Symphony Orchestra
Tchaikovsky Romeo and Juliet
Skilton Sunrise Song
Thomson Plough that Broke the Plain
Zimbalist American Rhapsody

New York, 23 January 1944
NBC Symphony Orchestra
Wagner Lohengrin Prelude
Wagner Wotan's Farewell (Walküre)
Hindemith Nobilissima Visione

New York, 30 January 1944
NBC Symphony Orchestra
Tchaikovsky Symphony No 6

New York, 6 February 1944
NBC Symphony Orchestra
Steuermann
Cesti Tu mancavi a tormentarmi
Schubert Symphony No 8
Schoenberg Piano Concerto

New York, 13 February 1944
NBC Symphony Orchestra
Debussy La cathédrale engloutie
Butterworth A Shropshire Lad
Antheil Symphony No 4

New York, 20 February 1944
NBC Symphony Orchestra
Rimsky-Korsakov Capriccio espagnol
Stravinsky Petrushka Suite
Amfitheatrof De profundis clamavi

New York, 27 February 1944
NBC Symphony Orchestra
Brahms Symphony No 3
Bach Passacaglia & Fugue in C minor

New York, 15 February 1945
New York City SO
Dorsey
Programme included
Shilkret Trombone Concerto

New York, 26 February 1945
New York City SO
Programme included
Fuleihan Theremin Concerto
Los Angeles, 15 July 1945
Hollywood Bowl SO
Grainger
Bach Toccata and Fugue in D minor
Grieg Piano Concerto
Grainger Londonderry Air
Grainger Molly on the shore
Debussy Prélude à l'après-midi
Antheil Heroes of Today

Los Angeles, 22 July 1945
Hollywood Bowl SO
M.Koshetz
Liadov 8 Russian folksongs
Rimsky-Korsakov Tsar's Bride Overture
Shostakovich Prelude in E flat minor
Mussorgsky Gopak (Sorochinsky Fair)
Granados Goyescas
Délibes Flower Dance (Naila)
Debussy Soirée dans Grenade
Steinert Clarinet Rhapsody
Vocal items by Rimsky-Korsakov
    and Rachmaninov

Los Angeles, 29 July 1945
Hollywood Bowl SO
Seidel
Bach Prelude in E flat minor
Rosza Pastorale
Chausson Poème
Wagner Tristan Liebesnacht

Los Angeles, 5 August 1945
Hollywood Bowl SO
Ayres, Weinstine, Warner, Schaeffer,
Lohman, Lewin, Eustis, Chang
Purcell Trumpet Prelude
Frescobaldi Gagliarda
Gluck Ballet Suite
Vivaldi 4-Violin Concerto in A minor
Bach 4-Piano Concerto in C minor
Brahms Minuetto (Serenade No 1)
Chabrier Espana

Los Angeles, 12 August 1945
Hollywood Bowl SO
Bloch, Reher
Saint-Saens Le déluge
Mozart Clarinet Concerto
Dvorak Rondo
Mussorgsky Pictures from an
    exhibition

Los Angeles, 19 August 1945
Hollywood Bowl SO
Moscona
Bach Fugue
Haydn Serenade
Schubert Moment musical No 3
Scharf Palestine Suite
Respighi Pini di Roma
Vocal items by Verdi, Gounod and
    Boito

Los Angeles, 26 August 1945
Hollywood Bowl SO
Turner, Abato
Bach Prelude (Partita in E)
Scriabin Prelude in C sharp minor
Young Pearls on Velvet
Creston Saxophone Concerto
Strauss Rosenkavalier Waltzes
Vocal item by KFI Contest winner

New York, 18 December 1945
NYPSO
Westminster Choir
Tourel
Prokofiev Alexander Nevsky

Los Angeles, 2 September 1945
Hollywood Bowl SO
Stern
Schubert Marche militaire
Tchaikovsky Waltz (Serenade)
Lalo Symphonie espagnole
Herbert Indian Summer
Beethoven Moonlight Sonata
Brahms Finale (Symphony No 1)

Los Angeles, 11 July 1946
Hollywood Bowl SO & Chorus
Heidt, M.Koshetz, Vinay, Pease
Bizet Carmen

Los Angeles, 14 July 1946
Hollywood Bowl SO
Wicks
Kabalevsky Colas Breugnon Overture
Dvorak Largo (Symphony No 9)
Glinka Jota aragonesa
Wieniawski Violin Concerto No 2
Wagner Rhine Journey
Britten Passacaglia (Grimes)
Ravel Tzigane
Honegger Pacific 231

Los Angeles, 16 July 1946
Hollywood Bowl SO
Brahms Academic Festival Overture
Brahms Symphony No 3
Wagner Lohengrin Prelude
Wagner Tristan Act 3 Prelude
Wagner Tannhäuser Overture and
    Venusberg Music

Los Angeles, 21 July 1946
Hollywood Bowl SO
Grainger
Lalo Le roi d'Ys Overture
Griffes White Peacock
Grainger In a Nutshell
Benjamin From San Domingo
Tchaikovsky Casse noisette Suite
Kodaly Dances of Galanta
Grainger Danish Folksongs
Scott Hornpipe and Shanty

Los Angeles, 23 July 1946
Hollywood Bowl SO
Mussorgsky Khovanschina Prelude
Shostakovitch Symphony No 1
Rachmaninov Isle of the Dead
Tchaikovsky Francesca da Rimini

Los Angeles, 28 July 1946
Hollywood Bowl SO
Conner
Toch Pinocchio
Sibelius Swan of Tuonela
Rose Holiday for Strings
Rose As Kreutzer spins
Borodin Polovtsian Dances
Vocal items by Bachelet, Massenet
   and Puccini

Los Angeles, 30 July 1946
Hollywood Bowl SO
Mozart Don Giovanni Overture
Beethoven Symphony No 7
Montemezzi My Italy
Iturbi Soliloquy
Turina Danzas fantasticas

Los Angeles, 4 August 1946
Hollywood Bowl SO
Cherkassky
Thomas Raymonda Overture
Cesto Tu mancavi a tormentarvi
Tchaikovsky Piano Concerto No 2,
   2nd and 3rd movements
Wagner Siegfried Forest murmurs
Délibes Sylvia Suite
Antheil Over the Plains
Líszt Les Préludes

Los Angeles, 6 August 1946
Hollywood Bowl SO
Berlioz Benevuto Cellini Overture
Debussy Soirées dans Grenade
Hindemith Symphony in E flat
Strauss Dance of the 7 veils
Copland Quiet City
Wagner Tristan Prelude & Liebestod

Los Angeles, 11 August 1946
Hollywood Bowl SO
Stockton
Suppé Beautiful Galathea Overture
Purcell Trumpet Prelude
Bach Arioso
Weber Rondo in C
Brahms Hungarian Dance No 1
Tchaikovsky Valse-scherzo
Solis Malaga
Paganini Perpetuum mobile
Falla 3-Cornered Hat Suite

Los Angeles, 13 August 1946
Hollywood Bowl SO
Merriman
Rachmaninov Symphony No 2
Milhaud Saudades do Brasil No 2
Falla El amor brujo

Los Angeles, 18 August 1946
Hollywood Bowl SO
Totenberg
Wolf-Ferrari Segreto di Susanna
   Overture
Villa-Lobos 2 Bachianas brasilieras
Saint Bacchanale (Samson et Dalila)
Turina Oracion del torero
Tchaikovsky Violin Concerto,
   2nd and 3rd movements
Grieg Peer Gynt Suite No 1

Los Angeles, 20 August 1946
Hollywood Bowl SO
Vivaldi Concerto in D minor
Mozart Symphony No 41
Debussy Prélude à l'après-midi
Gliere Symphony No 3

Los Angeles, 25 August 1946
Hollywood Bowl SO
KFI Contest winners
Offenbach Orpheus in the
   Underworld Overture
Mendelssohn Scherzo (MND)
Cadman Dance of the Willow Wand
Cadman Sacrificial Dance
Tchaikovsky Piano Concerto No 1,
   1st movement
Alfven Midsommarvaka

Los Angeles, 27 August 1946
Hollywood Bowl SO
Handel Overture in D minor
Thomson The Plow that broke the Plains
Elgar Enigma Variations
Tchaikovsky Symphony No 5

Los Angeles, 29 August 1946
Hollywood Bowl SO
Chorus and soloists
Bach Saint Matthew Passion

Los Angeles, 1 September 1946
Hollywood Bowl SO
Eustis
Rossini Italiana in Algeri Overture
Dolan Waltz (Lady in the Dark)
Ravel Alborada del gracioso
Schumann Piano Concerto, 1st movement
Bizet L'Arlésienne Suite No 1

New York, 26-27 December 1946
NYPSO
Bach Wir glauben all an einen Gott
Brahms Symphony No 1
Sibelius Symphony No 1
Creston Frontiers
Wagner Parsifal Symphonic synthesis

New York, 29 December 1946
NYPSO
Bach Wir glauben all an einen Gott
Brahms Symphony No 1
Siegmeister Harvest Evening
Wagner Parsifal Symphonic synthesis
Tchaikovsky Francesca da Rimini

New York, 2-3 January 1947
NYPSO
Thibaud
Victoria Jesu dulcis memoria
Mozart Don Giovanni Overture
Hindemith Symphony No 1
Lalo Symphonie espagnole
Milhaud Saudades do Brasil
Debussy Prélude à l'après-midi

New York, 5 January 1947
NYPSO
Merriman, Thibaud
Victoria Jesu dulcis memoria
Mozart Don Giovanni Overture
Lalo Symphonie espagnole
Falla El amor brujo

New York, 9-12 January 1947
NYPSO
List
Kabalevsky Colas Breugnon Overture
Tchaikovsky Symphony No 6
Shostakovich Piano Concerto No 1
Rachmaninov Isle of the Dead

New York, 16-17 January 1947
NYPSO
Bach Fugue in G minor
Bach Brandenburg Concerto No 2
Bach Komm süsser Tod
Bach Passacaglia & Fugue in C minor
Beethoven Symphony No 8
Wagner Tristan Liebesnacht

New York, 18 January 1947
NYPSO
Bach Brandenburg Concerto No 2
Bach Komm süsser Tod
Beethoven Symphony No 8
Siegmeister Prairie Legend
Wagner Tristan Liebesnacht

New York, 19 January 1947
NYPSO
Bach Fugue in G minor
Bach Ich ruf' zu dir
Bach Brandenburg Concerto No 2
Bach Prelude in E
Bach Komm süsser Tod
Bach Passacaglia & Fugue in C minor
Wagner Tristan Liebesnacht
Wagner Götterdämmerung Immolation

New York, 20-21 February 1947
NYPSO
Monath
Bach Toccata and Fugue in D minor
Brahms Symphony No 3
Mozart Piano Concerto No 19
Wagner Lohengrin Prelude

New York, 22 February 1947
NYPSO
Sanroma
Bach Toccata and Fugue in D minor
Brahms Symphony No 3
Tchaikovsky Piano Concerto No 1
Sibelius Finlandia

New York, 23 February 1947
NYPSO
Sanroma
Mussorgsky Khovanschina Entr'acte
Tchaikovsky Piano Concerto No 1
Brahms Symphony No 3
Sibelius Finlandia

Worcester Massachusetss, 4 March 1947
NYPSO
Bach Toccata and Fugue in D minor
Bach Komm süsser Tod
Brahms Symphony No 3
Creston Frontiers
Wagner Tristan Liebesnacht

New York, 10 March 1947
NYPSO
Corigliano, Rose
Bach Prelude in E
Bach Mein Jesu was für Seelenweh
Haydn Serenade
Beethoven 3 Equali
Brahms Double Concerto
Saint-Saens Septet
Ravel Introduction and Allegro
Schmitt Poem
Striegler Timpani Concerto
Turner Fanfare, Chorale and Finale
Concert given in the Plaza Hotel

New York, 13-16 March 1947
NYPSO
Casadesus
Albeniz Fête-Dieu à Seville
D'Indy Symphonie montagnarde
Debussy Soirée dans Grenade
Messiaen Hymne pour orchestre
Franck Variations symphoniques
Ravel La valse

New York, 3-6 April 1947
NYPSO
Bach Christ lag in Todesbanden
Beethoven Symphony No 6
Still Festive Overture
Wagner Parsifal Good Friday Music
Rimsky-Korsakov Russian Easter Overture

New York, 5 April 1947
NYPSO
Childrens' concert
Bizet Carmen Prelude
Beethoven Turkish March
Bach Prelude (Partita in E)
Novacek Perpetuum mobile
Tchaikovsky Scherzo (Symphony No 4)
Mussorgsky Ballet of Unhatched Chicks
    (Pictures from an exhibition)
Villa-Lobos Little Train of Caipira

New York, 10-11 April 1947
NYPSO
Pension Fund benefit concert
Mussorgsky Night on Bare Mountain
Shostakovich Symphony No 6
Prokofiev Scythian Suite
Stravinsky Firebird Suite

New York, 12 April 1947
NYPSO
Westminster Choir
Boerner, Merriman, Dame, Duncan
Pension Fund benefit concert
Beethoven programme
Symphony No 8/Symphony No 9

New York, 13 April 1947
NYPSO
Glinka Spanish Overture
Mussorgsky Khovanschina Entr'acte
Shostakovich Symphony No 6
Tchaikovsky Solitude
Stravinky Firebird Suite
Prokofiev Scythian Suite

Baltimore, 14 April 1947
NYPSO
Bach Toccata and Fugue in D minor
Beethoven Symphony No 7
Debussy Prélude à l'après-midi
Stravinsky Firebird Suite
Tchaikovsky Solitude
Novacek Perpetuum mobile

New York, 20 March 1948
NYPSO
Westminster Choir
Sayao, Hobson, Pressler
Pension Fund benefit concert
Tchaikovsky Sleeping Beauty excerpts
Grieg Piano Concerto
Wagner Rienzi Overture
Debussy La demoiselle élue
Ravel Bolero

New York, 21 March 1948
NYPSO
Merriman
Dvorak Symphony No 9
Thomson The Seine at Night
Falla El amor brujo
Fernandez Batuque
Debussy Clair de lune

New York, 25-27 March 1948
NYPSO
Beethoven Leonore No 3 Overture
Mozart Symphony No 41
Vaughan Williams Tallis Fantasia
Wagner Parsifal Symphonic synthesis
Rimsky-Korsakov Russian Easter Overture

New York, 28 March 1948
NYPSO
Hindemith Concert Music
Mozart Symphony No 41
Vaughan Williams Tallis Fantasia
Wagner Parsifal Symphonic synthesis
Rimsky-Korsakov Russian Easter Overture

New York, 1-2 April 1948
NYPSO
Khachaturian Russian Fantasy
Tchaikovsky Symphony No 4
Sibelius Belshazzar's Feast
Stravinsky Concerto in D
Wagner Tristan Prelude & Liebestod

New York, 3 April 1948
NYPSO
Khachaturian Russian Fantasy
Tchaikovsky Symphony No 4
Barber Medea Suite
Wagner Tristan Prelude & Liebestod

Norfolk Virginia, 15 April 1947
NYPSO
Bach Fugue
Brahms Symphony No 1
Creston Frontiers
Wagner Tristan Liebesnacht

Richmond Virginia, 16 April 1947
NYPSO
Kabalevsky Colas Breugnon Overture
Tchaikovsky Symphony No 5
Siegermeister Prairie Legend
Wagner Parsifal Symphonic synthesis
Bach Prelude (Partita in E)

Raleigh NC, 17 April 1947
NYPSO
Bach Toccata and Fugue in D minor
Beethoven Symphony No 7
Debussy Prélude à l'après-midi
Stravinsky Firebird Suite

Durham NC, 18 April 1947
NYPSO
Bach Fugue
Brahms Symphony No 1
Creston Frontiers
Wagner Tristan Liebesnacht
Tchaikovsky Solitude

Spartanburg SC, 19 April 1947
NYPSO
Bach Fugue
Brahms Symphony No 1
Stringfield Mountain Song and
    Cripple Creek
Wagner Tristan Liebesnacht
Tchaikovsky Solitude

Atlanta, 20 April 1947
NYPSO
Bach Toccata and Fugue in D minor
Brahms Symphony No 1
Wagner Tristan Liebesnacht
Debussy Prélude à l'après-midi

Atlanta, 21 April 1947
NYPSO
Kabalevsky Colas Breugnon Overture
Tchaikovsky Symphony No 5
Siegmeister Prairie Legend
Wagner Parsifal Symphonic synthesis

New York, 3-10 October 1947
NYPSO
Westminster Choir
Bach Sinfonia (Cantata No 156)
Brahms Symphony No 2
Debussy 3 Nocturnes
Ravel Daphnis et Chloé, 2nd Suite

Hartford, 11 October 1947
NYPSO
Bach Sinfonia (Cantata No 156)
Brahms Symphony No 1
Debussy Nuages et fêtes (Nocturnes)
Stravinsky Pastorale
Ravel Daphnis et Chloé, 2nd Suite

New York, 12 October 1947
NYPSO
Westminster Choir
Programme as for 3-10 October

New York, 16-19 October 1947
NYPSO
Shostakovich Prelude in E flat minor
Tchaikovsky Symphony No 5
Khachaturian Masquerade Suite
Mussorgsky Boris Godunov excerpts

New York, 23-24 October 1947
NYPSO
Milstein
Bach Prelude in E flat minor
Mendelssohn Symphony No 3
Dvorak Violin Concerto
Tchaikovsky Francesca da Rimini

New York, 25 October 1947
NYPSO
Bach Prelude in E flat minor
Mendelssohn Symphony No 3
Copland Prairie Night & Celebration
    Dance (Billy the Kid)
Bauer Sun Splendour
Mussorgsky Boris Godunov excerpts

New York, 26 October 1947
NYPSO
Milstein
Programme as for 23-24 October

New York, 30-31 October 1947
NYPSO
Hess
Griffes The White Peacock
Siegmeister Symphony
Schumann Piano Concerto
Wagner Walküre Wotan's Farewell

New York, 1 November 1947
NYPSO
Griffes The White Peacock
Siegmeister Symphony
Messiaen L'Ascension
Wagner Walküre Wotan's Farewell

New York, 2 November 1947
NYPSO
Hess
Griffes The White Peacock
Siegmeister Symphony
Mozart Piano Concerto No 14
Wagner Walküre Wotan's Farewell

New York, 11-12 March 1948
NYPSO
Casadesus
Bach Wachet auf
Beethoven Symphony No 7
Fauré Ballade
Casadesus Piano Concerto
Wagner Götterdämmerung Siegfried's
    Rhine Journey

New York, 14 March 1948
NYPSO
Casadesus
Bach Wachet auf
Beethoven Symphony No 7
Casadesus Piano Concerto
Stravinsky Pastorale
Wagner Götterdämmerung Siegfried's
    Rhine Journey
Dello Joio Concert Music

New York, 18-19 March 1948
NYPSO
Merriman
Schuman American Festival Overture
Dvorak Symphony No 9
Thomson The Seine at Night
Falla El amor brujo
Debussy Clair de lune

New York, 4 April 1948
NYPSO
Tchaikovsky Symphony No 4
Stravinsky Concerto in D
Wagner Tristan Prelude & Liebestod

Princeton, 6 April 1948
NYPSO
Bach Wachet auf
Beethoven Symphony No 7
Khachaturian Russian Fantasy
Stravinsky Concerto in D
Thomson The Seine at Night
Wagner Tristan Prelude & Liebestod

New York, 10 April 1948
NYPSO
Childrens' concert
Short pieces by Bach, Ravel, C.Jones,
J.Andersen, Wagner, Weber, Debussy
and Khachaturian

Syracuse, 20 September 1948
NYPSO
Bach Fugue
Brahms Symphony No 1
Porrino Sinfonia per una fiaba
Thomson The Seine at Night
Wagner Parsifal Symphonic synthesis

Cleveland, 21 September 1948
NYPSO
Bach Fugue
Brahms Symphony No 1
Dubensky Fugue
Messiaen L'Ascension
Wagner Tristan Prelude & Liebestod

Detroit, 22 September 1948
NYPSO
Bach Toccata and Fugue in D minor
Beethoven Symphony No 7
Khachaturian Masquerade Suite
Thomson The Seine at Night
Wagner Tristan Liebesnacht

Chicago, 23 September 1948
NYPSO
Bach Fugue
Brahms Symphony No 1
Porrino Sinfonia per una fiaba
Thomson The Seine at Night
Wagner Tristan Symphonic synthesis

Chicago, 24 September 1948
NYPSO
Stravinsky Petrushka Suite
Messiaen L'Ascension
Debussy Clair de lune
Dubensky Fugue
Khachaturian Symphony No 2

Madison Wisconsin, 25 September 1948
NYPSO
Bach Toccata and Fugue in D minor
Beethoven Symphony No 7
Khachaturian Masquerade Suite
Copland Prairie Night & Celebration
    Dance (Billy the Kid)
Wagner Tristan Prelude & Liebestod

Milwaukee, 26 September 1948
NYPSO
Bach Toccata and Fugue in D minor
Brahms Symphony No 1
Porrino Sinfonia per una fiaba
Thomson The Seine at Night
Wagner Tristan Liebesnacht

East Lansing, 27 September 1948
NYPSO
Stravinsky Petrushka Suite
Messiaen L'Ascension
Debussy Clair de lune
Dubensky Fugue
Tchaikovsky Symphony No 4

Columbus, 28 September 1948
NYPSO
Bach Toccata and Fugue in D minor
Beethoven Symphony No 7
Khachaturian Masquerade Suite
Copland Prairie Night & Celebration
    Dance (Billy the Kid)
Wagner Parsifal Symphonic synthesis

Buffalo, 29 September 1948
NYPSO
Stravinsky Petrushka Suite
Messiaen L'Ascension
Debussy Clair de lune
Dubensky Fugue
Tchaikovsky Symphony No 4

Utica, 30 September 1948
NYPSO
Bach Toccata and Fugue in D minor
Beethoven Symphony No 7
Messiaen L'Ascension
Debussy Clair de lune
Wagner Tristan Prelude & Liebestod

Rochester, 1 October 1948
NYPSO
Bach Toccata and Fugue in D minor
Beethoven Symphony No 7
Khachaturian Masquerade Suite
Copland Prairie Night & Celebration
    Dance (Billy the Kid)
Wagner Parsifal Symphonic synthesis

Boston, 2 October 1948
NYPSO
Bach Toccata and Fugue in D minor
Brahms Symphony No 1
Thomson The Seine at Night
Messiaen L'Ascension
Wagner Parsifal Symphonic synthesis

Portland, 3 October 1948
NYPSO
Stravinsky Petrushka Suite
Dubensky Fugue
Khachaturian Masquerade Suite
Tchaikovsky Symphony No 4

New York, 13-14 January 1949
NYPSO
Wagner Holländer Overture
Brahms Symphony No 4
Hindemith Orchestral Variations
Weinberger Polka and Fugue

New York, 15-16 January 1949
NYPSO
Bach Wir glauben all an einen Gott
Bach Ich ruf' zu dir
Bach Nun komm der Heiden Heiland
Brahms Symphony No 4
Stravinsky Petrushka Suite
Menotti 2 Interludes (Island God)
Weinberger Polka and Fugue

New York, 20-21 January 1949
NYPSO
Firkusny
Muradeli Georgian Dance
Khachaturian Symphony No 2
Menotti Piano Concerto
Debussy Prélude à l'après-midi

New York, 22 January 1949
NYPSO
Schola cantorum
Graham
Griffes Pleasure Dome of Khubla Khan
Cowell American Piper
Baron Ode to Democracy
Saint-Saens Piano Concerto No 2
Khachaturian Symphony No 2

New York, 23 January 1949
NYPSO
Schola cantorum
Griffes Pleasure Dome of Khubla Khan
Luening Pilgrim's Hymn
Cowell American Piper
Baron Ode to Democracy
Debussy Prélude à l'après-midi
Khachaturian Symphony No 2

New York, 27-28 January 1949
NYPSO
Janis
Moeran In the Mountain Country
Vaughan Williams Symphony No 6
Gershwin Piano Concerto
Liszt Hungarian Rhapsody No 2

New York, 30 January 1949
NYPSO
Rose
Moeran In the Mountain Country
Muradeli Georgian Dance
Scott From the Sacred Harp
Bloch Schelomo
Debussy Nuages et fêtes (Nocturnes)
Vaughan Williams Symphony No 6

New York, 3-4 February 1949
NYPSO
Hess
Walton Spitfire Prelude and Fugue
Brahms Piano Concerto No 1
Schumann Symphony No 2

THE PHILHARMONIC-SYMPHONY SOCIETY
1842 OF NEW YORK 1878
CONSOLIDATED 1928

1948 ONE HUNDRED SEVENTH SEASON **1949**

Conductors: BRUNO WALTER — DIMITRI MITROPOULOS
CHARLES MUNCH — LEOPOLD STOKOWSKI
Assistant Conductor: WALTER HENDL

CARNEGIE HALL

THURSDAY EVENING, FEBRUARY 10, 1949, at 8:45
FRIDAY AFTERNOON, FEBRUARY 11, 1949, at 2:30

4686th and 4687th Concerts

Under the Direction of
LEOPOLD STOKOWSKI

PROGRAM

DYSON   Overture to the Cantata, "Canterbury Pilgrims"
("At the Tabard Inn")
(First performances in this country)

DEBUSSY   "La Cathédrale Engloutie"

HERRMANN   Suite from "The Devil and Daniel Webster"
1. "Mr. Scratch"
2. "Ballad of Springfield Mountain"
3. "Diabolical Sleigh-Ride"
4. "The Miser's Waltz"
5. "Swing Your Partners"
(First concert performances in New York)

INTERMISSION

*TCHAIKOVSKY   Symphony in B minor, No. 6
("Pathétique"), Op. 74
I. Adagio; allegro non troppo
II. Allegro con grazia
III. Allegro molto vivace
IV. Finale: Adagio lamentoso

ARTHUR JUDSON, BRUNO ZIRATO, **Managers**
THE **STEINWAY** is the Official Piano of The Philharmonic-Symphony Society
———— *COLUMBIA AND ‡VICTOR RECORDS ————

These concerts will end on Thursday at approximately 10:30 *P. M.*
and on Friday at 4:15 *P. M.*

THE PHILHARMONIC-SYMPHONY SOCIETY
1842 OF NEW YORK 1878
CONSOLIDATED 1928

1948	ONE HUNDRED SEVENTH SEASON	1949

Conductors: BRUNO WALTER — DIMITRI MITROPOULOS
CHARLES MUNCH — LEOPOLD STOKOWSKI
Assistant Conductor: WALTER HENDL

CARNEGIE HALL

THURSDAY EVENING, FEBRUARY 17, 1949, at 8:45
FRIDAY AFTERNOON, FEBRUARY 18, 1949, at 2:30

4690th and 4691st Concerts

Under the Direction of
LEOPOLD STOKOWSKI

Assisting Artist:
WILLIAM KAPELL, *Pianist*

PROGRAM

VIVALDI — Concerto Grosso in D minor, Op. 3, No. 11
    I. Maestoso
    II. Largo
    III. Allegro

MOZART — Deutsche Tänze (K. 605), No. 3

HAYDN — Symphony in D major (B. & H. No. 53), "Imperial"
    I. Largo maestoso; Allegro vivace
    II. Andante
    III. Menuetto-Trio
    IV. Presto
    (First performances by the Society)

INTERMISSION

RACHMANINOFF — Concerto for Piano and Orchestra
in D minor, No. 3, Op. 30
    I. Allegro ma non tanto
    II. Intermezzo
    III. Finale
WILLIAM KAPELL

ENESCO — Roumanian Rhapsody in A major, No. 1

ARTHUR JUDSON, BRUNO ZIRATO, Managers
Mr. Kapell plays the Steinway Piano
THE STEINWAY is the Official Piano of The Philharmonic-Symphony Society
————— *COLUMBIA AND ‡VICTOR RECORDS —————

These concerts will end on Thursday at approximately 10:45 P. M.
and on Friday at 4:25 P. M.

THE PHILHARMONIC-SYMPHONY SOCIETY
1842 OF NEW YORK 1878
CONSOLIDATED 1928

| 1948 | ONE HUNDRED SEVENTH SEASON | 1949 |

Conductors: BRUNO WALTER — DIMITRI MITROPOULOS
CHARLES MUNCH — LEOPOLD STOKOWSKI
Assistant Conductor: WALTER HENDL

CARNEGIE HALL

THURSDAY EVENING, MARCH 24, 1949, at 8:45
FRIDAY AFTERNOON, MARCH 25, 1949, at 2:30

4708th and 4709th Concerts

Under the Direction of
LEOPOLD STOKOWSKI

Assisting Artist:
JOHN CORIGLIANO, *Violinist*

PROGRAM

PANUFNIK   "Tragic" Overture
(First performances in New York)

THOMSON   "Wheat Field at Noon"
(First performances in New York)

SIBELIUS   Concerto for Violin and Orchestra
in D minor

    I. Allegro moderato
    II. Adagio di molto
    III. Allegro ma non tanto

JOHN CORIGLIANO

*KHACHATURIAN   Music from the Ballet, "Gayaneh"
    a) Lesghinka   b) Lullaby   c) Dance of the Kurds
      d) Adagio   e) Sabre Dance

INTERMISSION

BRAHMS   Symphony in F major, No. 3, Op. 90

    I. Allegro con brio
    II. Andante
    III. Poco allegretto
    IV. Allegro

ARTHUR JUDSON, BRUNO ZIRATO, **Managers**
THE **STEINWAY** is the Official Piano of The Philharmonic-Symphony Society
———— *COLUMBIA AND ‡VICTOR RECORDS ————

*These concerts will end on Thursday at approximately 10:40 P.M.
and on Friday at 4:25 P.M.*

THE PHILHARMONIC-SYMPHONY SOCIETY
1842 OF NEW YORK 1878
CONSOLIDATED 1928

1948	ONE HUNDRED SEVENTH SEASON	1949

Conductors: BRUNO WALTER — DIMITRI MITROPOULOS
CHARLES MUNCH — LEOPOLD STOKOWSKI
Assistant Conductor: WALTER HENDL

CARNEGIE HALL
SUNDAY AFTERNOON, APRIL 3, 1949, at 2:45
Broadcast at 3:00 P.M. over the Coast-to-Coast Network of the
Columbia Broadcasting System under the sponsorship of
Standard Oil Company (New Jersey)

4715th Concert

Under the Direction of
LEOPOLD STOKOWSKI

PROGRAM

PURCELL-WOOD   Suite
    I. Molto maestoso: Prelude to Act III of the Opera
      "Dioclesian"
    II. Molto moderato: Minuet from the Tragedy
      "The Princess of Persia"
    III. Largo: from the Fifth of the "Twelve Sonatas of
      III Parts" for Strings
    IV. Allegro: "Hark, How the Songsters" from the
      Masque in "Timon of Athens"
    V. Vivace: from the First of the "Twelve Sonatas of
      III Parts" for Strings
        EDOUARD NIES-BERGER at the Organ

MOZART   Symphony in G minor, No. 40 (K. 550)
    I. Allegro molto
    II. Andante
    III. Minuetto; Trio
    IV. Finale: Allegro assai

INTERMISSION

WAGNER   Excerpts from "Götterdämmerung"
    (a) Siegfried's Rhine Journey
    (b) Siegfried's Death
    (c) Brünnhilde's Immolation

ARTHUR JUDSON, BRUNO ZIRATO, **Managers**
THE STEINWAY is the Official Piano of The Philharmonic-Symphony Society
——————— *COLUMBIA AND †VICTOR RECORDS ———————

This concert will end at approximately 4:25 P.M.

The next and last concert in the even Sunday subscription series on April
17th, 1949 will begin at 3:00 P.M. instead of the usual time of 2:45 P.M.
There will be no intermission.

New York, 6 February 1949
NYPSO
Hess
Sibelius Pelleas and Melisande
Walton Spitfire Prelude and Fugue
Mozart Piano Concerto No 21
Schumann Symphony No 2

New York, 10-11 February 1949
NYPSO
Dyson Canterbury Pilgrims Overture
Debussy La cathédrale engloutie
Herrmann The Devil & Daniel Webster
Tchaikovsky Symphony No 6

New York, 12 February 1949
NYPSO
Farrell, Davenport, Rhodes
Pension Fund benefit concert
Wagner programme
Rheingold Entry of the Gods/Siegfried
Forest murmurs & Forging song/Tristan
Prelude & Liebestod/Walküre Wotan's
Farewell/Rheingold Erda's Warning/
Götterdämmerung Immolation scene

New York, 13 February 1949
NYPSO
Maganini 3 Early American pieces
Tchaikovsky Symphony No 6
Debussy La cathédrale engloutie
Herrmann The Devil & Daniel Webster

New York, 17-18 February 1949
NYPSO
Kapell
Vivaldi Concerto grosso in D minor
Mozart German Dance No 3
Haydn Symphony No 53
Rachmaninov Piano Concerto No 3
Enesco Rumanian Rhapsody No 1

New York, 20 February 1949
NYPSO
Kapell
Vivaldi Concerto grosso in D minor
Bach Prelude (Partita in E)
Bach Ich ruf' zu dir
Bach Nun komm der Heiden Heiland
Mozart German Dance No 3
Haydn Symphony No 53
Prokofiev Piano Concerto No 3
Enesco Rumanian Rhapsody No 1

New York, 12 March 1949
NYPSO
Young Persons' concert
Works by Gounod, Foster, Pierné,
Kleinsinger and Khachaturian

New York, 24-25 March 1949
NYPSO
Corigliano
Panufnik Tragic Overture
Thomson Wheat Field at Noon
Sibelius Violin Concerto
Khachaturian Gayaneh Suite
Brahms Symphony No 3

New York, 26-27 March 1949
NYPSO
Wummer, Cella
Wagner Rienzi Overture
Thomson Wheat Field at Noon
Hanson Serenade for flute and harp
Debussy Soirée dans Grenade
Khachaturian Gayaneh Suite
Brahms Symphony No 3

New York, 31 March-3 April 1949
NYPSO
Purcell/Wood Suite
Mozart Symphony No 40
Wagner Götterdämmerung excerpts

New York, 2 April 1949
NYPSO
Fitch Terra nova
Mozart Symphony No 40
Wagner Götterdämmerung excerpts

New York, 9 April 1949
NYPSO
Young Persons' concert
Works by Mozart, Vaughan Williams,
Kreutz, Tchaikovsky, Dubensky,
Taylor and M.L.Wesley

White Plains, 18 April 1949
NYPSO
Bach Wir glauben all an einen Gott
Brahms Symphony No 1
Tchaikovsky Francesca da Rimini
Thomson Wheat Field at Noon
Khachaturian Gayaneh Suite

Richmond, 19 April 1949
NYPSO
Programme as for 18 April

Columbia, 20 April 1949
NYPSO
Programme as for 18 April

Atlanta, 21 April 1949
NYPSO
Cowell American Pipers
Wagner Walküre Wotan's Farewell
Menotti 2 Interludes (Island God)
Enesco Rumanian Rhapsody No 1
Tchaikovsky Symphony No 6

Knoxville, 23 April 1949
NYPSO
Programme as for 21 April

Birmingham Alabama, 24 April 1949
NYPSO
Brahms Symphony No 1
Wagner Siegfried Forest murmurs
Wagner Rheingold Entry of the Gods
Sibelius Pelleas and Melisande
Bach Nun komm der Heiden Heiland
Bach Ich ruf' zu dir
Bach Wir glauben all an einen Gott

New York, 13-14 October 1949
NYPSO
Wagner Meistersinger Overture
Copland The Red Pony
Debussy La mer
Brahms Symphony No 1

New York, 16 October 1949
NYPSO
Liebermann Suite on Swiss Melodies
Brahms Symphony No 1
Chopin Mazurka in A minor

New York, 20-21 October 1949
NYPSO
Miaskovsky Slavic Rhapsody
Glière Symphony No 3
Mozart Serenade K286
Strauss Tod und Verklärung

New York, 23 October 1949
NYPSO
Beethoven Leonore No 3 Overture
Glière Symphony No 3
Mozart Serenade K286
J.Strauss An der schönen blauen Donau
J.Strauss G'schichten aus dem
   Wienerwald

New York, 27-28 October 1949
NYPSO
Lipton
Wagner Lohengrin Prelude
Schoenberg Song of the Wood Dove
   (Gurrelieder)
Beethoven Symphony No 6
Villa-Lobos Uirapuru

New York, 29 October 1949
NYPSO
Istomin
Arnell Black Mountain Prelude
Glière Symphony No 3
Mozart Piano Concerto No 9
Strauss Tod und Verklärung

New York, 30 October 1949
NYPSO
Lipton
Bach Sinfonia (Cantata No 156)
Bach Mein Jesu was für Seelenweh'
Beethoven Symphony No 6
Schoenberg Song of the Wood Dove
   (Gurrelieder)
Villa-Lobos Uirapuru

New York, 3-4 November 1949
NYPSO
Fournier
Dubensky Concerto grosso
Diamond Tempest Overture
Bloch Symphonic Interludes (Macbeth)
Schumann Cello Concerto
Haydn Symphony No 101

New York, 5 November 1949
NYPSO
Lincer
Porrino Sardegna
Rivier Viola Concertino
Bloch Symphonic Interludes (Macbeth)
Vivaldi Concerto grosso in D minor
Haydn Symphony No 101

New York, 6 November 1949
NYPSO
Fournier
Vivaldi Concerto grosso in D minor
Haydn Symphony No 101
Schumann Cello Concerto
Diamond Tempest Overture
Bloch Symphonic Interludes (Macbeth)

New York, 10-11 November 1949
NYPSO
Kapell
Gabrieli Canzon quarti toni a 15
Beethoven Piano Concerto No 2
Tchaikovsky Symphony No 5

New York, 12 November 1949
NYPSO
Moll, Paris, Conley, Bernauer
Pension Fund Benefit concert
Wagner programme
Tannhäuser Bacchanale/Tristan Scenes
from Act 2/Siegfried Closing scene

New York, 13 November 1949
NYPSO
Kapell
Ivanov-Radkevitch Russian Overture
Tchaikovsky Symphony No 5
Revueltas Sensemaya
Falla Noches en los jardines Espana

New York, 17-18 November 1949
NYPSO
Landowska
Aubert Offrande
Poulenc Concert champêtre
Messiaen 3 Petites liturgies
Handel Harpsichord Concerto No 4
Mozart Symphony No 35

New York, 19 November 1949
NYPSO
Landowska
Bach Sarabande
Bach Sinfonia (Cantata No 156)
Bach Bourrée
Mozart Symphony No 35
Handel Harpsichord Concerto No 4
Poulenc Concert champêtre
Carpenter Carmel Concerto

New York, 24-25 November 1949
NYPSO/Abram
Ruggles Organum
Prokofiev Symphony No 6
Britten Piano Concerto
Tchaikovsky Romeo and Juliet

New York, 26 November 1949
NYPSO
Abram
Bennett Overture to an Imaginary
    Dream
Prokofiev Symphony No 6
Britten Piano Concerto
Borodin Polovtsian Dances

New York, 27 November 1949
NYPSO
Abram
Mozart Eine kleine Nachtmusik
Schubert Symphony No 8
Britten Piano Concerto
Borodin Polovtsian Dances

New York, 1-3 December 1949
NYPSO
Stern
Riegger Canon and Fugue
Schubert Symphony No 8
Brahms Violin Concerto
Wagner Tristan Prelude & Liebestod

New York, 4 December 1949
NYPSO
Stern
Purcell Suite
Haydn Violin Concerto in C
Bach Passacaglia & Fugue in C minor
Prokofiev Symphony No 6

New York, 10 December 1949
NYPSO
Childrens' concert
Works by Bach, Schubert, Dubensky,
Stravinsky, Prokofiev, Wagner & Sousa

New York, 17 December 1949
NYPSO
Childrens' concert
Works by Tchaikovsky, Mozart, Haydn,
Hendl, Ippolitov-Ivanov and Jessel

New York, 30 March-2 April 1950
NYPSO
Bach Sinfonia (Cantata No 147)
Bach Es ist vollbracht
Bach Chaconne
Thomson The Mother of us all, Suite
Brahms Symphony No 2

New York, 6-9 April 1950
NYPSO
Schola cantorum, Westminster Choir
Gabrieli In ecclesiis benedicte domine
Mahler Symphony No 8

Houston, 4 December 1950
Houston SO
Programme included Ruggles Organum
and works by Wagner

Dallas, 9 December 1950
Dallas SO
Programme included
Liebermann Furioso

San Antonio, 16 December 1950
San Antonio SO
Programme included
Iglesias First Adventure of Don
   Quixote

Washington, 28 February 1951
National SO
Purcell Suite
Vaughan Williams Symphony No 6
Falla El amor brujo
Debussy La cathédrale engloutie
Tchaikovsky Romeo and Juliet

Washington, 6-7 March 1951
National SO
Wagner Rheingold Entry of the Gods
Wagner Meistersinger Act 3 Prelude
Wagner Tristan Liebestod
Liebermann Furioso
Riegger Symphony No 3
Wagner Parsifal Symphonic synthesis

Bristol, 27 April 1951
RPO
Wagner Tannhäuser Overture & Venusberg
Villa-Lobos Impressao Moura
Falla El amor brujo
Brahms Symphony No 4

Bournemouth, 28 April 1951
RPO
Berlioz Carnaval romain Overture
Ruggles Organum
Debussy Prélude à l'après-midi
Stravinsky Firebird Suite
Tchaikovsky Symphony No 5

Cardiff, 29 April 1951
RPO

Birmingham, 30 April 1951
RPO

Leicester, 1 May 1951
RPO

Hanley, 2 May 1951
RPO

Nottingham, 5 May 1951
RPO

Bradford, 6 May 1951
RPO
Berlioz Carnaval romain Overture
Ruggles Organum
Stravinsky Firebird Suite
Tchaikovsky Symphony No 5

Newcastle-upon-Tyne, 7 May 1951
RPO

Manchester, 8 May 1951
RPO

London, 16 May 1951
RPO
Wagner Tannhäuser Overture & Venusberg
Villa-Lobos Impressao Moura
Falla El amor brujo
Brahms Symphony No 4

Oxford, 17 May 1951
RPO

Southend, 20 May 1951
RPO

London, 27 May 1951
RPO
Berlioz Carnaval romain Overture
Debussy Prélude à l'après-midi
Prokofiev Scythian Suite
Riegger Symphony No 3
Bach Passacaglia & Fugue in C minor

London, 4 June 1951
RPO
Ruggles Organum
Schoenberg Chamber Symphony No 1
Wagner Tristan Prelude & Liebestod
Tchaikovsky Symphony No 5

London, 9 June 1951
BBC Symphony Orchestra
Bach Wachet auf
Beethoven Symphony No 7
Barber Adagio for strings
Stravinsky Le sacre du printemps

London, 10 June 1951
BBC Symphony Orchestra
Beethoven Symphony No 7
Barber Adagio for strings
Stravinsky Le sacre du printemps

Scheveningen, 27 June 1951
Residentie Orchestra
Bach Wachet auf
Beethoven Symphony No 7
Foss Recordare
Shostakovich Prelude in E flat
Tchaikovsky Romeo and Juliet

Amsterdam, 5 July 1951
Concertgebouw Orchestra
Berlioz Carnaval romain Overture
Debussy Prélude à l'après-midi
Falla El amor brujo
Barber Adagio for strings
Brahms Symphony No 2

Munich, 16 July 1951
Bavarian Radio SO
Ruggles Organum
Brahms Symphony No 2
Schoenberg Chamber Symphony No 1
Stravinsky Firebird Suite

Liverpool, 1 August 1951
RPO
Berlioz Carnaval romain Overture
Debussy Prélude à l'après-midi
Falla El amor brujo
Brahms Symphony No 4

Liverpool, 4 August 1951
RPO
Leighton Primavera romana
Schoenberg Chamber Symphony No 1
Wagner Tristan Prelude & Liebestod
Tchaikovsky Symphony No 5

Lucerne, 11 August 1951
Lucerne Festival Orchestra
Rimsky-Korsakov Russian Easter Overture
Mussorgsky Pictures from an exhibition
Tchaikovsky Symphony No 6

Salzburg, 22 August 1951
VPO
Shostakovich Prelude in E flat
Mussorgsky Pictures from an exhibition
Picha Stepancikovo Overture
Tchaikovsky Symphony No 5

Salzburg, 23 August 1951
VPO
Shostakovich Prelude in E flat
Mussorgsky Pictures from an exhibition
Stravinsky Pastorale
Tchaikovsky Symphony No 5

Lisbon, 20 October 1951
Lisbon Orchestra
Bach Passacaglia & Fugue in C minor
Beethoven Symphony No 7
Berlioz Carnaval romain Overture
Debussy Prélude à l'après-midi
Wagner Tristan Prelude & Liebestod

Pittsburgh, 23-25 November 1951
Pittsburgh SO
Handel Overture in D minor
Brahms Symphony No 2
Villa-Lobos Cello Fantasy
Wagner Tristan Prelude & Liebestod

Pittsburgh, 30 November-
2 December 1951
Pittsburgh SO
Stravinsky Firebird Suite
Carrillo Horizontes
Debussy Prélude à l'après-midi
Tchaikovsky Symphony No 6

Washington, 28 February 1951
National Symphony Orchestra
Purcell Suite
Vaughan Williams Symphony No 6
Falla El amor brujo
Debussy La cathédrale engloutie
Tchaikovsky Romeo and Juliet

Washington, 6-7 March 1951
National Symphony Orchestra
Wagner Rheingold Entry of the Gods
Wagner Meistersinger Suite
Liebermann Furioso
Riegger Symphony No 3
Wagner Parsifal Symphonic synthesis

Minneapolis, 12 February 1952
Minneapolis SO
Bach Passacaglia & Fugue in C minor
Brahms Symphony No 2
Carrillo Horizontes
Tchaikovsky Romeo and Juliet

Toronto, 19-20 February 1952
Toronto SO
Purcell Suite
Vivaldi Concerto grosso in D minor
Bach Passacaglia & Fugue in C minor
Rubbra Symphony No 5
Wagner Tristan Prelude & Liebestod

Washington, 11 March 1952
National Symphony Orchestra
Bach Passacaglia & Fugue in C minor
Brahms Symphony No 2
Carrillo Horizontes
Wagner Tristan Prelude & Liebestod

New York, 27 April 1952
CBS SO
Programme included
Goeb Symphony No 3
Haieff Piano Concerto

London, 21 May 1952
BBC Symphony Orchestra
BBC Chorus
Purcell Suite
Bach Ich ruf' zu dir
Bach Nun komm der Heiden Heiland
Vivaldi Concerto grosso in D minor
Debussy 3 Nocturnes
Rubbra Symphony No 5
Wagner Meistersinger Overture

Florence, 10 June 1952
Maggio musicale Orchestra

Florence, 17 June 1952
Maggio musicale Orchestra

Milan, 20 June 1952
La Scala Orchestra

Zürich, 24 June 1952
Tonhalle-Orchester

Milan, 1 July 1952
La Scala Orchestra

Hamburg, 7 July 1952
NWDR Orchestra
Berlioz Carnaval romain Overture
Falla El amor brujo
Raphael Jabonah
Tchaikovsky Symphony No 5

Düsseldorf, 8 July 1952
NWDR Orchestra
Programme as for 7 July

New York, 28 October 1952
His SO
Galjour
Ben Weber Blake Symphony
Programme included
Ben Weber Blake Symphony

Detroit, 20 November 1952
Detroit SO
Programme included
Avshalomov Taking of T'ung Kuan

Kansas City, 8 January 1953
Kansas City PO
Berlioz Carnaval romain Overture
Copland Lincoln Portrait
Falla El amor brujo
Brahms Symphony No 2

Kansas City, 10 January 1953
Kansas City PO
Bach Wir glauben all an einen Gott
Brahms Symphony No 2
Powell Weaver The Vagabond
Wagner Götterdämmerung Immolation

Buffalo, 18-20 January 1953
Buffalo PO
Bach Toccata and Fugue in D minor
Brahms Symphony No 2
Debussy 3 Nocturnes
Wagner Tristan Prelude & Liebestod

Houston, 27 January 1953
Houston SO
Berlioz Carnaval romain Overture
Debussy Prélude à l'après-midi
Falla El amor brujo
Elwell Ode for orchestra
Tchaikovsky Symphony No 4

New York, 22 February 1953
His SO
Hess
Programme included
Glanville-Hicks Letters from
    Morocco

The Pittsburgh Symphony Orchestra

LEOPOLD STOKOWSKI, Guest Conductor

Friday evening, February 12, 1954
Sunday afternoon, February 14, 1954

SYRIA MOSQUE

PROGRAM

Nussio ....Danze di Majorca*

Pizzetti ....Preludio a un Altro Giorno*

de Falla .... "El Amor Brujo"
(Complete Ballet—Orchestral Version)

1.	Introduccion y Escena	Introduction and Scene
2.	En la Cueva. La Noche	In the Gypsies' Cave. Night
3.	Cancion del Amor dolido	Song of unrequited Love
4.	El Aparecido	Apparition of the Lover
5.	Danza del Terror	Dance of Terror
6.	El Circulo Magico	The Magic Circle
7.	A Media Noche. Los Sortilegios	Midnight. Black Magic
8.	Danza Ritual del Fuego	Dance of Fire
9.	Escena	Scene
10.	Cancion del Fuego fatuo	Dance of Fireflies
11.	Pantomima	Pantomime
12.	Danza del Juego de Amor	Dance of Love-Play
13.	Las Campanas del Amanecer	The Bells of the Morning

INTERMISSION

Dvorak ....Symphony No. 5, in E minor ("From the New World")
Adagio; Allegro molto
Largo
Scherzo: Molto vivace
Allegro con fuoco

*First Performance in These Concerts

STEINWAY PIANO   CAPITOL RECORDS

**Sixty-ninth
Season of
Henry Wood
Promenade
Concerts**

**Tuesday 30 July
7.30 p.m.**

Passacaglia and Fugue in C minor...................*Bach*

Symphony No. 2 (Resurrection).......................*Mahler*

The Interval will be after the first movement of the Mahler

RAE WOODLAND (soprano)

JANET BAKER (contralto)

BBC CHORUS

BBC CHORAL SOCIETY

GOLDSMITHS' CHORAL UNION Conductor, Frederick Haggis

HARROW CHORAL SOCIETY
                              Hon. Conductor, Clarice Brooksbank

LONDON SYMPHONY ORCHESTRA Leader, Erich Gruenberg

LEOPOLD STOKOWSKI Conductor

Cleveland, 2-4 April 1953
Cleveland Orchestra
Bach Wachet auf
Bach Christ lag in Todesbanden
Bach Chorale from Easter Oratorio
Wagner Parsifal Good Friday Music
Rimsky-Korsakov Russian Easter Overture
Tchaikovsky Symphony No 5

Rome, 3-4 May 1953
Santa Cecilia Orchestra

Florence, 9-20 May 1953
Maggio musicale Orchestra

Lugano, 28 May 1953
Swiss Italian Radio Orchestra

Bergen, 8-9 June 1953
Bergen SO
Bach Wir glauben all an einen Gott
Bach Ich ruf' zu dir
Bach Nun komm der Heiden Heiland
Brahms Symphony No 2
Saeverud Song of Revolt
Valen Cemetery by the Sea
Tchaikovsky Romeo and Juliet

Helsinki, 17-18 June 1953
Helsinki City SO
Sibelius programme
Finlandia/Symphony No 1/Pelleas and
Melisande/Symphony No 7

New York, 16 October 1953
Stokowski SO and Chorus
Programme of Canadian music
Mercure Pantomine
Brott Violin Concerto
McPhee Tabuh-Tabuhan
Morel Antiphone
Ridout John Donne Songs
Willan Coronation Suite

New York, 24 December 1953
CBS Concert Orchestra & Choir
Farrell
CBS Christmas concert
Carols and orchestral pieces

Washington, 5-7 January 1954
National Symphony Orchestra
Blacher Orchestral Variations
Bondeville Ophélie
Herrmann Berceuse for the Fallen
Klami Karelian Rhapsody
Dvorak Symphony No 9

Minneapolis, 22 January 1954
Minneapolis SO
Saeverud Sons of Revolt
Hanson Pastorale
Klami Kalevela Suite
Bach Komm süsser Tod
Beethoven Symphony No 7

Saint Louis, 30-31 January 1954
Saint Louis SO
Beethoven Turkish March
Mozart Turkish March
Brahms Symphony No 2
Elwell Forever Young
Wagner Rheingold Entry of the Gods &
    Alberich's Curse
Wagner Tristan Liebestod

Pittsburgh, 12 February 1954
Pittsburgh SO
Nussio Danza da Majorca
Pizzetti Preludio a un altro giorno
Falla El amor brujo
Dvorak Symphony No 9

Pittsburgh, 13 February 1954
Pittsburgh SO and Chorus
Concert of Russian choral music

Pittsburgh, 14 February 1954
Pittsburgh SO
Programme as for 12 February

Toronto, 2-3 March 1954
Toronto SO
Mussorgsky Night on Bare Mountain
Tchaikovsky Symphony No 4
Morel Antiphone
Pelvincourt Pamir
Vaughan Williams Folk Song Suite

New York, 1 April 1954
Stokowski SO
Svendsen Carnival in Paris
Valen Cemetery by the Sea
Saeverud Ballad of Revaet
Grieg The Bell
Johansen Poetic Edda

London, 5 May 1954
BBC Symphony Orchestra
Hollweg
Arnold Beckus the Dandiprat Overture
Glière Concerto for coloratura
Beethoven Symphony No 5
Rawsthorne Symphonic Studies
Enesco Rumanian Rhapsody No 1

London, 7 May 1954
BBC Symphony Orchestra
TV concert introduced by Stokowski
Bach Toccata and Fugue in D minor
Bax Tintagel
Enesco Rumanian Rhapsody No 1
Purcell Suite

London, 9 May 1954
BBC Symphony Orchestra
Schuman Circus Overture
Vaughan Williams Dives and Lazarus
Bax Tintagel
Brahms Symphony No 2

Brussels, 14 May 1954
Belgian National Orchestra
Bach Toccata and Fugue in D minor
Beethoven Symphony No 7
Brahms Symphony No 2

Paris, 21 May 1954
Paris Opéra Orchestra
Brahms Symphony No 2
Wagner Tristan Prelude & Liebestod
Tchaikovsky Symphony No 4

Lugano, 27 May 1954
Swiss Italian Radio Orchestra
Leimer
Dvorak Symphony No 9
Leimer Piano Concerto
Tchaikovsky Capriccio italien

Baden-Baden, 6 June 1954
Südwestfunk Orchestra
Schuman Circus Overture
Milhaud Carnaval d'Aix
Copland Statements
Liebermann Furioso
Enesco Rumanian Rhapsody No 1
Blacher Paganini Variations
Falla 3 Dances from 3-Cornered Hat

Venice, 19 June 1954
La Fenice Orchestra and Chorus
Carturan, Tagliabue, Spina
Gabrieli Canzon del quarti toni a 15
Gabrieli In ecclesiis
Monteverdi Sonata sopra Sancta Maria
Vivaldi Beatus vir

Venice, 21 June 1954
La Fenice Orchestra
Vivaldi Concerto grosso in D minor
Beethoven Symphony No 7
Dvorak Symphony No 9

Venice, 22 June 1954
La Fenice Orchestra
Bach Toccata and Fugue in D minor
Brahms Symphony No 2
Dvorak Symphony No 9

Rome, 27 June 1954
Santa Cecilia Orchestra
Mussorgsky Night on Bare Mountain
Rimsky-Korsakov Scheherazade
Tchaikovsky Symphony No 4

Rome, 30 June 1954
Santa Cecilia Orchestra
Bach Toccata and Fugue in D minor
Beethoven Symphony No 7
Dvorak Symphony No 9

Florence, 8 July 1954
Orchestra and programme not known

New York, 26 October 1954
NYPSO
Graffman
Columbia University Bi-Centennial
Mason Chanticleer Overture
Luening Symphonic Fantasia No 1
MacDowell Piano Concerto No 2
Bartok Dance Suite
Moore Symphony No 2

Cleveland, 9-11 December 1954
Cleveland Orchestra
Purcell Suite
Vaughan Williams Symphony No 7
Debussy 3 Nocturnes
Wagner Tristan Prelude & Liebestod

Detroit, 17 February 1955
Detroit SO
Programme included
Hovhaness Vision from High Rock
Panufnik Symphony For Peace

Oklahoma City, 22 February 1955
Oklahoma SO
The Star-spangled Banner
Rimsky-Korsakov Dubinushka
Shostakovich Symphony No 10
Debussy Clair de lune
Wagner Tristan Prelude & Liebestod

Rome, 23-24 April 1955
Santa Cecilia Orchestra and Chorus
Bach Wachet auf
Bach Mein Jesu was für Seelenweh
Bach Wir glauben all an einen Gott
Beethoven Symphony No 9

Rome, 30 April 1955
RAI Roma Orchestra and Chorus
Tuccari, Falachi, Salvi, Pirino,
Oppicelli
Bach Ein' feste Burg
Bach Schafe können sicher weiden
Bach Ich ruf' zu dir
Bach Passacaglia & Fugue in C minor
Orff Carmina burana

Turin, 6 May 1955
RAI Torino Orchestra
Handel Overture in D minor
Beethoven Symphony No 5
Ibert Féerique
Gould Sinfonietta
Enesco Rumanian Rhapsody No 1

Turin, 8 May 1955
RAI Torino Orchestra
Dominguez
Handel Overture in D minor
Beethoven Symphony No 5
Falla El amor brujo
Wagner Meistersinger Overture

Baden-Baden, 15 May 1955
Südwestfunk Orchestra
Mussorgsky Khovanschina Entr'acte
Debussy Prélude à l'après-midi
Debussy 3 Nocturnes
Bach Toccata and Fugue in D minor

Stuttgart, 20 May 1955
SDR Orchestra
Mussorgsky Khovanschina Entr'acte
Debussy Prélude à l'après-midi
Bach Toccata and Fugue in D minor
Tchaikovsky Symphony No 5

Cologne, 25 May 1955
WDR Orchestra
Bach Ein' feste Burg
Bach Schafe können sicher weiden
Bach Wir glauben all an einen Gott
Brahms Symphony No 2
Hartmann Symphony No 2
Blacher Paganini Variations

Frankfurt, 31 May 1955
Orchestra of Hessischer Rundfunk
Messiaen Hymne pour orchestre
Krenek Cello Concerto
Stravinsky Mass
Hartmann Symphony No 2
Henze 4 poemi
Debussy Prélude à l'après-midi

Vienna, 5 June 1955
VPO
Bach Wachet auf
Bach Ich ruf' zu dir
Bach Wir glauben all an einen Gott
Mozart Symphony No 40
Brahms Symphony No 2

Vienna, 11 June 1955
VPO
Mussorgsky Khovanschina Entr'acte
Haager Chaconne
Wagner Tristan Prelude & Liebestod
Tchaikovsky Symphony No 5

Los Angeles, 30 August 1955
Hollywood Bowl SO
Wagner Chorale
Horne, Nixon, Robinson, Blankenburg
Prokofiev Romeo at Juliet's Tomb
Glière Symphony No 3
Orff Carmina burana

Santa Barbara, 10 September 1955
Pacific Coast Festival Orchestra
Handel Concerto grosso No 6
Bach Siciliano
Bach Mein Jesu was für Seelenweh
Bach Prelude in B minor
Bach Prelude (Partita in E)
Mozart Serenata notturna
Hovhaness Concerto No 5
Cowell Hymn and Fugue
Schoenberg Verklärte Nacht

Santa Barbara, 11 September 1955
Pacific Coast Festival Orchestra
Corelli Concerto grosso No 3
Cesti Tu mancavi
Vivaldi Concerto grosso No 11
Gluck Ballet Suite
Berger Malincolia
Bloch Concerto grosso No 2

Santa Barbara, 17 September 1955
Pacific Coast Festival Orchestra
Lawes 6-Part Fantasy and Air
Locke Suite No 1
Purcell King Arthur excerpts
Humphries Concerto in C minor
Rodrigo Sarabanda Lejane
Tchaikovsky Serenade for strings

Santa Barbara, 18 September 1955
Pacific Coast Festival Orchestra
Milhaud Concerto
Ives The Unanswered Question
Bartok Music for strings, percussion
  and celesta
Stravinsky Mass
Sibelius Berceuse (The Tempest)
Vaughan Williams Serenade to Music

Houston, 31 October 1955
Houston SO
Wagner Meistersinger Overture
Hovhaness Mysterious Mountain
Ravel Daphnis et Chloé, 2nd Suite
Brahms Symphony No 1

Houston, 8 November 1955
Houston SO
Berlioz Carnaval romain Overture
Charpentier Passacaglia (Medea)
Debussy Prélude à l'après-midi
Ives The Unanswered Question
Hartmann Dances (Esther)
Beethoven Symphony No 7

Houston, 14 November 1955
Houston SO
Bach Toccata and Fugue in D minor
Bach Suite No 2
Bach Passacaglia & Fugue in C minor
Cowell Symphony No 6
Tchaikovsky Romeo and Juliet

Houston, 22 November 1955
Houston SO
Firkusny
Smetana Bartered Bride Overture
Dvorak Symphony No 9
Hanson Piano Concerto
Wagner Tristan Prelude & Liebestod

Houston, 28 November 1955
Houston SO
Khachaturian Festive Poem
Shostakovich Symphony No 10
Riegger Dance Rhythms
Enesco Rumanian Rhapsody No 1

Houston, 6 December 1955
Houston SO
Houston Chorale
Sibelius programme
Finlandia/Swan of Tuonela/Berceuse
(The Tempest)/Hymn to the Earth /
Symphony No 2

Washington, 17-18 December 1955
National SO
Mozart programme
Ave verum corpus/Missa brevis K65,
excerpts/Kyrie K341/Flute and Harp
Concerto/Serenade No 10 for 13 wind

Houston, 23 January 1956
Houston SO
Schubert Rosamunde Overture
Mozart Symphony No 40
Bach Chaconne
Messiaen Reveil des oiseaux
Stravinsky Firebird Suite

Houston, 31 January 1956
Houston SO
Houston Chorale
Babikian, Brown, Thompson, Waggoner,
Gardner, Hartmann
Bach Wir glauben all an einen Gott
Beethoven Symphony No 1
Orff Carmina burana

Houston, 2 April 1956
Houston SO
Houston Chorale
Babikian, Lokey, Waggoner, Gardner
Mendelssohn Ruy Blas Overture
Schumann Symphony No 2
Orff Trionfo di Afrodite

Houston, 10 April 1956
Houston SO
Ravel L'éventail de Jeanne
Guarnieri Dansa negra
Espla Con Quijote velando las armas
Ravel Bolero
Holmes Fable
Tchaikovsky Symphony No 4

Madrid, 9 May 1956
Orquesta Sinfonica do Madrid
Iglesias
Rodrigo Homenaje a la tempranica
Espla El sueno de Eros
Del Campo Fantasia Castellana
Milhaud Botafago (Saudades do Brasil)
Tchaikovsky Symphony No 5
Gould Tango

Zagreb, 25 May 1956
Zagreb PO
Bach Ein' feste Burg
Bach Ich ruf' zu dir
Bach Wir glauben all an einen Gott
Brahms Symphony No 2
Ravel Bolero
Berce Sunny Fields
Wagner Tristan Prelude & Liebestod

Belgrade, 2 June 1956
Belgrade PO
Bach Ein' feste Burg
Bach Ich ruf' zu dir
Bach Wir glauben all an einen Gott
Konjovic Chestnut Wood (Kostana)
Ravel Bolero
Tchaikovsky Symphony No 5

Zürich, 26 June 1956
Tonhalle-Orchester
Leimer
Beethoven Leonore No 3 Overture
Mozart Symphony No 40
Leimer Left Hand Piano Concerto
Ravel Bolero

New York, 19 July 1956
Symphony of the Air
Orff Midsummer Night's Dream
Staged version of incidental music

New York, 4 October 1956
Symphony of the Air
Programme included
Heiden Memorial
Helps Adagio for orchestra
Hovhaness Symphony No 3
Kirchner Toccata
Martinu Piano Concerto No 4

New York, 14 October 1956
Symphony of the Air
Leimer
Programme included
Leimer Piano Concerto No 4

Houston, 30 October 1956
Houston SO
Handel Overture in D minor
Brahms Symphony No 2
Davies Solemn Melody
Rice Wind and Percussion Concerto
Wagner Tannhäuser Overture

Houston, 5 November 1956
Houston SO
Bach Ein' feste Burg
Bach Schafe können sicher weiden
Bach Ich ruf' zu dir
Bach Fugue in G minor
Mozart Symphony No 41
Tippett Ritual Dances
Tchaikovsky Swan Lake excerpts

Houston, 13 November 1956
Houston SO
Banke, Fliegel, Davies
Beethoven cycle
Symphony No 1/Triple Concerto/
Symphony No 2

Houston, 19 November 1956
Houston SO
Stokes
Beethoven cycle
Coriolan Overture/Piano Concerto No
4/Symphony No 3

Houston, 27 November 1956
Houston SO
Lack
Glière Symphony No 3
Prokofiev Violin Concerto No 2
Borodin Polovtsian Dances

Houston, 3 December 1956
Houston SO
Beethoven cycle
Leonore No 3 Overture/3 Equali/
Symphony No 4/Symphony No 5

Houston, 11 December 1956
Houston SO
Blackburn
Beethoven cycle
Egmont Incidental music/Symphony No 6

Houston, 17-19 December 1956
Houston SO
Houston Chorale
Likey, Townsend, Lloyd, Waggoner,
Dickinson, Maero, Sze
Hovhaness As on the Night
Berlioz L'enfance du Christ

New York, 20 January 1957
Symphony of the Air
Barenboim
Bach Passacaglia & Fugue in C minor
Mozart Symphony No 41
Prokofiev Piano Concerto No 1
Concert on 21 January included
Panufnik Sinfonia elegiaca

Houston, 4 March 1957
Houston SO
Francescatti
Beethoven cycle
Prometheus Overture/Violin Concerto/
Symphony No 7

Houston, 12 March 1957
Houston SO
Houston Chorale
Petzold, Porter, Messer, Bennick
Debussy La cathédrale engloutie
Franck Symphony in D minor
Hovhaness Ad Lyram
Respighi Pini di Roma

Houston, 18 March 1957
Houston SO
Weaver
Arnell Ceremonial and Flourish
Bender Oboe Soliloquy
Chavez Toccata
Wagner Lohengrin Prelude
Tchaikovsky Symphony No 5

Houston, 27 March 1957
Houston SO
Houston Chorale
Hinkle, Dinwoodey, Petrak, Froman
Beethoven cycle
Symphony No 8/Symphony No 9

Vienna, 8-9 May 1957
Vienna SO
Debussy Prélude à l'après-midi
Mozart Symphony No 41
Dvorak Symphony No 9

Berlin, 15-16 May 1957
BPO
Falla El amor brujo
Stravinsky Firebird Suite
Debussy Prélude à l'après-midi
Stravinsky Petrushka Suite

Vienna, 9 June 1957
Vienna SO/Leimer
Falla 3 Dances (3-Cornered Hat)
Debussy 3 Nocturnes
Leimer Piano Concerto No 4
Stravinsky Firebird Suite

London, 26 June 1957
LSO
Berlioz Carnaval romain Overture
Ravel Rapsodie espagnole
Debussy 3 Nocturnes
Prokofiev Scythian Suite
Stravinsky Firebird Suite

London, 30 June 1957
LSO
Schubert Rosamunde Overture
Vaughan Williams Symphony No 8
Schumann Symphony No 2

Houston, 28-29 October 1957
Houston SO
Bach Nun komm der Heiden Heiland
Bach Komm süsser Tod
Bach Mein Jesu was für Seelenweh
Bach Fugue in G minor
Sibelius Symphony No 7
Wagner Götterdämmerung Rhine Journey,
    Funeral March and Immolation

Houston, 4-5 November 1957
Houston SO
Pennario
Debussy Epigraphes antiques
Serebrier Symphony No 1
Rachmaninov Paganini Rhapsody
Mussorgsky Pictures at an exhibition

Houston, 11-12 November 1957
Houston SO
Aue
Orff Nänie und Dithyrambe
Vaughan Williams Symphony No 8
Krenek Cello Concerto
Panufnik Sinfonia elegaica

Houston, 18-19 November 1957
Houston SO
Schedrin Hump-backed Horse
Liadov Russian Folk Songs
Stravinsky Petrushka Suite
Tchaikovsky Symphony No 6

Chicago, 2-3 January 1958
Chicago SO
Bach 4 Transcriptions
Brahms Symphony No 2
Szabelski Toccata
Wagner Götterdämmerung Immolation

Milwaukee, 6 January 1958
Chicago SO
Programme as for 2-3 January

Chicago, 9-10 January 1958
Chicago SO
Shostakovich Prelude in E flat
Gliere Symphony No 3
Prokofiev Romeo & Juliet Suite
Tchaikovsky Swan Lake Suite

Houston, 17-18 March 1958
Houston SO
Milstein
Vivaldi Concerto grosso in D minor
Bach Violin Concerto in A minor
Haydn Symphony No 88
Mozart Adagio and Rondo
Barber Intermezzo from Vanessa
Wagner Tristan Liebesnacht

Houston, 24-25 March 1958
Houston SO
Revueltas Janitzio
Prokofiev Symphony No 5
Ravel Alborada del gracioso
Debussy Ibéria
Tchaikovsky Romeo and Juliet

Houston, 31 March-1 April 1958
Houston SO
2 Ancient Liturgical melodies
Mennin Symphony No 6
Rimsky-Korsakov Russian Easter Overture
Wagner Parsifal Prelude, Good Friday
    Music and Symphonic synthesis

Houston, 7-8 April 1958
Houston SO
Houston Chorale
Babikian, Waggoner, Gardner, Naron
Shostakovich Symphony No 11
Orff Carmina burana

Paris, 12 May 1958
Orchestre National
Bach Passacaglia & Fugue in C minor
Brahms Symphony No 1
Ibert Escales
Ravel Alborada del gracioso
Debussy Ibéria

New York, 25 September 1958
Stokowski SO
Orrigo-Salas Obertura festiva
Creston Toccata
Hovhaness Mysterious Mountain
Vaughan Williams Symphony No 9

Houston, 20-21 October 1958
Houston SO
Houston Chorale
Weber Euryanthe Overture
Beethoven Symphony No 7
Hovhaness Meditation on Orpheus
Wagner Tannhäuser Overture & Venusberg

Houston, 27-28 October 1958
Houston SO
Rimsky-Korsakov Overture on Russian
    themes
Mussorgsky Khovanschina Entr'acte
Rachmaninov Prelude in C sharp minor
Tchaikovsky Solitude
Prokofiev Romeo and Juliet excerpts
Khachaturian Symphony No 2

Houston, 3-4 November 1958
Houston SO
Houston Chorale
Bach Adagio
Handel Oboe Concerto
Schubert Symphony No 8
Debussy 3 Chansons for a capella
    chorus
Gastyne Atala
Ibert Escales

Houston, 10-11 November 1958
Houston SO
Creston Toccata
Vaughan Williams Symphony No 9
Tchaikovsky Overture, Entr'acte and
    Funeral March (Hamlet)
Strauss Tod und Verklärung

New York, 25 November 1958
Symphony of the Air & Chorus
Saygun Yunus Emre, oratorio

New York, 3 December 1958
Stokowski SO
Concert of contemorary works for the
Contemporary Music Society

New York, 12 December 1958
Stokowski SO
Del Monaco
Gabrieli Sonata pian e forte
Respighi Pini di Roma
Shostakovich Symphony No 11
Vocal items by Verdi and Wagner
**In 1958 Stokowski also toured the
USSR, conducting various Russian
orchestras: repertoire included
Prokofiev Symphony No 5, Shostakovich
Symphony No 11, Barber Adagio for
strings and Wagner Tristan Liebesnacht**

Houston, 16-17 March 1959
Houston SO
Bach O Haupt voll Blut und Wunden
Brahms Symphony No 3
Amirov Azerbaijan Mugams
Scriabin Poème de l'extase

Houston, 23-24 March 1959
Houston SO
Various choirs
Bernasconi
Gabrieli Benedictus
Frescobaldi Gagliarda
Menotti Piano Concerto
Wagner Parsifal Good Friday Music
    and Symphonic synthesis
Rimsky-Korsakov Russian Easter Overture

Houston, 30-31 March 1959
Houston SO
Senofsky
Muravlyev Legend of Azov Mountain
Khachaturian Violin Concerto
Tchaikovsky Symphony No 4

Houston, 6-7 April 1959
Houston SO
Houston Chorale
Schmoll, Townsend, Brydon, Wainner,
Treigle
Bach Mass in B minor

New York, 25 April 1959
Symphony of the Air
Childrens' concert
Bizet Carmen Prelude
Mozart German Dance No 3
Haydn Toy Symphony
Shostakovich Polka (Age of Gold)
Bender Childrens' Suite
Bach Fugue in G minor
Humperdinck Evening prayer (Hänsel
    und Gretel)

Leipzig, 31 May-1 June 1959
Leipzig Gewandhaus Orchestra
Leipzig Radio Chorus
Ravel Rapsodie espagnole
Debussy 3 Nocturnes
Shostakovich Symphony No 5

Berlin, 7-8 June 1959
BPO
Favre Choir
Ravel Rapsodie espagnole
Debussy 3 Nocturnes
Shostakovich Symphony No 5

London, 30 June 1959
LSO
Gabrieli Sonata pian e forte
Respighi Pini di Roma
Tchaikovsky Hamlet
Shostakovich Symphony No 5

New York, 25 July 1959
Symphony of the Air
Chorus and soloists
Bloch Cortège funèbre
Bach Passacaglia & Fugue in C minor
Brahms Symphony No 3
Stravinsky Oedipus Rex

New York, 30 July 1960
Stadium SO
Bach Wir glauben all an einen Gott
Bach Schafe können sicher weiden
Bach Fugue in G minor
Brahms Symphony No 2
Strauss Don Juan
Strauss Dance of the 7 veils

New York, 7 October 1959
New York City Opera
Orchestra, Chorus and soloists
Stravinsky Oedipus Rex
Orff Carmina burana
Further performances of this double
bill were probably given

Houston, 19-20 October 1959
Houston SO
Handel Water Music
Mozart Symphony No 25
Rachmaninov Symphonic Dances
Mussorgsky Pictures at an exhibition

Houston, 26-27 October 1959
Houston SO
Serkin
Brahms cycle
Academic Festival Overture/Piano
Concerto No 1/Symphony No 4

Houston, 2-3 November 1959
Houston SO
Gabrieli Sonata pian e forte
Villa-Lobos Modinha
Respighi Pini di Roma
Farberman Symphony
Cowell Orchestral Variations

Houston, 9-10 November 1959
Houston SO
Francescatti
Brahms cycle
Haydn Variations/Violin Concerto/
Symphony No 2

Philadelphia, 12-15 February 1960
Philadelphia Orchestra
Verrett
Mozart Nozze di Figaro Overture
Falla El amor brujo
Respighi Pini di Roma
Shostakovich Symphony No 5
Stokowski's return to Philadelphia

New York, 16 February 1960
Philadelphia Orchestra
Verrett
Programme as for 12-15 February

Philadelphia, 23 February 1960
Philadelphia Orchestra
Bach Nun komm der Heiden Heiland
Bach Ich ruf' zu dir
Bach Wir glauben all an einen Gott
Wagner Tristan Liebesnacht
Brahms Symphony No 1
Debussy Prélude à l'après-midi
Programme probably also repeated in
New York

New York, 3-6 March 1960
NYPO
Handel Water Music
Mozart Symphony No 40
Amirov Azerbaijan Mugams
Shostakovich Symphony No 1

Houston, 14-15 March 1960
Houston SO
Yardumyan Veni sancte spiritus
Beethoven Symphony No 6
Chopin Mazurka, Prelude and Waltz
Wagner Walküre Wotan's Farewell

Houston, 21-22 March 1960
Houston SO
Houston Chorale
Bible
Brahms cycle
Hungarian Dance No 1/Serenade No 1/
Alto Rhapsody/Symphony No 1

Houston, 28-29 March 1960
Houston SO
Newell
Canning Fantasia on Justin Morgan
Mozart Horn Concerto No 4
Cowell Symphony No 12
Bartok Concerto for orchestra

Also during 1960 performances of
Dallapiccola's Prigionero for New
York City Opera

Houston, 4-5 April 1960
Houston SO
Houston Chorale & University Choir
Endich, Ligeti
Brahms cycle
Ein deutsches Requiem

New York, 16 April 1960
Symphony of the Air
Keeshan
Childrens' concert
Programme included Prokofiev Peter
and the Wolf

London, 28 June 1960
LSO
Beethoven Egmont Overture
Brahms Symphony No 3
Bartok Concerto for orchestra

Houston, 17-18 October 1960
Houston SO
Bach Schafe können sicher weiden
Bach Aus tiefer Not
Bach Prelude (Partita in E)
Beethoven Symphony No 3
Blacher Orchestral Fantasy
Strauss Rosenkavalier Waltzes

Houston, 24-25 October 1960
Houston SO
Rachlin
Haydn Sinfonia concertante
Mozart Piano Concerto No 24
Kodaly Hary Janos Suite
Debussy Soirée dans Grenade
Ravel Rapsodie espagnole

Houston, 31 October-1 November 1960
Houston SO
Woolridge The Elizabethans
Britten Passacaglia (Peter Grimes)
Walton Partita
Tchaikovsky Symphony No 5

Houston, 7-8 November 1960
Houston SO
Stern
Bach Toccata and Fugue in D minor
Beethoven Violin Concerto
Shostakovich Symphony No 5

Chicago, 15-16 December 1960
Chicago SO
Frager
Smetana Bartered Bride Overture
Prokofiev Piano Concerto No 1
Kodaly Hary Janos Suite
Shostakovich Symphony No 5

New York, 24 February 1961
Metropolitan Opera Orchestra
and Chorus
Nilsson, Moffo, Corelli, Giaiotti
Puccini Turandot

New York, 4 March 1961
Metropolitan Opera Orchestra
and Chorus
Nilsson, Moffo, Corelli, Giaiotti
Puccini Turandot

Philadelphia, 7-10 March 1961
Philadelphia Orchestra
Temple University Choirs
Rankin, Zambrana, Petrack
Schoenberg Gurrelieder
Concert repeated in New York

New York, 9 March 1961
Metropolitan Opera Orchestra
and Chorus
Nilsson, Stratas, Corelli, Giaiotti
Puccini Turandot

New York, 13 March 1961
Metropolitan Opera Orchestra
and Chorus
Nilsson, Stratas, Corelli, Giaiotti
Puccini Turandot

Philadelphia, 21 March 1961
Metropolitan Opera Orchestra
and Chorus
Nilsson, L.Price, Corelli,
Wildermann

New York, 24 March 1961
Metropolitan Opera Orchestra
and Chorus
Nilsson, Amara, Corelli, Wildermann
Puccini Turandot

New York, 29 March 1961
Metropolitan Opera Orchestra
and Chorus
Nilsson, L.Price, Corelli/Gari,
Wildermann
Puccini Turandot

New York, 8 April 1961
Metropolitan Opera Orchestra
and Chorus
Nilsson, Albanese, Corelli, Giaiotti
Puccini Turandot

New York, 11 April 1961
Metropolitan Opera Orchestra
and Chorus
Nilsson, Moffo, Corelli, Giaiotti
Puccini Turandot

New York, 15 April 1961
Symphony of the Air
Childrens' concert

New York, 19 April 1961
Metropolitan Opera Orchestra
and Chorus
Nilsson, Amara, Corelli, Giaiotti
Puccini Turandot

Vienna, May 1961
LSO
Walton Symphony No 2
Strauss Tod und Verklärung
Shostakovich Symphony No 5

Berlin, 8 June 1961
BPO
Mozart Zauberflöte Overture
Handel Water Music Suite
Concert for Max-Planck-Gesellschaft

Berlin, 11-12 June 1961
BPO
Smetana Bartered Bride Overture
Tchaikovsky Romeo and Juliet
Kodaly Hary Janos Suite
Shostakovich Symphony No 1

London, 18 June 1961
Philharmonia Orchestra and Chorus
Giebel, Kuen, Cordes
Bach Toccata and Fugue in D minor
Stravinsky Firebird Suite
Orff Carmina burana

Edinburgh, 20 August 1961
LSO
Edinburgh Choral Union
Brouwenstijn, Rankin, McCracken,
Lanigan, Robinson, Lidell
Schoenberg Gurrelieder

Edinburgh, 22 August 1961
LSO
Gabrieli Sonata pian e forte
Tippett Concerto for double string
    orchestra
Liszt Mephisto Waltz
Shostakovich Symphony No 5

Milwaukee, 9 October 1961
Chicago SO
Bach Toccata & Fugue in D minor
Brahms Symphony No 4
Tcherepnin Georgiana Suite
Rimsky-Korsakov Capriccio espagnol

Chicago, 12–13 October 1961
Chicago SO
Programme as for 9 October

New York, 4 November 1961
**Metropolitan Opera Orchestra
and Chorus
Nilsson, Amara, Tucker, Flagello**
Puccini Turandot

New York, 7 November 1961
**Metropolitan Opera Orchestra
and Chorus
Nilsson, Amara, Tucker, Flagello**
Puccini Turandot

Chicago, 4–5 January 1962
**Chicago SO
Janis**
Mussorgsky Night on Bare Mountain
Tchaikovsky Piano Concerto No 1
Wagner Götterdämmerung excerpts

Chicago, 11–12 January 1962
Chicago SO
Mozart Nozze di Figaro Overture
Beethoven Symphony No 3
Khrennikov Much Ado About Nothing
Tchaikovsky Romeo and Juliet

Philadelphia, 20 January 1962
**Philadelphia Orchestra
Nilsson, London**
Wagner Rienzi Overture
Wagner Lohengrin Prelude
Vocal items by Mozart, Gounod, Verdi,
   Borodin and Wagner
Programme also included Haydn's Toy
Symphony conducted by Harpo Marx

Philadelphia, 6 February 1962
Philadelphia Orchestra
Gabrieli Sonata pian e forte
Bach Es ist vollbracht
Bach Ich ruf' zu dir
Bach Wir glauben all an einen Gott
Frescobaldi Gagliarda
Chopin Mazurka in A minor
Tchaikovsky Romeo and Juliet
Eichheim Japanese Nocturne
Rimsky-Korsakov Scheherazade

New York, 1–4 March 1962
NYPO
Kurka Julius Caesar
Vaughan Williams Tallis Fantasia
Wagner Parsifal Symphonic synthesis
Shostakovich Symphony No 5

Philadelphia, 16 March 1962
Philadelphia Orchestra
Webern Passacaglia
Sibelius Symphony No 4
Debussy Soirée dans Grenade
Mussorgsky Pictures at an exhibition

New York, 20 March 1962
Philadelphia Orchestra
Programme as for 16 March

Athens, August 1962
Greek State Orchestra

Rome, August 1962
Santa Cecilia Orchestra

Chicago, 4–5 October 1962
Chicago SO
Bach Ein' feste Burg ist unser Gott
Beethoven Symphony No 2
Shostakovich Prelude in E flat
Gliere Symphony No 3

Chicago, 6 October 1962
Chicago SO
Berlioz Carnaval romain Overture
Tchaikovsky Symphony No 4
Ravel Alborada del gracioso
Gliere Symphony No 3

New York, 15 October 1962
**American SO
Starr**
Gabrieli Sonata pian e forte
Bach Toccata and Fugue in D minor
Beethoven Piano Concerto No 1
Shostakovich Symphony No 6

New York, 30 October 1962
American SO Chamber Ensemble
Concert of contemporary works for the
Contemporary Music Society

New York, 5 November 1962
American SO
Cowell Symphony No 15
Tchaikovsky Francesca da Rimini
Wagner Tristan Prelude & Liebestod
Hindemith Mathis der Maler Symphony

New York, 3 December 1962
American SO
Albeniz Fête-Dieu à Seville
Brahms Symphony No 2
Debussy Epigraphes antiques
Martin Petite symphonie concertante

Philadelphia, 17 December 1962
Philadelphia Orchestra
Wagner Lohengrin Act 3 Prelude
Beethoven Symphony No 5
Revueltas Sensamaya
Ravel Alborada del gracioso
Stravinsky Petrushka Suite
Clarke Trumpet Voluntary
Could Guaracho
Rachmaninov Prelude in C sharp minor
Haydn Finale (Symphony No 45)

Philadelphia, 19 January 1963
Philadelphia Orchestra
Sutherland, Starr, Corelli
Verdi Forza del destino Overture
Rachmaninov Paganini Rhapsody
Strauss Dance of 7 veils (Salome)
Enesco Rumanian Rhapsody No 1
Vocal items by Giordano, Puccini
    and Donizetti

Philadelphia, 8 February 1963
Philadelphia Orchestra
Beethoven Leonore No 3 Overture
Brahms Symphony No 1
Ippolitov-Ivanov Caucasian Sketches
Wagner Tannhäuser Overture

New York, 25 February 1963
American SO
Mozart Nozze di Figaro Overture
Ginastera Variaciones concertantes
Poulenc Concert champêtre
Beethoven Symphony No 3

New York, 4 March 1963
American SO
Davrath, Ashkenasi
Elgar Violin Concerto, 1st movement
Ben Haim Invocation
Tchaikovsky Tatiana's Letter scene
    (Evgeny Onegin)
Stravinsky Petrushka Suite

New York, 11 March 1963
American SO
Schola cantorum
Sills, Parker, Petrak, Boucher,
Wiederanders
Bach Saint Matthew Passion

New York, 28 March 1963
American SO
Laredo, Harrell
Schuman American Festival Overture
Boccherini Cello Concerto
Hovhaness Symphony No 15
Mendelssohn Piano Concerto No 1
Stravinsky Petrushka Suite

New York, 15 April 1963
American SO
Bach Christ lag in Todesbanden
Wagner Parsifal Symphonic synthesis
Creston Lydian Ode
Rimsky-Korsakov Russian Easter Overture.
Brahms Symphony No 4

Allentown Pennsylvania, 30 April 1963
Philadelphia Orchestra
Beethoven Leonore No 3 Overture
Brahms Symphony No 1
Mussorgsky Pictures at an exhibition

Bowling Green State University,
7 May 1963
Philadelphia Orchestra
Programme as for 30 April

Robin Hood Dell, 21 June 1963
Philadelphia Orchestra
Dukas La péri
Debussy Prélude à l'après-midi
Kodaly Hary Janos Suite
Tchaikovsky Symphony No 5

Tokyo, 8 July 1965
Japan Philharmonic SO
Bach Passacaglia & Fugue in C minor
Ives The Unanswered Question
Shibata Sinfonia
Tchaikovsky Symphony No 4

Tokyo, 13 July 1965
Japan Philharmonic SO
Eto
Bach Toccata and Fugue in D minor
Beethoven Symphony No 5
Cowell Koto Concerto
Stravinsky Petrushka

London, 17 July 1963
LSO
LSO Chorus
Addison Carte blanche Suite
Vaughan Williams Tallis Fantasia
Holst The Planets

London, 23 July 1963
BBC Symphony Orchestra
Gabrieli Sonata pian e forte
Britten Young Person's Guide
Beethoven Symphony No 7
Mussorgsky Pictures at an exhibition

London, 30 July 1963
LSO
Various choirs
Woodland, Baker
Bach Passacaglia & Fugue in C minor
Mahler Symphony No 2

New York, 7 October 1963
American SO
Bach Ein' feste Burg
Bach Ich ruf' zu dir
Bach Wir glauben all an einen Gott
Beethoven Symphony No 7
Serebrier Poema elegiaca
  (American SO commission)
Villa-Lobos Modinha
Stravinsky Firebird Suite

Red Banks NJ, 9 October 1963
American SO
Programme as for 7 October

New York, 21 October 1963
American SO
Kay New Horizons
Wagner Meistersinger Act 3 Prelude
Mahler Adagio (Symphony No 10)
Handel/Beecham Amaryllis Suite
Vivaldi Concerto grosso in D minor
Bach Passacaglia & Fugue in D minor
This concert had previously been
performed on 19 October at another
location

New York, 11 November 1963
American SO
Rigai
Schubert Rosamunde excerpts
Mozart Sinfonia concertante K297b
Ben-Haim Piano Concerto
Kodaly Hary Janos Suite

New York, 25 November 1963
American SO
Madeira
Wagner Lohengrin Prelude
Bartok 2 Images
Falla El amor brujo
Shostakovich Symphony No 5
Wagner Götterdämmerung Funeral March

A concert at Adelphi College with
American SO also took place during
1963, in which Stokowski accompanied
Lauritz Melchior in works by Grieg
and Wagner

New York, 10 December 1963
Philadelphia Orchestra
Bach Wachet auf
Beethoven Symphony No 3
Wagner Götterdämmerung excerpts

Philadelphia, 13 December 1963
Philadelphia Orchestra
Programme as for 10 December

Washington, 25 January 1964
American SO
Britten Passacaglia (Peter Grimes)
Sibelius Symphony No 2
Wagner Walküre Ride of the Valkyries
Bass Song of Hope
Strauss Tod und Verklärung

New York, 27 January 1964
American SO
Programme as for 25 January

Flushing NJ, 9 February 1964
American SO
Programme included
Sibelius Symphony No 2

New York, 24 February 1964
American SO
Rutgers University Choir
Rankin
Gabrieli Canzon quarti toni a 15
Bach Es ist vollbracht
Haydn Symphony No 88
Mozart Adagio and Fugue in C minor
Prokofiev Alexander Nevsky

Boston, 6-10 March 1964
Boston
Gabrieli Canzon quarti toni a 15
Vivaldi Concerto grosso in D minor
Mozart Sinfonia concertante K297b
Hovhaness Prelude & Quadruple Fugue
Rorem Eagles
Stravinsky Petrushka Suite

New York, 6 April 1964
American SO
Brearley School Chorus
Laredo
Dukas La péri
Debussy 3 Nocturnes
Barber Violin Concerto
Tchaikovsky Symphony No 4

New York, 20 April 1964
American SO
Beethoven Egmont Overture
Martin Petite symphonie concertante
Wagner Siegfried Idyll
Brahms Symphony No 1

New York, 22 April 1964
American SO and Chorus
Mozart Regina coeli K276
Wagner Siegfried Idyll
Brahms Schicksalslied
Brahms Symphony No 1

Berkshire, 21 August 1964
Boston SO
Mozart Sinfonia concertante K297b
Strauss Tod und Verklärung
Hovhaness Prelude & Quadruple Fugue
Rorem Eagles
Stravinsky Petrushka Suite

London, 15 September 1964
BBC Symphony Orchestra
Lane
Vaughan Williams Symphony No 8
Falla El amor brujo
Sibelius Symphony No 2

London, 17 September 1964
LSO
Mussorgsky Night on Bare Mountain
Novacek Perpetuum mobile
Tchaikovsky Francesca da Rimini
Shostakovich Symphony No 5
Vaughan Williams Greensleeves

New York, 5 October 1964
American SO
Handel Concerto grosso in D minor
Brahms Symphony No 3
Hovhaness Mountain Bell
Varèse Ionisation
Ravel Daphnis et Chloé, 2nd Suite

New York, 21 October 1964
London Symphony Orchestra
Serkin
Pierre Monteux Memorial concert
Beethoven Choral Fantasy
Shostakovich Symphony No 5

New York, 9 November 1964
American SO
Bach Wachet auf
Bach Schafe können sicher weiden
Schuman Symphony No 7
Satie Gymnopédies
Bartok Concerto for orchestra

New York, 22-23 November 1964
American SO
Iturbi
Beethoven Prometheus Overture
Mozart Piano Concerto No 20
Debussy Fantasy for piano & orchestra
Elgar Enigma Variations

New York, 7 December 1964
American SO and Chorus
Corelli Concerto da chiesa
Mennin Symphony No 3
Holst The Planets

London, 22 December 1964
LSO
Mussorgsky Night on Bare Mountain
Novacek Perpetuum mobile
Rimsky-Korsakov Scheherazade
Broadcast concert introduced by
Stokowski

Philadelphia, 28 December 1964
Philadelphia Orchestra
Smetana Sarka (Ma Vlast)
Sibelius Symphony No 2
Cowell Koto Concerto
Wagner Meistersinger Suite

New York, 29 December 1964
Philadelphia Orchestra
Programme as for 28 December

Baltimore, 6 January 1965
Philadelphia Orchestra
Programme as for 28 December

New York, 18 January 1965
American SO
Glinka Kamarinskaya
Tchaikovsky Serenade for strings
Shostakovich Symphony No 10

New York, 1 February 1965
American SO
Brahms Serenade No 1
Schubert Symphony No 8
Stravinsky Le sacre du printemps

Philadelphia, 4 February 1965
Philadelphia Orchestra
Gabrieli Sonata pian e forte
Vivaldi Concert grosso in D minor
Mozart Sinfonia concertante K297b
Shostakovich Symphony No 5

Boston, 12-13 March 1965
Boston SO
Bach Passacaglia & Fugue in C minor
Schubert Symphony No 8
Gluck Dance of the Blessed Spirits
Shostakovich Symphony No 5

New York, 4-5 April 1965
American SO
Westminster Choir
Boatwright, Allen
Creston Corinthians XIII
Mahler Symphony No 2

New York, 10 April 1965
American SO
Concert in Brooklyn College
Programme as for 4-5 April

New York, 26 April 1965
American SO
Schola cantorum
Serebrier, Katz
Wagner Holländer Overture
Sibelius Swan of Tuonela
Ives Symphony No 4
Beethoven Symphony No 5

Robin Hood Dell, 21 June 1965
Philadelphia Orchestra
Bonazzi
Wagner Holländer Overture
Enesco Rumanian Rhapsody No 1
Persichetti Hollow Man
Shostakovich Scherzo (Symphony No 10)
Prokofiev Alexander Nevsky

Berkshire, 15 August 1965
Boston SO
Bach Passacaglia & Fugue in C minor
Schubert Symphony No 8
Shostakovich Symphony No 5

London, 13 September 1965
New Philharmonia Orchestra
Beethoven Egmont Overture
Debussy La cathédrale engloutie
Tchaikovsky Sleeping Beauty Suite
Nielsen Symphony No 6

London, September 1965
New Philharmonia Orchestra
Tchaikovsky Swan Lake Suite
Mussorgsky Pictures at an exhibition
TV concert

New York, 4 October 1965
American SO
Star-Spangled Banner
Copland Orchestral Variations
Thomson The Seine at Night
Gershwin Porgy and Bess Suite
Brahms Symphony No 4

New York, 25 October 1965
American SO
Weber Oberon Overture
Beethoven Symphony No 2
Rimsky-Korsakov Capriccio espagnol
Mussorgsky Pictures at an exhibition

New York, 7-8 November 1965
American SO
Lowenthal
Gluck Ballet Suite
Mozart Symphony No 40
Bartok Piano Concerto No 1
Wagner Parsifal Symphonic synthesis

New York, 23 November 1965
Philadelphia Orchestra
Mozart Don Giovanni Overture
Beethoven Symphony No 7
Prokofiev Stone Flower excerpt
Stravinsky Firebird Suite

New York, 19-20 December 1965
American SO
Schola cantorum
Bach Christmas Oratorio excerpts
Purcell Trumpet Prelude
Barber Die natale
Honegger Symphony No 3

New York, 9-10 January 1966
American SO
Senofsky
Beethoven Symphony No 6
Prokofiev Violin Concerto No 2
Stravinsky Petrushka Suite

New York, 24 January 1966
American SO
Telemann Overture in G minor
Webern 6 Pieces
Strauss Dance of 7 veils (Salome)
Tchaikovsky Symphony No 6

Chicago, 24-25 March 1966
Chicago SO
Bach Passacaglia & Fugue in C minor
Beethoven Symphony No 8
Shostakovich Symphony No 10

New York, 16 April 1966
**Metropolitan Opera Orchestra
and Chorus**
Wagner Tannhäuser Entry of the Guests
Opening item in a farewell gala
performance in the old Metropolitan
Opera House

New York, 18 April 1966
American SO
Piston Concerto for orchestra
Schumann Symphony No 2
Ravel Pavane pour une infante défunte
Debussy Prélude à l'après-midi
Wagner Tristan Prelude & Liebestod

New York, 8-9 May 1966
American SO
Dessoff Choir
Mendelssohn Ruy Blas Overture
Haydn Symphony No 31
Orff Carmina burana

London, June 1966
New Philharmonia Orchestra
Vivaldi Le 4 stagioni
Radio broadcast

London, 10 September 1966
New Philharmonia Orchestra
Rosen
Rimsky-Korsakov Russian Easter Overture
Liszt Piano Concerto No 1
Ravel Daphnis et Chloé, 2nd Suite
Tchaikovsky Symphony No 5
Mussorgsky Khovanschina Entr'acte

New York, 10 October 1966
American SO
Diamond Tempest Overture
Beethoven Symphony No 4
Wagner Götterdämmerung excerpts

Philadelphia, 14 October 1966
Philadelphia Orchestra
Diamond Tempest Overture
Beethoven Symphony No 7
Mussorgsky Khovanschina Entr'acte
Stravinsky Petrushka Suite

New York, 23-24 October 1966
American SO
Puyana
Bach Brandenburg Concerto No 4
Haydn Harpsichord Concerto
Martin Harpsichord Concerto
Honegger Symphony No 3

New York, 20-21 November 1966
American SO
Watts
Hovhaness Mysterious Mountain
MacDowell Piano Concerto No 2
Brahms Symphony No 1

New York, 10 December 1966
American SO
Zaremba
Polish Academic Hymn
Chopin Piano Concerto No 2
Panufnik Sinfonia sacra
Polish Commemoration concert

New York, 18-19 December 1966
American SO
Schola cantorum
Ives Robert Browning Overture
Cowell Thanksgiving Psalm
Respighi Adoration of the Magi
Borodin Prince Igor excerpts
Rachmaninov 3 Russian songs
Mussorgsky Boris Godunov excerpts
Russian Christmas music

Bucharest, 19 January 1967
Bucharest SO
Bach Toccata and Fugue in D minor
Beethoven Symphony No 7
Mussorgsky Khovanschina Entr'acte
Stravinsky Petrushka Suite

Budapest, 2 February 1967
Hungarian State SO
Programme as for 19 January

Budapest, February 1967
Hungarian State SO
Kodaly Hary Janos Suite
Radio broadcast in presence of
composer

New York, 26-27 February 1967
American SO
Silverstein
Mennin Canto
Brahms Violin Concerto
Prokofiev Symphony No 5

New York, 3 April 1967
American SO
Godoy
Villa-Lobos Bachianas Brasilieras
    Nos 1 & 5
Ibert Escales
Ravel Scheherazade
Bernstein Jeremiah Symphony

New York, 7-8 May 1967
American SO
Wagner Rienzi Overture
Tchaikovsky Swan Lake excerpts
Enesco Rumanian Rhapsody No 1
Dvorak Symphony No 9

New York, 21-22 May 1967
American SO
Westminster Choir
Kusmin, Stanford, Kolk, Hayes
Gabrieli In ecclesiis
Lynn Gettysburg Address
Beethoven Symphony No 9

Paris, 3-5 June 1967
Premier Prix Orchestra
Beethoven Egmont Overture
Brahms Symphony No 1
Ravel Rapsodie espagnole
Shostakovich Symphony No 1

London, 15 June 1967
LSO
Lindholm
Mussorgsky Night on Bare Mountain
Tchaikovsky Marche slave
Stravinsky Firebird Suite
Wagner Götterdämmerung Rhine Journey,
    Funeral March and Immolation

Monte Carlo, 26 July 1967
Monte Carlo Opera Orchestra
Bach Toccata and Fugue in D minor
Beethoven Symphony No 5
Rimsky-Korsakov Scheherazade

Copenhagen, 4 August 1967
Danish Radio Orchestra
Nielsen Symphony No 2
Tchaikovsky Romeo and Juliet
Mussorgsky Khovanschina Entr'acte
Stravinsky Petrushka Suite

Stockholm, 9 August 1967
Stockholm Radio Orchestra
Bach Toccata and Fugue in D minor
Beethoven Symphony No 7
Mussorgsky Khovanschina Entr'acte
Stravinsky Petrushka Suite

Oslo, 18 August 1967
Oslo Radio Orchestra
Programme as for 9 August

London, 19 September 1967
LSO
LSO Chorus
Harper, Watts, Young, McIntyre
Meistersinger Overture and Suite
Beethoven Symphony No 9

Croydon, 23 September 1967
LSO
LSO Chorus
Harper, Watts, Young, McIntyre
Programme as for 19 September

New York, 16-17 October 1967
American SO
Various choirs
Buckingham
Ives 4 Pieces
Boito Mefistofele Prologue
Brahms Symphony No 2

New York, 7 November 1967
Philadelphia Orchestra
Singing City Choirs
Tyler, Godoy
Bach Magnificat excerpts
Mahler Symphony No 2

New York, 19-20 November 1967
American SO
Falla 3 Dances (3-Cornered Hat)
Ravel Rapsodie espagnole
Debussy Ibéria
Glière Symphony No 3

New York, 3-4 December 1967
American SO
Shapiro
Ruggles Sun Treader
Bloch Schelomo
Tchaikovsky Symphony No 5

New York, 17-18 December 1967
American SO
Camerata Singers
Gossec Nativity excerpts
Handel Pastoral Symphony (Messiah)
Verdi Te Deum
Schoenberg Friede auf Erden
Ives Symphony No 4

Providence, 11 January 1968
Boston SO
Mozart Don Giovanni Overture
Beethoven Symphony No 7
Tchaikovsky Hamlet
Mussorgsky Boris Godunov excerpts

Boston, 12-13 January 1968
Boston SO
Programme as for 11 January

Philadelphia, 30 January 1968
Boston SO
Programme as for 11 January

New York, 3 February 1968
American SO
Lowenthal
Bach Fugue in G minor
Beethoven Leonore No 3 Overture
Barber Adagio for strings
Schubert Symphony No 8
Rachmaninov Paganini Rhapsody
Ravel Bolero
Opening concert in Madison Square
Gardens new building

Chicago, 15-16 February 1968
Chicago SO
Shostakovich Age of Gold Suite
Shostakovich Symphony No 6
Khachaturian Symphony No 3

New York, 11-15 April 1968
NYPO
Rimsky-Korsakov Russian Easter Overture
Shostakovich Symphony No 6
Thomson Shipwreck and Love Scene
Wagner Parsifal Symphonic synthesis

New York, 28-29 April 1968
American SO
Entremont
Stringfield Mountain Song
Bernstein Symphony No 2
Beethoven Symphony No 3

New York, 5-6 May 1968
American SO
Bach Wachet auf
Bach Mein Jesu was für Seelenweh
Bach Prelude in B minor
Beethoven Symphony No 5
Wagner Tristan Symphonic synthesis

New York, 9 May 1968
American SO and Chorus
In memoriam Zoltan Kodaly
Kodaly Te Deum

New York, 19-20 May 1968
American SO
Dessoff Choirs
Bach Suite No 2
Martin Les 4 eléments
Prokofiev Alexander Nevsky

London, 18 June 1968
New Philharmonia Orchestra
Wagner Rienzi Overture
Scriabin Poème de l'extase
Berlioz Symphonie fantastique

Montreux, 11 September 1968
Suisse Romande Orchestra
Beethoven Egmont Overture
Schumann Symphony No 4
Tchaikovsky Romeo and Juliet
Mussorgsky Boris Godunov Symphonic
    synthesis

New York, 7-13 October 1968
American SO
Riegger Passacaglia and Fugue
Barber Mutations from Bach
Surinach Melorhythmic Dramas
Brahms Symphony No 1

Sunday 15 June 1969 at 7.30 p m

Royal Philharmonic Orchestra

Leader: Neville Taweel

Musorgsky	A Night on the Bare Mountain
Glinka	Kamarinskaya
Shostakovich	Prelude in E flat minor
Stravinsky	Pastorale.
Tchaikovsky	Overture '1812'

INTERVAL

Scryabin	Poem of Ecstasy
Lyadov	Russian Folksongs
Borodin	Polovtsian Dances

Conductor

Leopold Stokowski

John Alldis Chorus
(Conductor: John Alldis)

Welsh National Opera Chorale
(Conductor: James Lockhart)

Band of the Grenadier Guards
(By permission of Colonel A. N. Breitmeyer, Lieutenant Colonel Commanding the Regiment

LEOPOLD STOKOWSKI

WAGNER

Overture, Rienzi

SKRYABIN

Le Poème de l'Extase

BERLIOZ

Symphonie Fantastique

New Philharmonia Orchestra
Leader Carlos Villa

ROYAL FESTIVAL HALL
General Manager John Denison CBE
Tuesday 18 June 1968 at 8
Programme Two Shillings

New York, 27-28 October 1968
American SO
Beethoven Egmont Overture
Weigl Symphony No 5
Tchaikovsky Romeo and Juliet
Wagner Siegfried Idyll

New York, 17-18 November 1968
American SO
Diaz
Panufnik Epitaph for the Victims of
    Katyn
Ginastera Ollantay
Villa-Lobos Guitar Concerto
Rodrigo Adagio & Allegro (Guitar
    Concerto)
Debussy 3 Nocturnes

New York, 22-23 December 1968
American SO
Mendelssohn A Midsummer Night's
    Dream Overture
Josten Concerto sacro No 1
Hovhaness Praise the Lord
    (American SO commission)
Shostakovich Symphony No 1

Baltimore, 29-30 January 1969
Baltimore SO
Bach Ein' feste Burg
Beethoven Symphony No 7
Tchaikovsky Romeo and Juliet
Stravinsky Petrushka Suite

New York, 8 February 1969
NYPO
Bach Fugue in G minor
Stokowski's final appearance with the
New York Philharmonic, in the course
of a Young Peoples' concert conducted
by Bernstein

Philadelphia, 13 February 1969
Philadelphia Orchestra
Palestrina Adoramus te
Victoria Jesus dulcis memoria
Bach Chaconne in D minor
Mussorgsky Boris Godunov Symphonic
    synthesis
Stravinsky Petrushka Suite
Wagner Tristan Prelude & Liebestod
Haydn Andante cantabile
Stokowski's final appearance with
the Philadelphia Orchestra

New York, 9-10 March 1969
American SO
Wild
Gershwin/Kostelanetz Promenade
Copland Music for a Great City
Liszt Hungarian Fantasia
Tchaikovsky Hamlet
Mussorgsky Boris Godunov Symphonic
    synthesis

New York, 23-24 March 1969
American SO
Kim
Bach Passacaglia & Fugue in C minor
Mozart Symphony No 40
Beethoven 3 Equali
Vieuxtemps Violin Concerto No 4
Gutche Genghis Khan
Haydn Andante cantabile

New York, 4-5 May 1969
American SO
Bach Prelude (Partita in E)
Beethoven Symphony No 7
Ravel Bolero
Ives The Unanswered Question
Mussorgsky Pictures at an exhibition

New York, 18-19 May 1969
American SO
Westminster Choir
Labunski Canto di aspirazione
Bartok Miraculous Mandarin Suite
Orff Carmina burana

London, 15 June 1969
RPO
RPO Chorus
Mussorgsky Night on Bare Mountain
Glinka Kamarinskaya
Shostakovich Prelude in E flat minor
Stravinsky Pastorale
Tchaikovsky 1812 Overture
Scriabin Poème de l'extase
Liadov Russian folksongs
Borodin Polovtsian Dances

Paris, 26 June 1969
Orchestre de Paris
Janis
Beethoven Coriolan Overture
Brahms Piano Concerto No 1
Tchaikovsky Romeo and Juliet
Stravinsky Petrushka Suite

St Moritz, 30 August 1969
International Festival Youth
Orchestra
Di Carli
Bach Passacaglia & Fugue in C minor
Beethoven Symphony No 7
Mozart Piano Concerto No 20
Tchaikovsky Romeo and Juliet

Croydon, 8 September 1969
LPO
Mozart Serenata notturna
Beethoven Symphony No 5
Schubert Symphony No 8
Wagner Tristan Prelude & Liebestod

New York, 6-12 October 1969
American SO
Hines
Rimsky-Korsakov Dubinushka
Mussorgsky Boris Godunov excerpts
Gottschalk Symphony No 2
Barber Adagio for strings
Liszt Hungarian Rhapsody No 2

New York, 26-27 October 1969
American SO
Ogdon
Beethoven Coriolan Overture
Brahms Piano Concerto No 1
Tchaikovsky Francesca da Rimini
Rimsky-Korsakov Capriccio espagnol

Baltimore, 12 November 1969
Baltimore SO
Virizlay
Bach Passacaglia & Fugue in C minor
Beethoven Symphony No 2
Bloch Schelomo
Wagner Tristan Prelude & Liebestod

New York, 23-24 November 1969
American SO
Read
Telemann Overture in D
Bach Concerto in D minor
Handel Water Music
Rieti Harpsichord Concerto
Respighi Pini di Roma

New York, 7-8 December 1969
American SO
Lindholm
Wagner programme
Lohengrin Prelude/Wesendonk-Lieder/
Siegfried Forest murmurs/Tristan
Liebestod/Götterdämmerung Rhine
Journey, Funeral March & Immolation

New York, 14-15 December 1969
American SO
Gutman
Stravinsky Mass
Eichheim Japanese Nocturne
Bloch Schelomo
Borodin Polovtsian Dances
Prokofiev Cello Concertino
Rimsky-Korsakov Polonaise (Christmas
Eve)

New York, 18-19 January 1970
American SO
Rampal
Haydn Symphony No 60
Mozart Andante & Rondo (Flute Cto.)
Khachaturian Flute Concerto
Rimsky-Korsakov Coq d'Or Suite
Stravinsky Pastorale

Syracuse, 4-6 March 1970
Syracuse SO
Miller
Bach Fugue in G minor
Beethoven Symphony No 5
Tchaikovsky Romeo and Juliet
Rimsky-Korsakov Russian Easter Ov.
(vocal version)

New York, 13 March 1970
Juilliard Orchestra
Bach Toccata and Fugue in D minor
Schumann Symphony No 2
Schimmel Portrait No 1
Rimsky-Korsakov Capriccio espagnol

Atlanta, 2-4 April 1970
Atlanta SO
Bach Ein' feste Burg
Beethoven Symphony No 5
Hovhaness Mysterious Mountain
Stravinsky Petrushka Suite

New York, 15 April 1970
American SO
Sills, Serkin
Beethoven Leonore No 3 Overture
Bach Toccata and Fugue in D minor
Beethoven Piano Concerto No 5
Vocal items by Rossini, Bellini and
Donizetti
Salute to Pablo Casals: concert
concluded with Casals conducting 100
cellists in 2 of his own compositions

New York, 26-27 April 1970
American SO
Maehashi
Frescobaldi Gagliarda
Paganini Violin Concerto No 1
Berlioz Symphonie fantastique

New York, 3-4 May 1970
American SO
Westminster Choir
Thomson Sea Piece with Birds
Ginastera Creole Faust Overture
Beethoven Symphony No 9

New York, 8 May 1970
American SO
Barber Adagio for strings
Bach Chaconne in D minor
Handel Funeral March (Saul)
Bach Prelude in E flat minor
Scriabin Etude in C sharp minor
Bach Komm süsser Tod
Chopin Funeral March
Casals O vos omnes
Unrehearsed impromptu concert in
memory of students who died at Kent
State University

London, 18 June 1970
LSO
LSO Chorus
Messiaen L'Ascension
Ives 2nd Orchestral Set
Debussy La mer
Ravel Daphnis et Chloé, 2nd Suite
Berlioz Dance of the Sylphs

Croydon, 20 June 1970
LSO
LSO Chorus
Programme as for 18 June

Amsterdam, 20 August 1970
Hilversum Radio Orchestra
Van Sante
Ravel L'éventail de Jeanne
Franck Symphony in D minor
Prokofiev Alexander Nevsky

Rotterdam, 22 August 1970
Hilversum Radio Orchestra
Van Sante
Programme as for 20 August

New York, 6-11 October 1970
American SO
Wild
Handel Overture in D minor
Menotti Triple Concerto
Paderewski Piano Concerto
Schumann Symphony No 2
Schubert Moment musical No 3

New York, 19 October 1970
American SO Brass ensemble
Westminster Choirs
arr.Vaughan Williams Old 100th
Bach Singet dem Herrn excerpt
Panufnik Universal Prayer
Gabrieli In ecclesiis

New York, 1-3 November 1970
American SO
Szeryng
Herrmann Berceuse for the Fallen
Sibelius Violin Concerto
Franck Symphony in D minor
Satie Gymnopédies

New York, 15-17 November 1970
American SO and Chorus
Silberstein
Cowell Largo and Allegro
Ives Symphony No 4
Popper Cello Concerto
Strauss Also sprach Zarathustra

New York, 13-15 December 1970
American SO and Chorus
Rung, Riegel, Stilwell, Devlin
Berlioz L'enfance du Christ

New York, 14-16 January 1971
American SO
Beaux Arts Trio
Beethoven programme
Prometheus Overture/Triple Concerto/
Symphony No 3

New York, 21-23 March 1971
American SO
Masselos
Mozart Zauberflöte Overture
Strauss Rosenkavalier Waltzes
Josten Jungle
Mayer Octagon for piano & orchestra
Stravinsky Petrushka Suite
Tchaikovsky Chant sans paroles

New York, 4-6 April 1971
American SO
Westminster Choir
Moody, Parker

Shostakovich Prelude in E flat minor
Mahler Symphony No 2

New York, 25-27 April 1971
American SO
Debussy Prélude à l'après-midi
Mozart Symphony No 41
Wagner Meistersinger Act 3 Prelude
   and Dance of the Apprentices
Tchaikovsky Symphony No 4

Cleveland, 13-15 May 1971
Cleveland Orchestra
Bach Toccata and Fugue in D minor
Beethoven Symphony No 7
Sibelius Swan of Tuonela
Glière Symphony No 3

Twickenham, 20 June 1971
Halsey Singers
Cantelo, Watts, Partridge, Stalman
Panufnik Universal Prayer
Also recorded for television

New York, 12-17 October 1971
American SO
Bolet
Rimsky-Korsakov Ivan the Terrible
   Act 3 Prelude
Prokofiev Piano Concerto No 2
Brahms Symphony No 4

New York, 14-16 November 1971
American SO
Jung
Wagner programme
Walküre Ride of the Valkyries/
Wesendonk-Lieder/Holländer Overture/
Tristan Liebestod/Siegfried Forest
murmurs/Götterdämmerung Immolation

New York, 12-14 December 1971
American SO and Chorus
R.Ricci, G.Ricci
Bamert Mantrajana (American SO tenth
   anniversary commission)
Brahms Double Concerto
Ives Symphony No 4

Washington, 18-20 January 1972
National Symphony Orchestra
Mozart Nozze di Figaro Overture
Beethoven Symphony No 7
Borodin Steppes of Central Asia
Mussorgsky Pictures at an exhibition

New York, 26-28 March 1972
American SO
Masselos
Moe Fanfare (dedicated to Stokowski)
Rogers Fantasia
Beethoven Piano Concerto No 5
Tchaikovsky Capriccio italien
Dvorak Slavonic Rhapsody

New York, 23-24 April 1972
American SO
Yale Glee Club
Bach Ein' feste Burg
Bach Prelude in E flat minor
Bach Passacaglia & Fugue in C minor
Beethoven Symphony No 9

New York, 7-9 May 1972
American SO
Perlman
Mussorgsky Khovanschina Entr'acte
Tchaikovsky Violin Concerto
Shotakovich Symphony No 5
Encores by Chopin and Duparc
Stokowski's final concert in USA

London, 14 June 1972
LSO
Markovici
Stokowski 60th anniversary concert
Wagner Meistersinger Overture
Debussy Prélude à l'après-midi
Glazunov Violin Concerto
Brahms Symphony No 1
Tchaikovsky Marche slave

London, 15 June 1972
LSO
Markovici
Programme as for 14 June but with
additional encore pieces

Prague, 7–8 September 1972
Czech PO
Bach Toccata and Fugue in D minor
Bach Prelude (Partita in E)
Bach Mein Jesu was für Seelenweh
Bach Passacaglia & Fugue in C minor
Bach Sinfonia (Easter Oratorio)
Elgar Enigma Variations
Scriabin Poème de l'extase
Encore pieces by Rachmaninov,
    Tchaikovsky and Dvorak

London, 11 January 1973
New Philharmonia Orchestra
Beethoven Egmont Overture
Beethoven Symphony No 7
Rimsky-Korsakov Capriccio espagnol
Elgar Enigma Variations
Encore pieces by Bach, Wagner and
    Berlioz

Croydon, 21 April 1973
LSO
Tchaikovsky Symphony No 6
Encore pieces by Bach & Tchaikovsky
Additional item conducted by Handley

London, 25 April 1973
LSO
Vered
Beethoven Leonore No 3 Overture
Rachmaninov Paganini Rhapsody
Tchaikovsky Symphony No 6

London, 7 June 1973
New Philharmonia Orchestra
Beethoven Egmont Overture
Brian Symphony No 28*
Dvorak Symphony No 9
Radio broadcast

London, 19 August 1973
International Youth Orchestra
Tchaikovsky Symphony No 5
Other items conducted by Kosler

London, 30 September 1973
RPO
Mozart Nozze di Figaro Overture
Schubert Symphony No 8
Wagner Rienzi Overture
Wagner Walküre Wotan's Farewell
Wagner Meistersinger Suite
Wagner Tristan Prelude & Liebestod

London, 4 November 1973
LPO
LPO Chorus
Brahms Academic Festival Overture
Brahms Song of Destiny
Brahms Haydn Variations
Tchaikovsky Casse noisette Suite
Tchaikovsky Capriccio italien
Tchaikovsky Polonaise (Eugene Onegin)

London, 7 January 1974
LSO
Bach Ein' feste Burg
Bach Siciliano
Bach Chaconne in D minor
Tchaikovsky Serenade for strings
Tchaikovsky Francesca da Rimini

London, 10 February 1974
LSO
Beethoven programme
Coriolan Overture/Symphony No 8/
Symphony No 3

London, 14 May 1974
New Philharmonia Orchestra
Klemperer Merry Waltz
Vaughan Williams Tallis Fantasia
Ravel Rapsodie espagnole
Brahms Symphony No 4
Stokowski's final British appearance

Vence, 22 July 1975
Rouen Chamber Orchestra
Bach Prelude (Partita in E)
Bach Air (Suite No 3)
Bach Prelude in B minor
Bach Siciliano
Bach Fugue in G minor
Other works not conducted by Stokowski
Stokowski's final public appearance

See also list of works given their first performances by Stokowski on page 273

THE STOKOWSKI TRANSCRIPTIONS

This appendix lists currently available recordings of Stokowski's orchestral transcriptions as performed by other artists. At the time of writing, further such recordings are understood to be in the pipeline, signifying a veritable surge of interest in the art of Stokowski the transcriber. Those of us with memories which stretch back into the LP era will recall that, with barely any exceptions, the only recordings of these transcriptions once available were Stokowski's own versions.

ALBENIZ/Fête-Dieu à Seville (Ibéria)

1987	Cincinnati Pops Orchestra Kunzel	CD: Telarc CD 80129/CD 80338
1994	BBC PO Bamert	CD: Chandos CHAN 9349

BACH/Adagio (Organ Toccata, Adagio and Fugue in C)

1990	Sydney SO Pickler	CD: Chandos CHAN 6532
1993	BBC PO Bamert	CD: Chandos CHAN 9259

BACH/Air from Suite No 3

1993	BBC PO Bamert	CD: Chandos CHAN 9259

BACH/Christ lag in Todesbanden

1990	Sydney SO Pickler	CD: Chandos CHAN 6532
1993	BBC PO Bamert	CD: Chandos CHAN 9259

ENTR'ACTE
TO
KHOVANTCHINA

MUSORGSKY-STOKOWSKI

Sostenuto assai [♩ = about 58]

BACH/Ein' feste Burg ist unser Gott

1995	Philadelphia Orchestra Sawallisch	CD: EMI CDC 555 5922

BACH/Komm süsser Tod (Schemellis Gesangbuch)

1990	Sydney SO Pickler	CD: Chandos CHAN 6532
1993	BBC PO Bamert	CD: Chandos CHAN 9259

BACH/Mein Jesu, was für Seelenweh' (Schemellis Gesangbuch)

1993	BBC PO Bamert	CD: Chandos CHAN 9259

BACH/Organ Fugue in G minor "Little"

1987	Cincinnati Pops Orchestra Kunzel	CD: Telarc CD 80129/CD 80338/CD 80401
1990	Sydney SO Pickler	CD: Chandos CHAN 6532
1993	BBC PO Bamert	CD: Chandos CHAN 9259

BACH/Passacaglia and Fugue in C minor

1990	Sydney SO Pickler	CD: Chandos CHAN 6532
1993	BBC PO Bamert	CD: Chandos CHAN 9259

BACH/Prelude in B minor (Wohltemperiertes Klavier Book 1)

1993	BBC PO Bamert	CD: Chandos CHAN 9259

BACH/Schafe können sicher weiden (Cantata No 208)

1993	BBC PO Bamert	CD: Chandos CHAN 9259
1995	Philadelphia Orchestra Sawallisch	CD: EMI CDC 555 5922

BACH/Siciliano from Violin and Clavier Sonata No 4

1993	BBC PO Bamert	CD: Chandos CHAN 9259

BACH/Toccata and Fugue in D minor

1987	Cincinnati Pops Orchestra Kunzel	CD: Telarc CD 80129/CD 80338
1990	Sydney SO Pickler	CD: Chandos CHAN 6532
1993	BBC PO Bamert	CD: Chandos CHAN 9259
1995	Philadelphia Orchestra Sawallisch	CD: EMI CDC 555 5922
1995	New Zealand SO Sedares	CD: Koch 3-7344-2

BACH/Wachet auf, ruft uns die Stimme (Cantata No 140)

1995	Philadelphia Orchestra Sawallisch	CD: EMI CDC 555 5922

BACH/Wir glauben all' an einen Gott

| 1990 | Sydney SO
Pickler | CD: Chandos CHAN 6532 |
| 1993 | BBC PO
Bamert | CD: Chandos CHAN 9259 |

BEETHOVEN/First movement from the Moonlight Sonata

1987	Cincinnati Pops Orchestra Kunzel	CD: Telarc CD 80129/CD 80338
1994	BBC PO Bamert	CD: Chandos CHAN 9349
1995	Philadelphia Orchestra Sawallisch	CD: EMI CDC 555 5922

BOCCHERINI/Minuetto (Quintetto in E)

| 1987 | Cincinnati Pops
Orchestra
Kunzel | CD: Telarc CD 80129/CD 80338 |
| 1995 | Philadelphia
Orchestra
Sawallisch | CD: EMI CDC 555 5922 |

BRAHMS/Hungarian Dance No 6

| 1993 | Cincinnati Pops
Orchestra
Kunzel | CD: Telarc CD 80338 |

CHOPIN/Prelude in E minor

1995	Philadelphia	CD: EMI CDC 555 5922
	Orchestra	
	Sawallisch	

CHOPIN/Funeral March (Piano Sonata No 2)

1994	BBC PO	CD: Chandos CHAN 9349
	Bamert	

CLARKE/Trumpet Voluntary

1994	Addinall	CD: Chandos CHAN 9349
	BBC PO	
	Bamert	

DEBUSSY/La cathédrale engloutie

1987	Cincinnati Pops	CD: Telarc CD 80129/CD 80338
	Orchestra	
	Kunzel	
1995	Philadelphia	CD: EMI CDC 555 5922
	Orchestra	
	Sawallisch	

DEBUSSY/Clair de lune

1987	Cincinnati Pops	CD: Telarc CD 80129/CD 80338
	Orchestra	
	Kunzel	
1995	Philadelphia	CD: EMI CDC 555 5922
	Orchestra	
	Sawallisch	

DEBUSSY/La fille aux cheveux de lin (Préludes)

1994	BBC PO	CD: Chandos CHAN 9349
	Bamert	

FRANCK/Panis angelicus

| 1994 | BBC PO
Bamert | CD: Chandos CHAN 9349 |
| 1995 | Philadelphia
Orchestra
Sawallisch | CD: EMI CDC 555 5922 |

GABRIELI/Sonata pian e forte (Sacrae symphoniae)

| 1994 | BBC PO
Bamert | CD: Chandos CHAN 9349 |

HANDEL/Overture in D minor (Chandos Anthem No 2)

| 1994 | BBC PO
Bamert | CD: Chandos CHAN 9349 |

MATTHESON/Air (Harpsichord Suite No 5)

| 1994 | BBC PO
Bamert | CD: Chandos CHAN 9349 |

MOZART/Turkish March (Piano Sonata No 11)

| 1994 | BBC PO
Bamert | CD: Chandos CHAN 9349 |

MUSSORGSKY/Pictures at an exhibition

1995	BBC PO Bamert	CD: Chandos CHAN 9445
1995	New Zealand SO Sedares	CD: Koch 3-7344-2
1995	Cleveland Orchestra Knussen	DG awaiting publication

MUSSORGSKY/Great Gate of Kiev (Pictures at an exhibition)

| 1993 | Cincinnati Pops
Orchestra
Kunzel | CD: Telarc CD 80338 |

MUSSORGSKY/Night on Bare Mountain

1987	Cincinnati Pops Orchestra Kunzel	CD: Telarc CD 80129/CD 80338
1995	BBC PO Bamert	CD: Chandos CHAN 9445
1995	New Zealand SO Sedares	CD: Koch 3-7344-2

MUSSORGSKY/Boris Godunov, Symphonic synthesis

| 1995 | BBC PO
Bamert | CD: Chandos CHAN 9445 |

MUSSORGSKY/Khovantschina, Act 4 Entr'acte

| 1995 | BBC PO
Bamert | CD: Chandos CHAN 9445 |

RACHMANINOV/Prelude in C sharp minor

| 1987 | Cincinnati Pops
Orchestra
Kunzel | CD: Telarc CD 80129/CD 80338 |
| 1995 | Philadelphia
Orchestra
Sawallisch | CD: EMI CDC 555 5922 |

SCHUBERT/Ständchen

| 1994 | BBC PO
Bamert | CD: Chandos CHAN 9349 |

SHOSTAKOVICH/United Nations March

| 1994 | BBC PO
Bamert | CD: Chandos CHAN 9349 |

SOUSA/Stars and stripes forever

| 1994 | BBC PO
Bamert | CD: Chandos CHAN 9349 |

TCHAIKOVSKY/Andante cantabile (String Quartet in D)

| 1994 | BBC PO
Bamert | CD: Chandos CHAN 9349 |
| 1995 | Philadelphia
Orchestra
Sawallisch | CD: EMI CDC 555 5922 |

TCHAIKOVSKY/At the ball

| 1995 | Lipovsek
Philadelphia
Orchestra
Sawallisch | CD: EMI CDC 555 5922 |

RUSSIAN CHRISTMAS MUSIC/attributed to Ippolitov-Ivanov

1994	BBC PO	CD: Chandos CHAN 9349
	Bamert	

SELECTION OF WORKS GIVEN THEIR FIRST PERFORMANCES BY LEOPOLD STOKOWSKI
These were either world or American premieres

Amirov	Azerbaijan Mugam	Cowell	Koto Concerto
	Azerbaijan Mugam, Suite		Hymn and Fuguing Tune
Amfiteatrov	De profundis clamavi		Pastoral & Fiddler's
Antheil	Heroes of Today		Delight
	Symphony No 4		Symphony No 6
Arbos	Guajiras		Symphony No 12
Atterberg	Symphony No 2		Synchrony
	Symphony No 4		Tales of our Countryside
Aubert	Offrande		Variations for orchestra
Avshalomov	The Taking of T'ung Kuan	Davies	Parthenia Suite
Barlow	Babar		Solemn Melody
Barth	Quartertone Concerto	Dawson	Negro Folk Symphony
Bauer	Sun Splendor	Dubensky	Concerto grosso
Bender	San Luis Rey		Fugue for 18 violins
	Oboe Soliloquy		The Raven
Ben-Haim	Piano Concerto		Tom Sawyer Overture
Bennett	Abraham Lincoln Symphony	Eichheim	Bali
Berg	Wozzeck	El-Dabh	Fantasia Tahmeel
Berger	Malincolia	Elgar	Symphony No 2
Bliss	Introduction & Allegro	Enesco	Second Orchestral Suite
	Melée fantasque	Espla	Don Quijote velando las
Braunfels	Fantastic Variations		armas
Brian	Symphony No 28	Falla	El amor brujo
Brooks	Three Units	Fitch	Terra nova
Bruch	Double Piano Concerto	Fitelberg	Polish Rhapsody
Busoni	Indian Fantasy	Fuleihan	Theremin Concerto
Carpenter	Carmel Concerto	Gastyne	Atala
	A Pilgrim Vision	Glanville-	
Carrillo	Concertino	Hicks	Letters from Morocco
	Horizontes	Glière	Sirenen
	Sonido 13	Goeb	Symphony No 3
Chasins	Piano Concerto No 2	Gould	Chorale & Fugue in Jazz
Chavez	Horsepower	Gretchaninov	Symphony No 5
Chou	To a Wayfarer	Grieg	The Bell
Copland	Dance Symphony	Griffes	Bacchanale
Coppola	Burlesque		Clouds
			Notturno
			The White Peacock

Gutche	Genghis Khan	Malipiero	Pause del silenzio
Haieff	Piano Concerto	Martinu	Piano Concerto No 4
Harrison	Violin & Piano Concerto	Mason	Symphony No 1
Hausegger	Wieland der Schmied	Mayer	Octagon
Heiden	Memorial	McDonald	2-Piano Concerto
Helps	Adagio for orchestra		Symphony No 1
Henze	4 poemi		Symphony No 2
Hindemith	Nuschi-Nuschi Tänze		Festival of the Workers
Holmes	Fable	McPhee	Nocturne
Hovhaness	Ad lyram	Medtner	Piano Concerto No 1
	Meditation on Orpheus	R.Mengelberg	Scherzo sinfonico
	Meditation on Zeami	Menotti	Triple Concerto
	Mysterious Mountain	Messiaen	Réveil des oiseaux
	Praise the Lord with		Hymne
	Psaltery		3 petites liturgies
	Symphony No 3	Miaskovsky	Slavic Rhapsody
	Visions from High Rock		Symphony No 5
Iglesias	First Adventures of Don		Symphony No 6
	Quixote		Symphony No 10
Illiashenko	Suite de danses antiques	Moe	Fanfare
Ivanov-		Moeran	In the Mountain Country
Radkevitch	Russian Overture	Montemezzi	My Italy
Ives	Second Orchestral Set	Nordoff	Fugue
	Robert Browning Overture	Orff	Midsummer Night's Dream
	Symphony No 4		Nänie und Dithyrambe
Johansen	Voluspaa, excerpt		Trionfo di Afrodite
Khachaturian	Festive Poem	Ornstein	Piano Concerto No 2
	Russian Fantasy	Paderewski	Symphony in B minor
	Symphony No 3	Panufnik	Epitaph
Khrennikov	Symphony No 1		Sinfonia elegiaca
Kirchner	Toccata		Symphony for Peace
Leighton	Primavera romana		Universal Prayer
Leimer	Piano Concerto No 4	Ponce	Chapultepec
Liebermann	Furioso	Porrino	Sardegna
	Swiss Folk Melody Suite	Prokofiev	Alexander Nevsky
Levidis	Poème symphonique		Le pas d'acier
Lourié	Sinfonia dialectica		Symphony No 6
Mahler	Das Lied von der Erde	Rabaud	Symphony No 2
	Symphony No 8		

Stokowski premieres/concluded

Rachmaninov	Piano Concerto No 4	Sibelius	Hymn to the Earth
	Paganini Rhapsody		Symphony No 5
	Symphony No 3		Symphony No 6
	The Bells		Symphony No 7
	Russian Folksongs	Siegmeister	Prairie Legend
Ravel	Piano Concerto in G		Symphony No 1
Rice	Concerto for winds and	Steinert	Clarinet Rhapsody
	percussion	Still	Symphony in G minor
Riegger	Study in Sonority	Strauss	An Alpine Symphony
	Symphony No 3	Stravinsky	Le sacre du printemps
Rimsky-Korsakov	Invisible City of Kitezh, excerpts		Les noces
			Oedipus rex
Rouseel	Evocation No 2		Le chant du rossignol
Ruggles	Organum		Symphonies of Winds
Saint-Saens	Marche héroique	Szymanowski	Symphony No 3
Saygun	Yunus Emre		Violin Concerto No 1
Schelling	Victory Ball	Tansman	Ouverture symphonique
Schmitt	Rapsodie viennoise	Thomson	Shipwreck & Love scene
Schoenberg	Die glückliche Hand	Tippett	Ritual Dances
	Gurrelieder	Varèse	Amériques
	Kammersymphonie		Arcana
	Piano Concerto	Vaughan Williams	Symphony No 9
	Orchestral Variations		
	Violin Concerto	Villa-Lobos	Danzas caracteristicas
Scott	Piano Concerto	B.Weber	Symphony on Blake Poems
Scriabin	Symphony No 3	Webern	Passcaglia
Serebrier	Poema elegiaca	Weigl	Symphony No 5
	Symphony No 1	Weill	Lindbergh's Flight
Shchedrin	Humpback Horse Suite	Widor	Symphony No 6
Shilkret	Trombone Concerto	Zemachson	Chorale and Fugue
Shostakovich	Piano Concerto No 1		
	Symphony No 1		
	Symphony No 3		
	Symphony No 6		
	Symphony No 11		

Discographies

The Furtwängler Sound, 5th edition
Composer and chronological discographies,
300 pages
Price £22 (£28 outside UK)

Teachers and pupils
Schwarzkopf / Ivogün / Cebotari /
Seinemeyer / Welitsch / Streich / Berger
7 separate discographies, 400 pages
Price £22 (£28 outside UK)

The post-war German tradition
Kempe / Keilberth / Sawallisch /Kubelik /
Cluytens
5 separate discographies, 300 pages
Price £22 (£28 outside UK)

Mid-century conductors
and More Viennese singers
Böhm / De Sabata / Knappertsbusch / Serafin /
Krauss / Dermota / Rysanek / Wächter /
Reining / Kunz
10 separate discographies, 420 pages
Price £18 (£22 outside UK)

Tenors in a lyric tradition
Fritz Wunderlich / Walther Ludwig /
Peter Anders
3 separate discographies, 350 pages
Price £22 (£28 outside UK)

Makers of the Philharmonia
Galliera / Susskind / Kletzki / Malko / Matacic /
Dobrowen / Kurtz / Fistoulari
8 separate discographies, 300 pages
Price £22 (£28 outside UK)

A notable quartet
Janowitz / Ludwig / Gedda / Fischer-Dieskau
4 separate discographies, 600 pages
Price £20 (£25 outside UK)

Musical knights
Wood / Beecham / Boult / Barbirolli /Goodall /
Sargent
6 separate discographies, 400 pages
Price £20 (£25 outside UK)

Prices include postage
order from: John Hunt, Flat 6,
37 Chester Way, London SE11 4UR

CREDITS

Valuable help in the preparation of
these discographies came from:

Richard Chlupaty, London
Dennis Davis, London
Clifford Elkin, Glasgow
Mathias Erhard, Berlin
Edward Johnson, London
Alan Newcombe, Hamburg
Alan Sanders, Richmond
Malcolm Walker, Harrow